AF327179

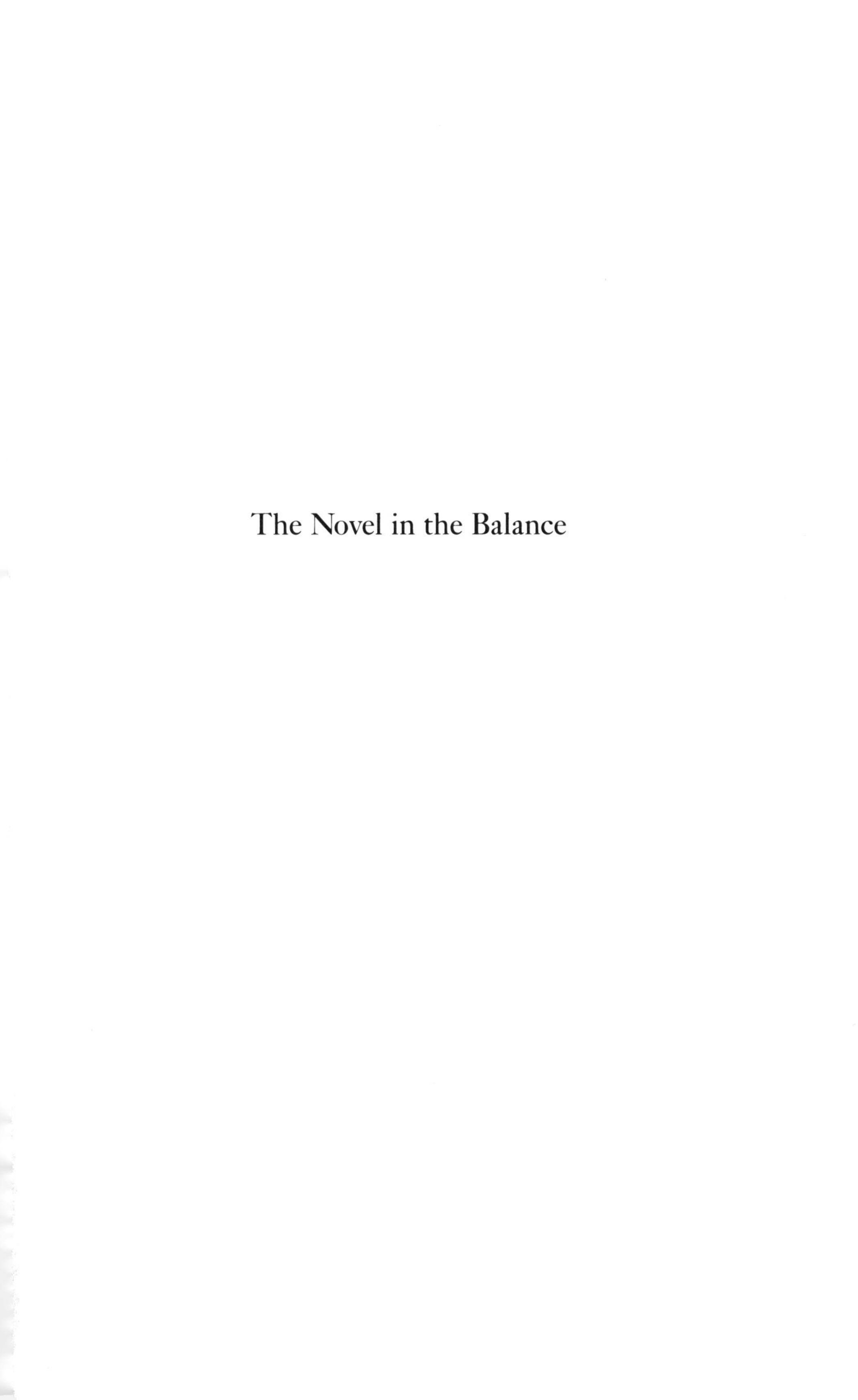

The Novel in the Balance

THE NOVEL IN THE BALANCE

Arthur M. Saltzman

University of South Carolina Press

Published in Columbia, South Carolina, by the
University of South Carolina Press

Manufactured in the United States of America

Library of Congress Cataloging-in-Publication Data

Saltzman, Arthur M. (Arthur Michael), 1953–
The novel in the balance / Arthur M. Saltzman.
p. cm.
Includes bibliographical references and index.
ISBN 0–87249–960–X
1. American fiction—20th century—History and criticism.
I. Title.
PS379.S24 1993
813′.5409—dc20 93–14192
CIP

For Elizabeth
and the gift of wonder
you have, you are

Contents

Acknowledgments

A portion of chapter 3 originally appeared in *Since Flannery O'Connor: Essays on the Contemporary American Short Story* (1987), ed. Loren Logsdon and Charles W. Mayer; an early version of chapter 8 was published in the winter 1990 issue of *Contemporary Literature* (31, no. 4). I appreciate the opportunity to have tried out my ideas in those sources and to reprise that material here. I also wish to recognize Missouri Southern's Faculty Development Program, whose financial support helped to defray reprint expenses. My gratitude goes to Jerome Klinkowitz and R. Baird Shuman, who provided generous encouragement of the project in its initial stages, as well as to two anonymous manuscript readers and to Warren Slesinger of the University of South Carolina Press for their sound advice. Nor can I forget to mention Milo Kaufmann, who some fifteen years ago intrigued me with the question of where the forest became the field, for I think of that conversation as the moment when the spell of indeterminate zones was cast upon me. And for Marla Marantz there is everything that all too often goes without saying, offered here: my love and thanks.

I wish also to thank the following publishers and authors of copyrighted works who have generously granted permission to use quotations that are not clearly governed by fair-use standards:

From *Heaven and Earth: A Cosmology*, by Albert Goldbarth. Copyright 1991 by the University of Georgia Press. Reprinted by permission of the author.

From *Hybrids of Plants and Ghosts*, by Jorie Graham. Copyright 1980 by Princeton University Press. Reprinted by permission of Princeton University Press.

From *Erosion*, by Jorie Graham. Copyright 1983 by Princeton University Press. Reprinted by permission of Princeton University Press.

From *Collected Poems*, by Robert Hayden, edited by Frederick Glaysher. Copyright 1985 by Erma Hayden. Reprinted by permission of Liveright Publishing Corporation.

From *Death of a Naturalist*, by Seamus Heaney. Copyright 1966 by Faber and Faber Ltd. Reprinted by permission of Faber and Faber Ltd.

From *Spectral Emanations: New and Selected Poems*, by John Hollander. Copyright 1978 by John Hollander. Reprinted by permission of the author.

From *Middle Passage*, by Charles Johnson. Copyright 1989 by Charles Johnson. Reprinted by permission of Atheneum Publishers, an imprint of Macmillan Publishing Company.

From *Plus*, by Joseph McElroy. Copyright 1976 by Joseph McElroy. Reprinted by permission of Alfred A. Knopf, Inc.

From *Housekeeping*, by Marilynne Robinson. Copyright 1980 by Farrar, Straus and Giroux, Inc. Reprinted by permission of Farrar, Straus and Giroux, Inc.

From *Ceremony*, by Leslie Marmon Silko. Copyright 1977 by Leslie Marmon Silko. Reprinted by permission of Viking Penguin, a division of Penguin Books USA Inc.

From *Wrinkles*, by Charles Simmons. Copyright 1978 by Farrar, Straus and Giroux, Inc. Reprinted by permission of Farrar, Straus and Giroux, Inc.

From *Collected Poems*, by Wallace Stevens. Copyright 1923, 1947, 1950, 1951 by Wallace Stevens and renewed 1970 by Holly Stevens. Reprinted by permission of Alfred A. Knopf, Inc.

From *The Universe, and Other Fictions*, by Paul West. Copyright 1988 by Paul West. Reprinted by permission of the Overlook Press, Woodstock, N.Y. 12498.

From *Paterson*, by William Carlos Williams. Copyright 1958 by William Carlos Williams. Reprinted by permission of New Directions Publishing Corporation.

From *Collected Poems*, by W. B. Yeats. Copyright 1933 by Macmillan Publishing Company and renewed 1961 by Bertha Georgie Yeats. Reprinted by permission of Macmillan Publishing Company.

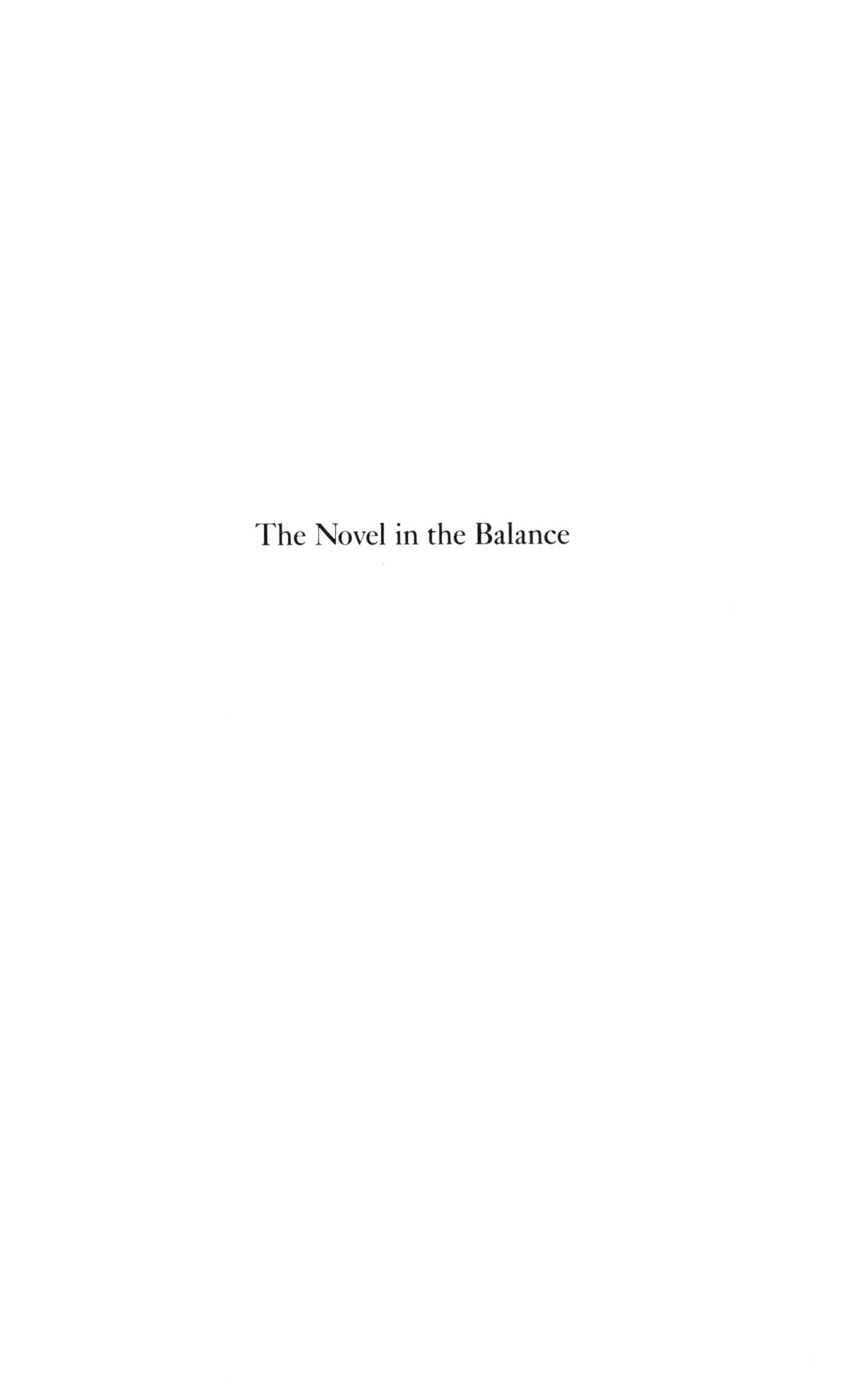

The Novel in the Balance

1

INTRODUCTION

Views from the Brink

If I have a faith it is something like this: this ordering
of images
within an atmosphere that will receive them, hold them
in solution, unsolved.

—Jorie Graham, "The Lady and the Unicorn and Other Tapestries"

He was a staple of the vaudeville circuit and *The Ed Sullivan Show*—a little man, all earnestness and optimistic rush, whose talent was to get a row of dinner plates spinning atop an anchored row of flexible rods. One by one he would start them by hand, a matter of coddling and delicacy, until each responded sufficiently for him to go on to another plate. The trick, of course, not to mention the primary source of entertainment, was that he had to contend with the waning energy of the first vertical even as he busied himself with the next, the result being that he would continually have to return to wrist additional encouragement into the old rods while setting about initiating the new. As the stakes increased with more and more plates aloft, the equilibrium artist grew feverish, then manic. Yet his private regimental galaxy shivered into being: the trembling axes, the lowing audience following his own perpetual motion, with which he hoped to imbue the ever-evolving project. (Surely his cartoon anxiety was part of the performance, but great art can cause even the jaundiced eye to flash. We were eager accomplices.)

Out of those turbulent stresses arose a gratifying arrangement, "a wavering, lurching, animating harmony" imitating Nature's own eccentricities and subtly insistent as a weather system (Gleick, Text to *Nature's Chaos* 16). What mesmerized us was the blessed riddance of earthly drag and bother, the sense of an instant, however fleeting, of lofted emportraiture, of dreamy unindebtedness. The performance did not actually end per se. Rather, at that instant when all ten plates were successfully revolving and the air was fully inhabited, when all was suspended between erection and deterioration, he would scamper out for his applause, which rang out even with the crashing return of gravity and the sober world.

Let this fellow be the muse and his restless architecture the model for this study.

The title *The Novel in the Balance* may initially sound like a belated contribution to the bidding for autopsy rights that has occasionally characterized literary criticism for better than a generation now. Variously charged with negligence, fecklessness, irrelevance, or downright immorality, contemporary fiction is seen from this perspective as a gasping aberration in the otherwise robust and honorable history of the genre.[1] We are familiar with the guiding myth of the crisis mentality, which goes something like this: around 1960 a band of vandals posing as novelists upset the applecart, leaving the truly civic-minded among us to mutter over the bruised fruit. In fact, one of the main instigations behind my writing *Designs of Darkness in Contemporary American Fiction* (1990) was to respond to the consternation (urbane alarm may be more like it) of so many excellent readers when faced with recent texts by suggesting that these were works that deliberately seek to redraw the standard contracts among reader, author, and book. The "integrity of irresolution" that identifies the fictions I investigated forces a self-conscious reexamination, if not a repudiation, of such fundamental matters as epiphanic closure, the steady development and imparting of hierarchic order, and linguistic groundings. Obviously, those readers dedicated to driving home their points from the right side of the road, who are accustomed to having their forests groved, and who prefer that passages lead through books as conclusively as they do through government buildings are going to be impatient when faced with these adjustments. Nevertheless, the result of such interrogations has not been to lay waste to the possibilities of fiction but, rather, simply to point out the insufficiencies, and perhaps the potential tyrannies, inherent in totalizing conventions.

The thrust of *The Novel in the Balance* is quite literal, in that this is a study of how the concept of balance inheres in a variety of contemporary fictions. My intention is to provide a second, complementary slant on the ways in which these fictions accentuate the interrogative: whereas *Designs of Darkness* concentrated on works committed to the exposure and subversion of revelatory motives, the analysis at hand shifts the focus from tactics of rupture to tactics of consolidation. Certainly, words like *reconciliation*, *intersection*, *alliance*, and *equilibrium* appear with regularity in the current study; it is full of lucent thresholds and shimmering borders—all sites of delicate negotiation. But, just as an either-or division between textual breakdown and repair is too facile, so too is the equation between final draft and mission accomplished deceptive, for the texts I survey in *The Novel in the Balance* effect their balances furtively, provisionally, performing "brink jobs," as it were. Each finished book manifests a tentative reign, and that very tentativeness, often as not, is the subject of the narrative. "I will continue to proceed with an irregular consistency," declares the narrator of Brad Leithauser's *Hence*, "which is to say, with that unflinching comprehensiveness accessible only to paradox. I would bring you (let the phrase be underlined, and later recalled) *something knotted up, and fantastical and stubbornly indirect*" (29). Or, as Theodore Roethke, that prescient equilibrium artist, wrote in "The Waking," "This shaking keeps me steady" (l. 16). Paradox is at once a philosophical premise and a formal principle of the works under discussion; their favored territory is the transitional, where balance is hard to perfect, harder perhaps to justify.

In using balance as my theme and guide, I do not mean to campaign for its particular ingenuity. Obviously, balancing the world's and the word's respective requirements and offerings—the task of referentiality like a yearly audit or some literal correspondence course countering the imagination's levitating strains—has always been central to successful writing. The novel has always been set, and flourished in, the space between given and if. But the striking feature of the balances found in these fictions is that they deliberately—one might say unavoidably—retain and reflect the competing motions out of which they arise and which they have been presumably summoned to answer. Like the fretted descent of Duchamp's nude on the staircase, these are works concerned with whatever is still falling in a pause.[2] Our reading experience corresponds to Seamus Heaney's confrontation in "Waterfall":

> My eye rides over and downwards, falls with
> Hurtling tons that slabber and spill,
> Falls, yet records the tumult thus standing still.
>
> (ll. 10–12)

Here is the torsion between tide and undertow made apparent; here the water waits, while the field streams.

The compensations of art that so eagerly enlists oxymorons and that always proceeds under the watch of disclaimers are subtle, but they are more profound than those who mourn the absent heft of solid theses acknowledge. If there is any consistent message conveyed in the fictions covered in *The Novel in the Balance*, it is in the slippages. As William Carlos Williams advises in *Paterson:*

> Dissonance
> (if you are interested)
> leads to discovery.
>
> (176)

Meaning teeters on the verge of its displacement; it is posited in the shadow of that awareness. Whatever is most genuine here takes the form of the propitious, magnetized hush—some marvel caught at the top of its arc. The artist's emphasis is not so much on a rescue from flux or an extraction of stable images from contingency and dross but, instead, on a recognition (and perpetuation) of mutualities that exist between created and inherited realities.

For some this is just an elaborate way of talking about postmodernism. Indeed, however one chooses to define this loose, baggy term, his or her definition will undoubtedly include something about postmodern art's penchant for muscling in on its own critical reception. Linda Hutcheon names this the mode of "complicitous critique," whereby every stance seems to contain its compromise: "Postmodernism's distinctive character lies in this kind of wholesale 'nudging' commitment to doubleness, or duplicity. In many ways it is an even-handed process because postmodernism ultimately manages to install and reinforce as much as undermine and subvert the conventions and presuppositions it appears to challenge" (1–2). It is not my goal in *The Novel in the Balance* to enlist in the seemingly interminable discussion of what postmodernism is or whether in fact it merits a designation apart from modernism—whether, to adapt from John Donne's "A Valediction: Forbidding Mourning," postmodernism is not "a breach, but an expansion, / Like gold to airy thinness beat" (ll. 23–24).[3] I am not attempting to map out the entire landscape in this book—to be sure, some will question my selections—but to make observations along what seems to me to be a particularly interesting and rewarding road that goes through it.

On that subject I might also address my chapter-by-chapter method of juxtaposing texts. To some degree this is a cosmetic means of reinforcing the sense of the title throughout the book, but, more important, I hope that this argumentative structure will establish a kind of oscillation, or dialogue, in the reader's mind, as "reciprocal" texts establish and refine interpretive grounds for one another. In *Second Skin* and *Housekeeping* the two respective narrators must reconcile their desires to edit and constrain experience with the inevitable fluidity and traumatic content of that experience. But unlike, say, Cleanth Brooks, for whom the creative imagination is bent upon quelling and harmonizing "the discordant and contradictory" (qtd. in van Delden 127), John Hawkes and Marilynne Robinson share a nonauthoritarian vision, whereby the tensions and inconsistencies that awaken artistic impulses are still evident in the artistic product. In this sense, reconciliation of "warring elements" is also, and self-evidently, reconciliation *to* warring elements—or, looking forward to my adaptation of Eliot's imagery, the still point does not vanquish the turning world but, rather, admits it into a complicated, still-moving balance.

I trace this paradox into the schizophrenic form of the short story cycle in *Lives of the Poets: Six Stories and a Novella* and *The Things They Carried*. The notion of an achieved vision is particularly elusive in the context of a cycle, in which the textual product continues to betray the process of its development and in which the integration of parts is ostensibly less "committed" than in a conventional novel, yet whose components are definitely affiliated more strongly than a mere chronological collection of short stories would imply. Both E. L. Doctorow and Tim O'Brien find the cycle format hospitable to their efforts to examine events without domesticating them, and what resolutions they construct are set upon gap-riddled foundations.

The Universal Baseball Association and *The Music of Chance* exhibit a somewhat different balance between craft and accident. For Robert Coover and Paul Auster circumstances that drive the hero into recoil infiltrate the ludic refuge. Yet, ironically, while too much reality forecloses possibility and chokes off play, without some legislative presence the game grows pallid and seems little more than an indiscretion; illusion melts into shapeless caprice, which no longer entices or restores the player in the text or the reader of the text. Risk coupled with restraint is progressive; improvisation thrives only inside the baselines. Enchantment must contend with awareness of its privilege and its price: "In the expression of this irony there is joy, but it is the harsh, pyrrhic joy of consciousness triumphant over its own creative powers" (Boyers 749). The "counternarrative" that the artist-gambler creates is not seamless. Again, as is so often the case in *The Novel in the Balance*, qualified abandonment is the order of the day.

Ratner's Star and *Plus* take these issues to the cosmos. Don DeLillo and Joseph McElroy, two of our most erudite, venturesome novelists, are concerned with the appeal and the fallibility of systems of thought themselves. "Mathematics, rightly viewed, possesses not only truth, but supreme beauty," writes Bertrand Russell, who goes on to worship its capacity for evincing "stern perfection such as only the greatest art can show" (qtd. in Peterson 288). The sublimity of such discoveries, however, and the myth of exactitude they extend warp against the brute confusion of the physical realities they are summoned to explain. Even as it appears to concede to our forays, chaos yawns wider than the virile new poetry of circuits and theorems can accommodate. Is the universe set like a table for discerning company, or does randomness also teasingly include occasional pockets of order? "Even starlight, that most diaphonous stuff, has its formal qualities," reasons poet Alice Fulton, "though they prove too cagey, too wayward for calibration from earth" (53).[4] Grand unifying gestures do not fully transcend us, yet we continue to launch analogies and try to colonize the sky.

Flaubert's dream of a novel sustained by nothing other than its style seems to have captivated a great many contemporary American writers. But reputations for baroque, self-consultive, or antimimetic art aside, it is the resiliency of referential tethers, not their absence, upon which verbal "worlds elsewhere" prove to depend. (The hypothetically pure metafiction would be something akin to a cake that returned to flour, sugar, and water in one's hands, and which could hardly calm the appetite.) In *Prisoner's Dilemma* and *The MacGuffin* the mental precincts in which Eddie Hobson and Bobbo Druff, respectively, prefer to reside are inescapably conjoined to the secular. Familial demands, historical forces, moral obligations, and remembered debts and enthusiasms find their way through the barricades. Happily, at least in Richard Powers's and Stanley Elkin's examples, attachment is enrichment—a fortunate fall into healthful equilibrium. This serves as a standard of style for the authors as well as a standard of living for the characters: lyrical flights regularly depart from realistic terminals. A measured rapture prevails.[5]

Segregative tactics also fail in the political sphere. *Ceremony* and *Middle Passage* demonstrate that unadulterated racial and cultural legacies are false claims. When they seek to establish identities for themselves, Leslie Marmon Silko's Native American and Charles Johnson's African American discover that emergence from the Other must be tempered by the unavoidability (and perhaps the value) of mergence with the Other. Oppression must be resisted, of course, but it cannot be disavowed, for that would result in stasis. The polytropic resolve that enables both of the novels' heroes to survive defines them as moving, growing hybrids. In this sense political and psychic balances interanimate one another; new mythic strains evolve to contend successfully with the multiplicities of American society.

The final chapter of the book uses a somewhat wider lens to look at the conventional boundaries between story and novel. Minimalism is a favorite target of disdain these days, and even those critics who do approve of contemporary literature tend to haul their crafts alongside the "big books" for a flensing—*Gravity's Rainbow*, *The Public Burning*, and *LETTERS* are among the most celebrated prey—and ignore smaller game. My strategy in "Maximalist Stories, Minimalist Novels" is to complicate this sort of reflex categorization by thinking of minimalism in terms of how it asks questions and how, by abrading fiction to its conceptual grain, it refocuses the issue of scope from width to depth. The novels I select to represent the border between forms—Alf MacLochlainn's *Out of Focus*, Nicholson Baker's *The Mezzanine*, Charles Simmons's *Wrinkles*, Renata Adler's *Speedboat*, Stephen Dixon's *Work*, and Ronald Sukenick's *The Endless Short Story*—bear witness to what turns out to be a productive tension between serial and procedural requirements[6] and, as they undertake some of the same philosophical challenges as their megalithic counterparts, reinforce the status of fiction in a minor scale.

In her poem "Two Lengths has every Day" Emily Dickinson wonders about the character of eternity; she determines that it will be either "Velocity or Pause" (l. 6). In *The Novel in the Balance* I presume to defend a combined fate. By attempting to describe the flair behind his or her fitfulness, the flexibility of his or her qualified functions, I hope to define and defend for the equilibrium artist a place on the stage of contemporary fiction.

Notes

1. My introduction to *Designs of Darkness in Contemporary American Fiction* ("A De-Meaning Poetics") samples representative complaints against the contemporary American literary scene by critics who seem to have ground their axes at the same stone (1–7).
2. From André Breton's second "Surrealist Manifesto" comes another deposition from the visual arts in support of the harnessing of opposites as a productive aesthetic destiny: "Everything leads one to believe that there exists a certain state of mind where life and death, the real and the imaginary, the past and the future, the communicable and the uncommunicable, the heights and the depths cease to be seen as contradictory. In fact it would be pointless to look for anything else in surrealism, but the hope of clearing up this point" (qtd. in Weelen 9).
3. One particular modern novel that strikes me as compatible with the "postmodern" theme of this book is *As I Lay Dying* (1930). The "rigid terrific hiatus" of Jewel and his horse (12) and the river current's "fury in itself quiet with stagnation" (156) are but two suggestions of the paradoxical balances at work in Faulkner's novel. My study of recent American fiction is not meant to treat its symptoms as exclusive, although it does suggest that this theme has special prominence among contemporary authors.

4. In her commentary on the generation of her poem "Everyone Knows the World Is Ending" Fulton prefaces this statement by referring to the atmospheric and perceptual distortions that make "coherent starlight" (the astronomical term for when starlight is at the top of our atmosphere so that "its waves are in harmony") a troubling concept at best (52).
5. I first introduced this phrase in regard to William Gass, another author who openly and consistently tests this tension, in "Where Worlds Dwell Adored" (12).
6. I import these terms from Joseph M. Conte's *Unending Design: The Forms of Postmodern Poetry*, in which he explores the relationship between discontinuous elements and a designated system of arbitrary restraints in the given space of the work of art.

2

STILL POINT AND TURNING WORLD

Second Skin and *Housekeeping*

I

> Only by the form, the pattern,
> Can words or music reach
> The stillness, as a Chinese jar still
> Moves perpetually in its silence.
> —T. S. Eliot, *Burnt Norton*

For all his blundering, for all his obstinate innocence and self-justifying manipulations of his so-called "naked history," John Hawkes's Skipper in *Second Skin* (1964) is typically viewed by critics as an artist whose transcendence of the vile contingencies of his past and escape to a serene golden island represent the triumph of the imagination over brute and brutal facticity. Donald G. Greiner's polarization of the lacerating realities of *Second Skin* and its narrator's lyrical alternative is representative. Greiner concludes that "Skipper successfully erects the pleasures of the imagination against the indignities of a world that deliberately hurts him" (13). Susan Sontag is no less definitive in her review of the novel, saying that "it is, in short, about horror surmounted by lushness and love" (3), and Tony Tanner concurs: "He is transposing his life by describing it in his chosen way. Thus he is able to make whatever was negative in the past into something more healing and affirmative by submitting it to his own stylistic and rhetorical translations" (227).[1] Accordingly, Skipper's self-anointment at the beginning of *Second Skin* glorifies that translation, even as it subtly conflates his many motives:

> I will tell you in a few words who I am: lover of the hummingbird that darts to the flower beyond the rotted sill where my feet are propped; lover of bright needlepoint and the bright stitching fingers of humorless old ladies bent to their sweet and infamous designs; lover of parasols made from the same puffy stuff as a young girl's underdrawers; still lover of that small naval boat which somehow survived the distressing years of my life between her decks or in her pilothouse; and also

> lover of poor dear black Sonny, my mess boy, fellow victim and confidant, and of my wife and child. But most of all, lover of my harmless and sanguine self. (1)

Nevertheless, this remarkable welcome is by no means as open-handed as the buoyant tone suggests. Skipper's designs are at once "sweet and infamous," patterns riddled with suspicion; he likens himself to one of nature's generative geniuses, the hummingbird, while he himself is an artificial inseminator, a servicer of cattle, master of surrogacy. He champions his "harmless and sanguine self," but he is exposed throughout the novel as a hapless catalyst of catastrophe—he is Papa Cue Ball, a shatterer and randomizer of the arrangements he enters—and he is haunted by the miseries he attends to (family deaths) or is victimized by (Tremlow's betrayal). Indeed, he is a "still lover," his constancy more a matter of passivity or utter absorbency, a fat target for snowball barrages or more profound treacheries; the phrase also confesses a love of stillness, a yearning to settle urgencies and dissolve his bad dreams through an art of selective remembrance which indulges those psychological needs.

There is no question that the disasters Skipper attempts to deflect are extraordinary. His avuncular tone at the beginning of the novel—itself a triumph of art—as he dreamily recollects from his tropical vantage point vividly contrasts with the series of personal devastations that marked his journey there. His father, a mortician, and his faithless wife commit suicide, both of them having been more driven than deterred by Skipper's cloying love. His daughter punishes him for his smothering affections with assorted outrages, ranging from having Skipper submit to a horrifying tattooing to engaging in random promiscuity; she, too, kills herself by leaping from a lighthouse. His son-in-law, a larcenous pervert procured by Skipper himself, is viciously murdered during the honeymoon. And, perhaps most traumatic of all, he suffers a mutiny and rape at the hands of Tremlow, whose name and image hover over the narrative, gathering imminence and precision from their recurring invasions of his consciousness. During each catastrophe Skipper waits in stuporous attendance, his ineffectuality at once his limitation and his exemption from responsibility. The structural logic of *Second Skin* complements this paradox by featuring alternations of settings between past disturbances and the Edenic present on Catalina Kate's island, which are complicated by Skipper's psychological baffles, allusive fertility, and surreal recreations. Thus, the novel thickens more than it progresses, its plot movements defused by densely poetic interludes and hazy reverberations.

In short, this ostensibly winsome narrator is a congeries of oppositions whose invocation of the narratival privilege to select or stifle at his discretion confesses, and therefore gives access to, the ignominies he means to dispose of; although it is the beauties beyond the rotting sill and not the sill itself that he chooses as his emblems, both are undeniable presences in his life. He "skips" what disturbs the serenity of his idyllic outpost on his "wandering island," but the novel is littered with images that challenge the purity of his productions.

Wallace Stevens anticipates the rewards of tampering with reality in "On the Road Home":

> It was when I said,
> "There is no such thing as truth,"
> That the grapes seemed fatter.
>
> (ll. 1–3)

Or, as Skipper himself later puts it, when contrasting his present circumstances to the bleakness of Miranda's "scum-washed black island in the Atlantic," "the golden wheel of my hot sun" guarantees that "the light of my triumph must shine through" (48). That "must" marks him as the craftsman and custodian of his past, for, as Hawkes himself attests, "there is nothing else in the world except what he creates and the figures he discovers in his creation" ("Response to Richard Yarborough" 64). But Hawkes is guilty in this declaration of promoting the same sort of pretense that his narrator does, and Hawkes's and Skipper's aesthetic creeds prove far less absolute in their opposition of imaginative alternatives to worldly realities than they are reputed to be.

This approach to the novel enables us to view it as Hawkes's deposition in the modernism/postmodernism debate. If we generalize and postulate modernism as an effort to transcend the circumstances of its generation, to found an "aura of achieved certainty" purged of randomness and contingency (Attridge); if we then consider postmodernism, on the contrary, as a recognition of the embeddedness of art in those circumstances, an aesthetic that tolerates, even celebrates, the felicitous conjunction between the work of art and the accidents of experience, Skipper's narrative fits into the sleeve between them. It is simultaneously, to borrow Alan Wilde's terms, fiction as an "enclave of value" in place of the world *and* in face of the world (*Horizons of Assent* 148). In other words, we might say that Skipper initially appears to be a modernist, but, while purporting to coerce a significant subjugation of convulsive materials, he creates an open-ended postmodern text despite himself. As Wendy Steiner maintains, "Rather than maniacally synthesizing allusive fragments into a coherent—if difficult—aesthetic whole, postmodernism basks in heterogeneity, in the vertigo of historical disjunction and interpretive indeterminacy" (63). The failure to construct an exclusionary, imperial interpretation proves fortunate in the sense that a totalized interpretive network would rigidify and foreclose Skipper's experience. Therefore, the ungraspability of the story's elements—their defiance of forged connection, as well as Skipper's abdication of the narrator's conventional responsibility to establish it—serves to protect Skipper from any absolute verdict regarding his role in the deaths that crowd his history. The performative flexibility of fiction making provides Skipper with improvisational options for renewal, however many corpses litter the stage.

The modernist goal of artifactive arrest and the promise of a stable depth at the center of shifting surfaces could define Skipper as victim or villain. As a result, Skipper counts on the fact that his retrospective assaults on Truth never attain authority. Imagination's second skin is neither uniform nor impermeable; the modernist agenda and world/word oppositions notwithstanding, *Second Skin* operates in accordance with William James's contentions that "truth . . . is not a stagnant property" and that there is no such thing as "Reality with the big R, reality that makes the timeless claim, reality to which defeat can't happen" ("Pragmatism and Radical Empiricism" 312; "Pragmatism and Humanism" 458).

Greiner and Tanner imply that reformulating reality to feature and forgive him- or herself is the artist's province. But what sort of artist *is* Skipper? In what has become the most frequently quoted of Hawkes's comments on his aesthetic principles, the author appears to be vindicating the way his own narrator operates:

> I began to write fiction on the assumption that the true enemies of the novel were plot, character, setting, and theme, and having once abandoned these familiar ways of thinking about fiction, totality of vision or structure was really all that remained. And structure—verbal and psychological coherence—is still my largest concern as a writer. Related or corresponding event, recurring image and recurring action, these constitute the essential substance or meaningful density of my writing. ("John Hawkes: An Interview" 149)

Much has been made of the dismissal of realistic conventions and of the variety of forms that this dismissal takes in Hawkes's novels. No less controversial, however, is the exaltation of "totality of vision" which succeeds it. While it is likewise tempting to assign Hawkes's priorities to his narrator in *Second Skin*, we might contend that this pronouncement conceals important contradictions, much the same way as does Skipper's introduction to his handiwork. Moreover, totality of vision, with its connotations of completeness and composure, evolves from artistic precepts that Skipper flouts throughout his chronicle.

We may begin by examining the false equation of "totality of vision" and "verbal and psychological coherence" which Hawkes proposes. Whereas the former phrase smacks of Modernist supremacy and ultimate consolidation—Yeats's "artifice of eternity," say, in "Sailing to Byzantium" (l. 24) or Eliot's recognition in "*Ulysses*, Order, and Myth" of Joyce's having imposed "a way of controlling, of ordering, of giving a shape and a significance to the immense panorama of futility and anarchy which is contemporary history" (177)—the latter is far less ambitious, or rather, its ambitions proceed in a different direction. Skipper exploits language to redeem his fears and failures, and in doing so he learns that language simultaneously invokes and subdues; indeed, for him, psychological coherence often necessitates the sacrifice of verbal coherence, in that too clear a rendering of events such as the encounter with the "kissing bandits" or the outrages on the *Starfish* would cause him to relive and to authenticate those traumas. Therefore, Skipper chooses to baffle vision with structural shuffling, to poeticize the past so as to elude the brunt of clarity. He resists the confinement of closure, endlessly deferring final interpretation of any incident. We recall the agony he endures while being branded with the name of Cassandra's husband at the infernal tattoo parlor: in a sense this could be said to exemplify the tyranny of a definitive signature—specifically here, a "green lizard that lay exposed and crawling on my breast" (20)—which rivets him to the insult and fatal error of promoting Fernandez as a son-in-law. *Second Skin* is not an alternative explanation so much as an alternative *to* explanation, a refusal of fixity.[2] The sacrifice of reductive sense for aesthetic satisfaction must be understood on Skipper's terms—namely, that freedom from implication either in the catastrophes he has left in his wake or in any other closed historical account is not negotiable.

In light of these priorities consider Skipper's descriptions early in the novel of the deaths of his father and mother. The suicide of Skipper's father, done behind the bathroom door while his plump, hopeless son tries to cajole him with cello playing on the other side, "had begun my knowledge of death as a lurid truth" (8). Skipper directs us to focus on his own culpability in this instance, calling himself both "witness and accomplice" to "that uncensored scene" (7), and this attitude neatly coincides with his unnatural willingness to absorb pain and humiliation on behalf of Cassandra (who, of course, finds his capacity for abuse exasperating). But no less important is the fact that Skipper is associating "knowledge" and "Truth" with terror. When, on the other hand, he recounts the details of his mother's death—she deafened herself against her husband's gunshots by pouring melted wax in her ears—he openly recognizes the compatibility of their respective efforts to combat the intensity of knowledge. "A waxen tableau," he terms it, "no doubt the product of a slight and romantic fancy. Yet I prefer this vision to my father's death" (9). "Vision" is a softer sense of things—vision described the images "lying closest to the peaceful center of my childhood" (6)—and it is set against "knowledge" as a less formidable obstacle to his "sanguinity." Furthermore, his mother's death is extolled for having "extended" the "lurid truth" precipitated by his father's death "toward the promise of mystery" (8). The promise of mystery is the assurance of ambiguity and its unbounded options.[3]

Finally, Skipper's insertion of "I prefer" in conjunction with his mother's death contaminates his "naked history" with intention, but it is a circumspect, irregular intention, erratic as the flight of the hummingbird he claims as his aesthetic standard. Thus, we return to that phrase "still lover": like the hummingbird, whose apparent stillness is an illusion created by super-swift fluttering of its wings, Skipper would combine the solidity of a stationary remove with the vitality and open-endedness of unresolved readings. On those occasions when images or occurrences prove too much for his imagination to revise according to preference, the system shuts down. For instance, encountering the mutilated corpse of Fernandez, Skipper muses briefly on whether or not Tremlow could be either the second dead man (Harry) on the flophouse floor or the hideous murderer of both men, but he quickly scuttles the investigation: "I could not be sure and was careful that I never would know" (158).

The same sort of deflection is evident on several occasions on Miranda's island. When Miranda leaves the malignant symbol of the sliced rubber nipples of Pixie's baby bottles for Skipper to stumble upon, he automatically throws up his hands: "I could make nothing of this sad vehement litter" (61); the oppressive interior of rust, rubbish, and mold summons to mind "nothing that I could see to fear" (60); even the dressing dummy, a maimed, hermaphroditic torso wearing Skipper's naval uniform and splashed with "blood" does not engage awareness: "But of course I ignored it as best I could, tried to overlook the fresh dark gouts of ketchup she had flung down the front of that defiled figure, and merely shut my door"

(67). The same reflex deflects any understanding of Miranda's hideous parting "gift" of the dead fetus in a fruit jar—memento and motive of Cassandra's suicide. Skipper's incuriosity is so effective a shield, we might be moved to call it intrepid: "What was she trying to tell me? And then suddenly I knew the first thing I had to do, and I did it. I simply reached out my hand, picked up the package, put it to my ear and shook it. But there was no sound. And I could tell nothing by the weight. It was a fruit jar, just as she said, but whether it contained anything or was empty, I did not know" (202). Nor does he look. Miranda savages the "old fool" for his daughter's suicide, but its harrowing insights are negated by the same refusal to see: "I won't ask why, Cassandra. Something must have spoken to you, something must have happened. But I don't want to know, Cassandra. So I won't ask . . ." (199).

Similar evasions mark Skipper's degradation by the invidious Tremlow, the memory of which permeates the novel but which only comes into focus two-thirds of the way through. Not only does Skipper cling to inaction, despite Sonny's warnings that a mutiny is in the making, but he "still missed the idea, the plan, which was surely riding far forward by then in Tremlow's eye," (146) at the moment of the assault and rape. His mouth leaking blood from Tremlow's blows, Skipper ludicrously sputters on about duty; caught in a tangled pile of bodies in the lifeboat, Skipper remains in the dark: his mind is elsewhere, on the gentle moon's pulse as it flashes through the star-shaped hole in the tarpaulin. "I must have moaned," he reasons, and he considers that "there seemed to be a purpose in that struggle, but still it escaped me" (146–47).

"Forever in the darkness" even as he is being assaulted—the word *darkness* appears six times within the page-long description of the rape scene—Skipper responds by letting his assailants escape: "They disappeared like three drops of milk dissolving in a creamy soup, those three boats" (148). This image recalls the way time works on events "like water on old knots" (4), taking the stiffness out of history, subverting its hold. Allowed to dissolve into the general slough of vagaries that blanket consciousness like a steady sleep, Tremlow loses his sharp contours—"the terrible bones of his hips" (145) soften and disintegrate. (Later, by virtue of his own angling of his hipbone into the blow, Skipper will win the belly-bumping contest, as though performing a comic reversal of the ignominy at Tremlow's hands.) The hole in the lifeboat tarpaulin, a "great star" that will be imitated in the hole in the roof of Skipper's hut on his wandering island, is like a flaw in the fabric of the story he weaves which ensures that no closure is obtainable.

Skipper's porous story leaves many openings for escape. We need only contrast Skipper's art with the art practiced by the tattooer, whose scalding needles leave absolute, intransigent designs—we are reminded of Kafka's Penal Colony, in which the supreme punishment is to have the definition of one's crimes clawed onto his skin by a diabolical contraption of harness, rack, and needles—to appreciate the preservation of artificing alternatives that Skipper's selective method provides. A comparable distinction can be seen in Skipper's distancing from the machinations of Miranda, which are delivered in terms of necromancy. Her infernal asthma powders are choking, her sewing dummy full of pins implies voodoo at Skipper's expense, and her very description bristles with cutting consonants and the hiss and smack of menace: "Slacks. Canary yellow slacks. Soft thick canary yellow slacks tight at the ankles, and binding the long thighs, binding and so tight on the hips—yellow smooth complicated block of flesh and bone—that she could only force the tips of her long fingers into the slits of the thin-lipped and slanted pockets. Slacks and square white jaw and great nest of black hair strapped in an emerald kerchief" (59). Tremlow, the tattoo artist, and Miranda are all threats and edges; meanwhile, Skipper is consistently depicted in terms of tender, unguarded flesh, ripe for the vicious inscriptions a harsh environment regularly imposes (Chénetier 168–70). Skipper's stitching together of a second skin, however, not only suggests protection and healing, but it also affords elasticity that soon seems as natural as the original it covers.

As Skipper tries to retool himself through rendition, revising cowardice as courageousness, cloyingness as reliability, lugubriousness as grace, he laces his fiction—a second skin of altered conditions superimposed upon his past—with all sorts of yoked opposites, such as "aggressive . . . serenity" and "locomotion of peace," which further illustrate the suspensive quality of his tale (Robertson 433–34). These are rehearsals, if you will, for the principal oxymorons of artificial insemination and the wandering island, whose unstable solutions Skipper is devoted to keeping intact but unsettled, thereby accommodating his contradictory desires for stable moorings and freedom from contingency.

In other words, Skipper assumes the privilege of discretion against a rigidified truth, whether that truth be discovered or created. Hawkes's desire to "hold in balance poetic and novelistic methods in order to make the novel a more valid and pleasurable experience" can be compared to the uneasy mixture of imaginative and empirical impulses that contend in *Second Skin* ("John Hawkes: An Interview" 149). It is significant to note that this is in fact a balance that Hawkes means to effect, rather than a prelude to the domination of a new regimental interpretation of experience by the imagination. As Robert Scholes argues, Hawkes chooses "valid" over "real" or "true" as his litmus test for the work of art because he abjures absolutes; he is after "a less comprehensive kind of accuracy, suggesting an internal coherence rather than a correct statement about something outside the work itself" (70). Skipper, too, despite his claims to the contrary, would forestall "dead reckoning" as a narrative aim. Even as he denies the possibility that his record is trivial or defeatist, he shuns any formula that will contradict it absolutely: "Say, rather, that it is the chronicle of recovery, the history of courage, the dead reckoning of my romance, the act of memory, the dance of shadows. And all the earmarks of pageantry, if you will, the glow of Skipper's serpentine tale" (Hawkes, *Second Skin* 162). For Skipper romance by its very nature countermands static readings: dead reckoning is reckoning with death, then reckoning as death, the dead end of knowledge, whereas romance is an island that wanders, after all. Therefore, he immediately undermines the effect of phrases like "history of courage" and "dead reckoning of my romance" with "the act of memory," which emphasizes the active, fluid nature of his own brand of historical enterprise, and "the dance of shadows," which further attenuates his findings. The stalwart quality of "Say, rather" is exchanged for the tentativeness of "if you will."

Skipper's island reign, then, is no resolution; it is no Byzantium where his loose ends are finally tied into "the artifice of eternity," despite his frequent heralding of the "sweet timeless time" he enjoys there (171).[4] (Yeats's frozen artifice more accurately recalls the "desperate honeycomb of dead time" or "the glazed eye of time"—stagnant versions of his mortifying experience which Skipper condemns for their lack of malleability, their immunity to imaginative manipulation.) Nor is Skipper a Prospero with his prowess guaranteed, his Miranda in tow, his Calibans fixed and at bay. Instead, his status on the gentle island is consistently questioned. Sonny openly urinates against the side of his "chief's" hut, for example, and Catalina Kate, who busies herself by washing out Sonny's drawers, may have betrayed her master sexually, however less dire the consequences of treachery here may be than they were on the *Starfish*.

This is no final resting place for contrarieties but, instead, a "grove of perpetuation" (169), where realities proliferate; it is a domain of the perpetually in-process which brings to mind Robert Coover's island of endless invention in his story "The Magic Poker." "I wander the island, inventing it," begins Coover's narrator, embarking upon the page like a pioneer and, like Skipper, conditioning his art to accept the competing requirements of an open design: "I impose a hot midday silence, a profound and heavy stillness. But anything can happen" (20).

In much the same way Skipper discovers on his island groundedness without commitment, and our reading experience parallels this inconclusive conclusion as we "experience the conditions of meaning if not the meaning itself" of the novel's complex proceedings (Robertson 450). Here his "brand"—the tattooed name of his dead son-in-law—is bleached by the sun, but it is not eliminated completely; the ghastly blackbirds of Miranda's island are redeemed somewhat as "night angels" attending Skipper, Sonny, and the native women during their "fête with the dead" even as they retain their malignant allusiveness. Throughout the novel Hawkes teases us with image patterns that resist the consistency that their prominence implies, or he seduces us with conventional symbols only to complicate or reverse their associations (for instance, in his corruption of "green," typically suggestive of fertility and growth, by connecting that color with the tattoo, Fernandez's guitar, the muck surrounding the *Peter Poor*, and other festering, forbidding images). Skipper's second skin, therefore, is not a hermetic seal but, rather, a selectively permeable filter; Skipper is an editor who revises more than he retracts.

The concept of a wandering island—to be sure, many readers suspect that this place is entirely a product of Skipper's imagination—offers permanence and portability, while it requires little more than sublime indolence from its monarch. An elastic pastoral, a fluid idyll: Skipper's paradise refines and locates his competing penchants for uninhibited motion (the artist's creative freedom, the editor's authority) and for solid footing (a staked claim in a sea of nebulous, yet disturbing, memory).[5] As Gertrude Stein explains while reminiscing about "getting acquainted with pictures," "This sounds as if it might have been an end of something as being in the nature of a solution but it was not it was just something going on" ("Pictures" 77–78). In this forever-inchoate domain Skipper's ineffectuality is without consequence. He may fail to wrestle a monstrous lizard off of Catalina Kate's back, but it eventually slides harmlessly away; his sexual vagueness throughout the novel, which is still implied by the steer that bears his name on this island, is trumped by his role of artificial inseminator—a potent potentate, indeed! Never mind that "his" son by Catalina Kate favors Sonny's coloring more than his own or that, when Kate busies herself by washing out Sonny's drawers, we wonder what other intimacies they have shared. Skipper is satisfied to have found a place where his ignorance is bliss.

The concluding scene of *Second Skin* finds the cozy population of the wandering island presiding over what at first appears to be a symbolic reconciliation of the contrarieties that have caused Skipper such difficulty throughout the novel.[6] The birthday celebration in the graveyard is a kind of refutation of the dismal heritage of this mortician's son and a late vindication of the deaths he has witnessed, as well as an ironic employment of Wallace Stevens's pronouncement in "Sunday Morning" that "death is the mother of beauty" (l. 63). Whereas Skipper's cello playing outside the door failed to stop his father's suicide, the art he practices now is soothing, even though the imagination from which it springs seems somewhat frail and insubstantial against the burden of death and regret. It is positive, yet indistinct, like "the light of a candle" sustained against "my loud wandering night" (210). If the tattoo artist's productions were bloodlettings, his punctures "fast as the sting of artificial bees" (19), the efforts of the artificial inseminator, which are provisional, take root less painfully. On Skipper's island silhouettes glide through a casual dimness, and every venture bears fruit.

The last lines of *Second Skin*, therefore, constitute a parting duplicity. Taken at face value, they confirm the perception that Skipper has found sanctuary in a fortress of the imagination and has drawn up the gate against an injurious, time-bound world: "Because now I am fifty-nine years old and I knew I would be, and now there is the sun in the evening, the moon at dawn, the still voice. That's it. The sun in the evening. The moon at dawn. The still voice" (210). The "still voice" brings us full circle from the "still lover" of the novel's opening paragraph and apparently seals Skipper safely inside his artifice. Indeed, this final synthesis seems to parallel the epiphanic "still point of the turning world" described by Eliot in *Burnt Norton* (2.16), as well as Lily Briscoe's aesthetic destination in Virginia Woolf's *To the Lighthouse* (1927): "She looked at the steps; they were empty; she looked at her canvas; it was blurred. With a sudden intensity, as if she saw it clear for a second, she drew a line there, in the centre. It was done; it was finished. Yes, she thought, laying down her brush in extreme fatigue, I have had my vision" (310).

In *Second Skin*, of course, the "achievement" of the lighthouse, which is the setting for Cassandra's suicide, stands in forbidding contrast to its representation of artistic fulfillment in Woolf's novel; obviously, achievement as such cannot be countenanced. Furthermore, the vision that concludes Hawkes's novel only masquerades as a Modernist frozen vantage, all exactitude and hammered gold. For, as we have seen, vision in *Second Skin* is always beset by linguistic and psychological tensions; to equate Skipper's lush, abiding isle with, say, Yeats's Byzantium would be to dismiss these contradictions and to forget the postmodern quality of Skipper's aesthetic, which interrogates and disrupts its constructions in the name of free play. A more precise resonance may be discovered in one of Gertrude Stein's *Portraits and Prayers* (1934): "To finish a thing, that is to keep on finishing a thing, that is to be one going on finishing so that something is a thing that any one can see is a finished thing is something" ("Manguin a Painter" 54).

Raymond Federman, in his essay entitled "Fiction in America Today or the Unreality of Reality," effectively summarizes how the radical indecisiveness of someone like Hawkes's narrator may actually be understood in terms of a political creed: "It denounces the fixation of desire in language," and, by dismantling terminal, restrictive orders, works of art that derive from it may "neutralize the fiasco of reality and the imposture of history" (15, 16). Because they are both so intransigent, a fixed history and a frozen art are equally unsupportable. According to this logic, there is really only a superficial difference between the golden birds of Byzantium, "More miracle than bird or handiwork, / Planted on the starlit golden bough" (ll. 18–19), and the ragged prowler that Skipper sees framed by his bedroom window at Miranda's: "I watched a single hungry bird hang itself on the wet rising wind and, battered and crescent-shaped and angry, submit itself endlessly to the first raw gloom of day in the hopes of spying from on high some flash of food in the dirty undulating trough of a wave" (51). Like the "immobile frenzy" of the scenes in the chapter entitled "The Brutal Act" (161)—the phrase equally applies to the crystallized nightmares of his father's suicide, to Fernandez's mutilation and murder, and to the tidal trap of bodies piled upon Skipper in the *Starfish* lifeboat—this scene of arrested development suffocates him. Faced with unyielding images, Skipper feels helpless and dissociated, and he is rendered a grotesque "phantom accomplice" to the brutalities he dumbly endures (160). Much better to achieve suspension through one's own perpetual motion, like the hummingbird Skipper prizes, than to starve optionless in the grip of life *or* art.

Clearly, Skipper does not display Federman's "on to the barricades" tone, but in his own shambling manner he does neutralize the fixities both of his past and of the imagination's gilded offerings. His "That's it" merely parodies Lily Briscoe's "It was done; it was finished," and there is in that seemingly inconspicuous phrase as much self-approval and exposure of the in-the-making nature of his vision as there is a sense of completed mission. Skipper does not replace the world with his world, nor does he evacuate the past. What he does is to spread the contamination of narrative unreliability and thereby steep all events in the same haze. As the title of this chapter implies, his is no either-or division between desert of ruination and oasis of vision, no simple exchange of old scrip for new. It is still point *and* turning world together. His improbable victory in *Second Skin* is that, as the robust, laughing master of a free-floating yet dependably entrenched island, Skipper has it both ways.

II

> The human soul is an amphibian, and I have touched its sides.
>
> —Saul Bellow, *Herzog*

Like John Hawkes, her onetime mentor, Marilynne Robinson is a verbal impressionist whose voluptuous, often hallucinatory prose style similarly softens the knots that situate and stabilize the realistic novel.[7] The title *Housekeeping* (1980) may designate a common stay against confusion—the maintenance of domestic symmetries—but Robinson's novel reveals that, just as the Foster house is founded on floodwaters and just as the entire town of Fingerbone, Idaho, rides unsteadily on the lip of a glacier, so too are the trappings of control which housekeeping connotes thwarted by example upon example of transience and perishability.

In fact, terms like *housekeeping* and *household* are under implicit indictment throughout the novel, whose prevailing images deny the possibility of such security. The Foster family is built upon a shifting, shadowy foundation. At the heart of *Housekeeping* is a host of fundamental, and occasionally sensational, departures. Ruth's grandfather, Edmund Foster, ends fantastically and unobserved when his train leaves the tracks one night and plunges into Lake Fingerbone "like a weasel sliding off a rock" (6), where his mystery persists beneath the glassy, impenetrable surface. Ruth's mother, Helen, commits suicide with silent deliberation, driving a borrowed car off a cliff as though completing the day's last errand. Sylvia, the widowed grandmother, having learned long ago "that love was half a longing of a kind that possession did nothing to mitigate" (12), treats Edmund's death like a defection from the virtues of ordinariness and domesticity, "and she whited shoes and braided hair and turned back bedclothes as if re-enacting the commonplace would make it merely commonplace again" and heal the breach the way the lake itself closed after the derailed train (25); regardless, after her own death the "habits and patterns and properties" that constituted her turn liquid (27), her assets and accomplishments proving as miscible as her husband and daughter, who have been claimed by the lake. And when their grandmother dies Ruth and Lucille find her in a final pantomime of the presumed postures of Edmund and Helen: "It was as if, drowning in air, she had leaped toward ether" (164).

All structure is deception; each heartbeat sends its echo into the waiting void. Even the house itself, which periodically swells with floodwater and in whose humid interior, at once ark and womb, the family members ride out their days, accentuates the instability of fate and forms. Like all of the relations set within it, the Foster house is waterlogged; accordingly, Ruth's book is a water log, respectful and reflective of the impermanance it depicts. What Robinson calls "the implicit numinousness of every human object" not only validates the rapt, lyrical, meditative style of the novel (Interview by Bonetti); it also confirms the untrustworthiness of its contours and contents, all of which are subject to dissolution through the liquefaction of her prose.

The Modernist approach to these conditions might well be to erect aesthetic designs that negate, or at least deflect, the ravenous pillaging of time. Robinson herself declares that Eden represents a locus of fullness, composure, and completeness which is not compatible with existence of and in time (Interview), and the impulse to create an aesthetic realm that provides these guarantees—a Byzantium—may be seen in Lucille, "fiercely neat, stalemating the forces of ruin" (216) with her precise hair and attention to the subtleties of assimilation.

Interestingly, Lucille initially reveals a kinship of personality with the sister and aunt whom she will later repudiate. When, for example, she is wrongly accused of cheating on a history test what most provokes her is the "violation of her anonimity" (78), a response in keeping with the way Ruth and Sylvie ultimately rebel against the clinical, constrictive attentions of the sheriff and of those zealous women, credentialed by talk of salvation and sheer officiousness, who come to paw about "the labyrinths of our privacy" (182). But soon, charmed by the comforts of propriety, Lucille finds herself encamped as an intermediary between "those demure but absolute arbiters who continually sat in judgment of our lives" (104) and the stubborn oddness of her family; eventually, resentful of humiliation, Lucille embraces conventionality with a vengeance. Seeing in everything—natural and family histories alike—"its potential for invidious change" (93), she shores the trappings of decorum against ruin. The orthodoxies of fashion, grooming, and deportment represent for Lucille moral exercises; with pinking shears and polishing cloths she directs "a fury of righteousness" against the indignities of randomness and loss (217). In the tighter braid, the trimmer hem, she establishes her defiance of the erratic and the perishable and, "forever pushing, nudging, coaxing," undertakes the task of pulling her sister into some likewise "seemly shape" (123). In a final rage of rectitude Lucille forsakes her aberrant aunt and sister for the promise of a precise life with her home economics teacher. (That Miss Royce is a furtive, "rabbity" creature—a woman given to "tense slumbers" (140)—betrays Lucille's trust in someone who has made a professional reputation out of keeping house.)

It is the light of conformity, then, which Lucille casts; meanwhile, Sylvie, faithful to the implications of her own name, offers a cloak of shadows like some primal glade. *Housekeeping* rests upon a delicate infrastructure of such opposites personified by the exacting, impatient Lucille on the one hand and Sylvie, the inveterate transient, on the other. After Lucille's abandonment Sylvie's influence upon Ruth becomes more and more pronounced. Ruth is ravished by darkness. She comes to accept the evanescence of all things, even to relish "the tingling seep of water through the seams" (93). As Sylvie reminisces about vagrant acquaintances, pulls decaying treasures from her trench coat pockets, or smiles over stories in the newspaper about eccentric or misbegotten characters, Ruth feels increasingly invisible, "incompletely and minimally existent," and discovers that there is something comforting about that: "I made no impact on the world, and . . . in exchange I was privileged to watch it unawares" (105–6). Ghostliness seems a virtue, corporeality awkward and gross. When Lucille disdainfully convicts her sister of being just like Sylvie, Ruth realizes that not only were Helen and Sylvie "long and narrow women like me, and nerves like theirs walk my legs and gesture my hands" (131), but she also is given to desultory meditations, long gazes out of windows. The same legacy of oblivion rules her too.

In fact, the preponderance of the evidence in *Housekeeping* seems to confirm the anarchic quality of natural phenomena and human experience alike. Sylvie is the very personification of dispossession, and her recollections are almost exclusively of other drifters and transients whose tenuous histories compound the sense that "every soul is put out of house" (179). Dissolution is the truth of us, mocking Sylvia Foster's devotion to maintenance of the ordinary and Lucille's to the industry of the self. The grandmother's own ceremonial deference to domesticity cannot stave off the inexorability of ruin. The house's furnishings and appointments, its piano and couch like statements of principle, its bookcases heavy with almanacs and classic novels, can only deceive so far. In the end the Fosters' "holdings" are illusory:

> For all the appearance these things gave of substance and solidity, they might better be considered a dangerous weight on a frail structure. I could easily imagine the piano crashing to the cellar floor with a thrum of all its strings. And then, too, our house should not have had a second story, for, if it fell while we were sleeping, we would plummet disastrously through the dark, knowing no more perhaps than that our dreams were suddenly terrible and suddenly gone. A small house was better. It broke gracefully, like some ripe pod or shell. . . . It is better to have nothing, for at last even our bones will fall. It is better to have nothing. (159)

The very landscape, honeycombed by caves and surrounded by the shadows of the woods, is a place of magnetic peripheries ripe with mystery and the promise of concealment. Were Ruth and Lucille to plummet into the depths of the old quarry, that "great and attractive terror," "the hoboes would find us. The bears would find us. *No* one would find us" (98). Truancy from school and domestic entropy are paralleled by the black holes of Fingerbone and the persistent, spectral company of transients. *Housekeeping* submits that the strongest forces we are prey to are centrifugal, migratory, expulsive. Floods and fires assail the town so regularly that "a diaspora threatened always," while the local population seems to be given over more and more to drifters "terrifying as ghosts because they were not very different from us" (178). "Like the dead, we could consider their histories complete," says Ruth, reinforcing the congruence between those within and without the census with that dangling construction, "and we wondered only what had brought them to transiency, to drifting, since their lives as drifters were like pacings and broodings and skirmishes among ghosts who cannot pay their way across the Styx" (179). They are the human residue of "the brisk and ruinous energies of the world" (163).

The insidiousness of drifting is the appeal of oblivion; Sylvie rests serenely in its soft folds. The darkness she inhabits and personifies is not purgatory but, rather, the peace of utter relinquishment:

> Evening was her special time of day. She gave the word three syllables, and indeed I think she liked it so well for its tendency to smooth, to soften. She seemed to dislike the disequilibrium

> of counterposing a roomful of light against a worldful of darkness. Sylvie in a house was more or less like a mermaid in a ship's cabin. She preferred it sunk in the very element it was meant to exclude. We had crickets in the pantry, squirrels in the eaves, sparrows in the attic. Lucille and I stepped through the door from sheer night to sheer night. (99)

Sylvie in a house is a refutation of its connotations, a smuggler of the gloom of deep woods and silent stretches of water. Her asceticism, for all its odd trappings—her pockets riddled with debris, her penchant for signature games of crazy eights and solitaire, her preternatural stillness—has the air of "that repose of grace that is beyond willing" (Updike 248). Thus, whereas mundane chores about the house are rendered ridiculous by Sylvie's supervision, and extravagant efforts to "air out" the house demonstrate her absent-mindedness more than her diligence (85–86), uncanny episodes seem virtually ritualistic. House, kitchen, bedroom, womb: these feminine spheres of influence are based on interiority. They are vessels that must be broken in order that Ruth achieve a rite of initiation into psychic adventure; indeed, Ruth needs to assert her *right to* initiation, which the traditional male literary hero evidently has made his exclusive province, relegating the female to confinement or, in fact, defining her *as* his confinement (Ravits 653, 664).

If the Foster house is the body, endlessly weathered, its fixities undone by bloat and decay, then Lake Fingerbone is the amniotic fluid of consciousness, in which memory and desire, past and present, heritage and identity, mix beyond distinction. Sylvie and Ruth's voyage out (chap. 8) features some of the most uncompromising examples of Robinson's incantatory prose style; the contents of the plot are suspended in aqueous solution. At first, roused from sleep so early, Ruth is miserable with cold, hunger, and exhaustion: "There was nothing out there—no smell of wood smoke or oatmeal—to hint at human comfort"; she tries to fend off these sensations, "crouched far inside myself, still sleeping" (144). The revelations that await her do not disturb her sleep so much as translate it: "I walked after Sylvie down the shore, all at peace, and at ease, and I thought, We are the same. She could as well be my mother. I crouched and slept in her very shape like an unborn child" (145).

Bettina Knapp's analysis of "alchemical theory" is relevant here, for it emphasizes the transmutational capacities of water as the key to becoming "reintegrated into the primordial unity." The evolution of personality (individuation, in Jungian terms) is a movement "from a stultified, congealed, or, in alchemical language, *fixatio* life experience, to *solutio*, or the dissolution of psychological and spiritual problems through the water ritual. Such a transformative process may lead to expanded consciousness and rebirth, or to the eclipse of the ego and its annihilation" (50). Water purges as it conducts the "encrusted" ego. As Knapp argues, "In these aqueous spheres, emotions are reshuffled and obstacles liquefied, bringing about alterations of outlooks, emphases, and attitudes" (56). Consequently, the expansion of the self (and, by extension, the expression of the self in words) begins with the release of the self as a discrete entity. Robinson represents Ruth's "absorption" into Sylvie as a prelude to a new birth, which is made explicit by the image of Ruth crawling "under her body and out between her legs" as they situate themselves in the boat (146). (The boat is headed for an abandoned homestead that lies in a deep valley between mountain ridges, thereby connoting a topographical complement to the pantomime of birth which Ruth and Sylvie enact.)

In this sense, too, Ruth's expanding relationship with Sylvie and its affinities with their environment seem to corroborate Keats's distinction between his own "chameleon Poet" and the Wordsworthian "egotistical sublime": "he has no Identity—he is continually in for—and filling some other Body—The Sun, the Moon, the Sea and Men and Women who are creatures of impulse are poetical and have about them an unchangeable attribute—the poet has none . . ." (*Letters* 1:387). Keats opposes the arrogance of translating the universe to feature the ego. As set forth in his famous definition of Negative Capability, Keats prefers the capacity "of being in uncertainties, Mysteries, doubts, without any irritable reaching after fact & reason" (193), whereby the undogmatic ego surrenders to the abyss and subdues its domineering tendencies. In her wakeful passivity Robinson's heroine exemplifies this "negative sublime."[8]

The boat, like the house, is suffused with the water that conducts it, which not only suggests why Sylvie occasionally comes home with fish in her pockets but also shows this to be an adventure marked by receptivity rather than appropriation—a passive initiation to the dark world. A desultory fisher of children, Sylvie confesses her rude plot to lure them from the woods with marshmallows and crackers. So, an hour away from the dawn of the "ordinary sun" and unencumbered by Lucille's charge (147), Sylvie indulges her impulses more freely and exposes her methods to Ruth in the course of enchanting her.

Ruth likewise abjures "dawn and its excesses," preferring the baptismal vortices of "this bitter, moon-pulled lake" and the circumambient disorder left by the "rampages of glaciers" to the "enameled sky" which she relates to the fixities of heaven, "where I have always known I would not be comfortable" (149–50). For her ancestors have not, after all, been transferred to some remote eternal distance. The lake, their grace, is a restless constant. They silently heave beneath her, riding the rhythms of the water, steadying and accompanying her initiation and asserting their ghostly presence like "a music I no longer heard, that rang in my mind, itself and nothing else, lost to all sense, but not perished, not perished" (160).

Ruth thinks that she would have made a snowwoman to commemorate this passage were snow available. Unlike the barren pillar of salt which Lot's wife became, a snowwoman would represent extravagant potentialities rather than mourning, a more suitable magnet for "such wild and orphan things" rumored to inhabit the landscape; but, like the snowwoman conjured by Ruth and Lucille in the wake of Sylvie's arrival at Fingerbone (61),[9] it is an unstable configuration, an amalgam of creation and dissolution which is melting even in its making. This is the inexorability of dilapidation and decline, the surrender of "outward forms" to "the unimaginable touch of Time" described in Wordsworth's "Mutability" (ll. 7, 14) and imitated in *Housekeeping* by the rusting hinges, chinked walls, and thinning bones that predict "wholesale obliteration" and the vanity of human effort (157), which nature's treacheries are destined to undo. We discover another parallel in the "Time Passes" intersection of Woolf's *To the Lighthouse*, where corruption snuffles at the roots of things; nor are the characters spared its persistence: "no image with semblance of serving and divine promptitude comes readily to hand bringing the night to order and making the world reflect the compass of the soul" (Woolf 193). The arthritic Mrs. McNab and Mrs. Bast take up brooms and brushes against the massive tides of war, nature, and age; Lucille has also enlisted in this operation, "stalemating the forces of ruin" and carrying on the assault "in a fury of righteousness, cleansing and polishing" (Robinson, *Housekeeping* 216–17). Still, despite their industry and despite their temporary triumph over split boards, cracked plaster, and choking dust, we suspect that the incursions of chaos will finally prove irresistible: "the house, sinking, falling, would have turned and pitched downwards to the depths of darkness" (Woolf 208).[10]

The search for lost children in *Housekeeping* becomes a rescue mission for the self, but Ruth comes to realize that this, too, is betrayed by flux—the "swim and flow" of all things and all enterprises (162). Conversely, during their silent vigil at the grave site of water, Ruth's wish "utterly to be elsewhere" is granted by the inherent and universal displacement that water effects (165). Its incursions into Ruth's consciousness reveal the essential equivalence of perceiver and perceived context, and we recall Andrew Marvell's metaphor from "The Garden":

> The mind, that ocean where each kind
> Does straight its own resemblance find;
> Yet it creates, transcending these,
> Far other worlds, and other seas,
> Annihilating all that's made
> To a green thought in a green shade.
>
> (ll.43–48)

Time escapes its marked contours; images from dreams and memories integrate and lose their distinctions, so that, Ruth says, "the wreck of my grandfather's train is more vivid in my mind than it would have been if I had seen it" (166), and she can gaze into a mirror (another reflective lake) and witness the superimposition of selves—the merging of Sylvie, Helen, Sylvie, and Ruth in the solvent of shared blood. And, as they wait beneath the bridge, a train rides over them as if to reflect the drowned train of Ruth's grandfather, which lies beneath them but which is still moving in the imagination, still imminent. Ruth confesses that she would not have been surprised at that moment to see her companion step over the boat and, her dress billowing around her, slide "through rifts of moonlight into the wintering lake" (168), the way Sylvie "had leaped toward ether" at her death. For in this world elsewhere the rigging of the ordinary frays to breaking, and the boundaries that separate fact and fancy, memory and desire, solid and fluid, definition and drift, are eliminated, or revealed as a trick of the plain light of day.

Thus, the fate of the Foster family replicates that of all mankind in the Bible. After the Flood "the waters were full of people," and nothing but narration can preserve them. Still, the generations are not lost in the water but, rather, are present, like vagabonds and like Ruth's mother and grandfather, "under an altered dispensation": "Looking out at the lake one could believe that the Flood had never ended. If one is lost on the water, any hill is Ararat. And below is always the accumulated past, which vanishes but does not vanish, which perishes and remains" (172).

This netherworld synthesis, "which vanishes but does not vanish, which perishes and remains," is Robinson's version of the paradoxical image process found in *Second Skin*. Like Skipper on his wandering island, Ruth inhabits a protean, floating world; like him, she is able to fashion a narrative that, by eschewing resolution, keeps mystery alive and her angels aloft. Skipper's editing "cues" were "Say, rather" or "I prefer," and Ruth's authorial prerogatives take a comparable form: "Say there were two or three inches of hard old snow on the ground" (16), she begins a description she requires; "Say that this resurrection was general enough to include my grandmother, and Helen, my mother" (96), she muses, opening a series of propositions ("Say that . . .") whose end is to reunite her family, if only in her own words; "Say that my mother was as tall as a man" (116), she starts again to grant the lost a measure of permanence; "Say that the water lapped over the gunwales, and I swelled and swelled until I burst Sylvie's coat" (162), she imagines, proposing more in the way of wondrous alternatives than of precise explantations. As narrator, Ruth can construct and distribute better destinies, or at least less restrictive ones, and conceive of a world that Robinson elsewhere describes as "cleansed . . . of its compromising historical particularity" ("Writers and the Nostalgic Fallacy" 34). Like Skipper, Ruth softens and slips the "knots" of objective accounting.

Numerous references to "hovering" in the novel correspondingly create an atmosphere of open-endedness and stave off the foreclosure of death:

> A narrow pond would form in the orchard, water clear as air covering grass and black leaves and fallen branches, all around it black leaves and drenched grass and fallen branches, and on it, slight as an image in an eye, sky, clouds, trees, our hovering faces and our cold hands. (5)

> The water bore him [the boy who discovers Edmund Foster's train in the lake] up. He said only that smooth surface, of all the things he touched, was not overgrown or hovered about like a cloud of something loose, like silt. (8)

> After their father's death, the girls hovered around her [Sylvia], watched everything she did, followed her through the house, got in her way. (10)

> But watching Sylvie seemed very much like dreaming, because the motion was always the same, and was necessary, and arduous, and without issue, and repeated, not as one motion in a series, but as the same motion repeated because here was the mystery, if one could find it. We only seemed to be tethered to the old wreck on the lake floor. It was the wind that made us hover there. (169–70)

The repetitions of motions described and of the descriptions themselves, as Ruth's sentences roll back upon themselves like waves do, further establish the sense of abeyance. All presences seem eerily insubstantial, while the absent are hauntingly real and available. Thanks to the written record before us, the dead are "at once dead and alive. Similarly, their construction and deconstruction in discourse are simultaneous" (Meese 65).

Housekeeping is all pregnant verges. In the darkness, "deprived of all perspective and horizon" (70), Ruth feels herself become nothing, then suspended in nothingness, poised. God Himself hovers—another water-walker, whose circuit of death and salvation indicates a hovering at the heart of all being. And, when Sylvie sets the house afire to escape with Ruth from the clutches of the prying world of sheriffs and truant officers and *Good Housekeeping* magazine, she leads Ruth over Lake Fingerbone, balancing on the suspended tracks, buoyed by the familiar ghosts below them (211).[11]

Housekeeping resembles *Second Skin* in that it also is situated in that slippery divide between still point and turning world. Considering an assortment of images of precarious balance—including a faith healer trying to walk across the water's surface, a horse galloping over the frozen lake, a leaf gleaming in the wind, and her Aunt Molly rescued both from ambiguity and from practicing bookkeeping—Ruth envisions a "harvest" that "would put an end to all anomaly": "There would be a general reclaiming of fallen buttons and misplaced spectacles, of neighbors and kin, till time and error and accident were undone, and the world became comprehensible and whole" (91–92). This is the artist's conventional faith in the arrival of order, which the artist deliberately imposes in lieu of such an arrival. Ruth calls it "a law of completion," which she prescribes as an antidote to the flux of experience: "For why do our thoughts turn to some gesture of a hand, the fall of a sleeve, some corner of a room on a particular anonymous afternoon, even when we are asleep, and even when we are so old that our thoughts have abandoned other business? What are all these fragments for, if not to be knit up finally?" (92). This is the domestication of misgivings and error and "misplaced spectacles," the storification of Fingerbone into a place of legible addresses, straight streets, and reliable itineraries. Enter the artist to qualify and consecrate. But, of course, the adoption of a law of completion does not come without compromise. "Ascension seemed at such times a natural law" as well (92). If completion suggests comprehension, ascension suggests whatever exceeds it; the former offers management, the latter elusiveness—but also imaginative range.

The combination results in hovering objects, suspensive personalities, and nonauthoritarian narrative. Once again William James offers a psychological confirmation of the wedding of fluidity and form by imaging the mind as a permeable bulwark in a turbulent sea of phenomena. This dual nature keeps us from being swamped by tides of perception on the one hand, but it also ensures opportunities for growth, assimilation of new data, and crucial remapping of our sensational lives on the other. In this way we can rely upon the organizing, clarifying habits of mind—specifically, the familiar fixities of words—without succumbing to petrifying stock conceptions. Or, to use James's terms, fresh "genius" protects us from the shoals of "old-fogeyism" (Ruddick, 339–40).[12]

When the Foster house collapses in flames the ashes rise; phoenix-like, Sylvie and Ruth pursue the compensations of dispossession. As the fire engulfs bundles of newspapers and magazines, a "furious ascending" is unleashed (199): "I saw the fiery transfiguration of a dog, and the bowl he ate from, and a baseball team, and a Chevrolet, and many hundreds of words. It had never occurred to me that words, too, must be salvaged, though when I thought about it, it seemed obvious. It was absurd to think that things were held in place, are held in place, by a web of words" (200). "Matter has its radiance and its darkness; it lifts and it buries," writes John Updike ("Packed Dirt" 253). In Robinson's novel burning returns things to their molecular level, making them easier to imaginatively transport and recombine. Even Ruth's language hovers: words are in one sense stolen by the artist, in another created by her; they are designed to salvage what they signify, yet they themselves require saving; they constitute a web, but they cannot hold things in place.[13]

In her diligence as narrator Ruth refuses and reverses the abandonment of her family; her devotion, however, is not at the expense of evanescence. Although Ruth supposes that "what perished need not also be lost" (124), her linguistic reclamation project is necessarily an ongoing negotiation between loss and recovery. The delights of surrender to darkness and drifting at the end of the novel compete with the possessive urgency that motivates its narrator. Consequently, *Housekeeping* concludes by respecting the dual nature of a "water log." The escape of Sylvie and Ruth from detection is a delicate journey, indeed: as they cross the bridge, feeling invisible in the enveloping night, the stars above are at once "dim as dust in their Babylonian multitudes" and "pulled through the dark along the whorls of an enormous vortex." In other words, they connote both fixity and disorder, freedom and compulsion. Meanwhile, the women must labor to maintain their footing so as not to succumb too completely to a dream of ascension and plummet. As Melville's Ishmael knew so well, there is a savage side to romantic release: aloft in the crow's nest, it is too easy to be mesmerized by the "inscrutable tides of God," whereupon one misstep, "and your identity comes back in horror. Over Descartian vortices you hover" (140).[14] The successful venturer, the successful artist, is one who acknowledges and respects the tension between ascension and completion, or substantial and sublime, which makes hovering possible.

The end is no ending. Death's dominion is really vitality at a remove. The rumor validated by the newspaper is LAKE CLAIMS TWO, but the metaphorical accuracy of the headline, in that Sylvie and Ruth have been possessed by the spirit of (and spirits in) the lake, underscores its empirical inadequacy. Indeed, "fact explains nothing. On the contrary, it is fact that requires explanation" (217), Ruth declares, impugning not only the construction of her story by local journalists but also the reliability of her own account of herself. Like Huck Finn, who had fabricated evidence of his own murder to live free of detection, Robinson's heroes elude society's attempts to bring them into custody. They take odd jobs—clerking, waitressing—whose "ceremonies of sustenance, of nurturing" (214), are undermined by the drifting that identifies and unites these women. Conversely, Ruth's solitude is not a total renunciation. We recall how Skipper's island embraced company and thereby revised a history of horrifying desertions. And, notwithstanding the legacy of Edmund and Sylvia, who were souls "all unaccompanied" (17), Ruth is not alone in her vagrancy. On the contrary, there is Sylvie, as well as the conjured presences of her ancestral past, to whose relentless currents Ruth moves.

There is also Lucille. Unfettered by either behavioral or journalistic custom, Ruth indulges in fictional alternatives instead of making inquiries into the fate of her sister. She first imagines Lucille home again—home made whole again—awaiting their return, only to find that she cannot understand the words Ruth and Sylvie utter, because they "are smothered, and their intervals swelled, and their cadences distended, like sounds in water" (217). Or she locates Lucille in a Boston restaurant, modestly exercising her desire for closure by trying with her thumb to complete the circle of a ring of water left by her glass. Meanwhile, Ruth's Lucille slips packets of oyster crackers into her handbag to feed the gulls, which suggests that she is unconsciously haunted by the ghosts of Sylvie and Ruth which arise in the involuntary gesture or pulse in the underside of the unadulterated personality Lucille has tried to craft for herself. "We are nowhere in Boston," Ruth admits, for she and Sylvie could only be spectral or irrelevant amid the gridded streets and tailored fashions; nevertheless, and despite Lucille's having put a continent between them, "There is remembrance, and communion, altogether human and unhallowed. For families will not be broken" (194).

By concluding with the "conquest" of Lucille, or at least the mitigation of Lucille's determination to extract herself from implication in her family, Ruth affirms connectedness and mutuality, even as she sounds in her book a profoundly poetic call for personal release. Separation and return constitute a kind of formal and psychological oscillation. A useful touchstone here can be found in Patricia Waugh's *Feminine Fictions*, which posits a description of women's fiction in opposition to the dominant culture of male writing in order to locate agency and historical dimension, boons that have traditionally been denied to women in literature and in society. The crucial difference, however, is that "much women's writing can, in fact, be seen not as an attempt to define an isolated individual ego but to discover a collective concept of subjectivity which foregrounds the construction of identity *in relationship*" (10). An authentic self need not be a finished, unitary one; on the contrary, it lives in shared process. Furthermore, in keeping with the overriding concept of hovering in *Housekeeping*, relationship exists *with* dispersal, change, and contingency, not by virtue of the elimination of those ruptures so as to reify an autonomous personality (Waugh 12–13).[15] Robinson gives us Ruth's emergence through her writing from Fingerbone and the trappings of convention; she gives us Ruth's mergence within her writing with her gathered ghosts.

The closing lines of the novel reinforce this duality with an image of Lucille occupying a crowded solitude: "No one watching this woman smear her initials in the steam on her water glass with her first finger, or slip cellophane packets of oyster crackers into her handbag for the sea gulls, could know how her thoughts are thronged by our absence, or know how she does not watch, does not listen, does not wait, does not hope, and always for me and Sylvie" (219). As a girl, Lucille prized anonymity as an escape from critical evaluation, but in this fabricated context her dismissal of Ruth and Sylvie cannot conceal a yearning for reconnection; the catalog of "nots" is contested by the affirmation of "always for me and Sylvie." Furthermore, her sister and her aunt are especially conspicuous in their absence, which suggests that Lucille, the most recalcitrant member of the house of Foster-Stone, is potentially available to transfiguration too. Significantly, the vision of Lucille trying to close the circle of water has been exchanged for one of trying to leave a trace of identity on the water. However refracted or frustrated this attempt to inscribe a self may be, both by the inevitable transcience of the inscription and by the negations that succeed it as the passage ends, Lucille has become another water-writer. This confirms the usurpation of her original intentions by Ruth and Sylvie, for not only do they continue to "throng her thoughts" but they also invade her behavior. If Ruth begins the novel by staking a claim to a self ("My name is Ruth"), Lucille concludes it the same way. Or, rather, Ruth makes a second, indirect claim through the fiction of Lucille she proposes. Evanescence humbles that claim, but familial continuity fortifies it. Between the equally compelling consequences of absence and presence, in compunction and celebration, dispossessed and self-possessed, the artist practices her precipitous art.

Notes

1. Tanner pursues a comparable direction in *The Reign of Wonder: Naivety and Reality in American Literature*, in which he discovers in American literature the pervasiveness of the "predilection for the strategy of the naive vision," which prefers "wonder over analysis" (11). From this perspective Hawkes's novel sustains Tanner's view of the American tradition of renunciation of a received, restrictive past in favor of present-tense imaginative explorations (14).
2. On this point we might also allude to "Jawing of Genesis," by Edwin Honig, the poet to whom Hawkes dedicates *Second Skin*. Skipper refracts what Honig calls "the thud of grim intelligence" which would have "slammed shut / The summer silence." The poem recognizes this "thud" as the inevitable, immediate result of the advent of linguistic consciousness and, hence, the ruination of paradise: "Up rose the wordy islet, / Awash with seas' first rocky stutterings."
3. An absolute, defined work of art represents a fatality for possibility. This is perhaps most evident in Hawkes's image of the "emportraited" suicide in *Adventures in the Alaskan Skin Trade*, who "thrust his head through an unfinished canvas and, wearing his rent canvas like a sumptuous ruff, shot himself in the temple" (13). More compatible with the "hovering" status of death which Skipper sustains is the death of Billy Boy in that same novel. His suicide on the tennis court is designed to preserve mystery: he is discovered "arrested in an unimaginable tableau that no one but Billy Boy himself could have created" and which is simultaneously "stunning" and "inexplicable" (321).
4. "I suffered each separate moment of my personal contribution to the obscene annals of naval history" (52), Skipper ruefully concludes. Part of the obscene

impact on him is due to the fact that separate moments can only be suffered; it requires a tapestry of timelessness to guard his scars and weather memory.

5. We recall from Greek mythology how the wandering isle of Delos offered refuge to Leto, who had been impregnated by Zeus and consequently rejected by all other communities for fear of their incurring the wrath of the betrayed Hera. As a result of this hospitality, Delos became magically anchored by undersea pillars, and what had previously been a windy, barren place was transformed into "the heaven-built isle": the birthplace of Phoebus Apollo (Hamilton 433–34). Likewise, Skipper, a contemporary if decadent sentinel of light, song, and the imagination (though conspicuously lacking Apollo's quality of self-knowledge), is redeemed on an island that flouts cartography and which prospers beneath "the golden wheel of my hot sun." (Skipper also emulates Apollo's characteristic remoteness; see Otto 64–67.) That Cassandra proves less fortunate than either Leto or Catalina Kate in locating suitable premises to accommodate her own scandalous birthing is but one of the novel's poignant ironies.
6. This reconciliation, however, is not necessarily a saving grace in Hawkes's other novels. Sybilline's "faint jazz step that kept her moving nowhere" is a prelude to disaster in *The Lime Twig* (144), in whose climax Michael is trampled by racehorses keeping a "pace so fast that it ceases to be motion" (171). Similarly, the so-called erotic triad offers a brace of invidious images which contests Skipper's implied faith in the healing power of the mobile/stationary complex: Hugh and Catherine's tour bus appears to be both agitated and mired in "the deep intestinal tug" of Illyria's excremental canal in *The Blood Oranges* (26–27); Allert senses that his ship seems now to drift, now to be becalmed, "rolling like a bottle lying on its side in a sea of oil," in *Death, Sleep & the Traveler* (2); and Papa orchestrates the "static movement" of the speeding car in *Travesty* to conclude in a deadly chaotic array (58). In these instances deferring or destabilizing devastation does not forestall its consequences.
7. In the Bonetti interview Robinson reflects on her apprenticeship with John Hawkes in his creative writing class at Brown University, as well as on the nineteenth-century American literature classes that "colonized my imagination forever." She credits Hawkes with being "very protective" of the "eccentric" elements of her prose style.
8. On the other hand, as a committed narrator, Ruth tempers her surrender with lyricism and remembrance. Keats may have been similarly conflicted. He belies his refusal of the "egotistical sublime" in the conclusion of that letter: "All I hope is that I may not lose all interest in human affairs—that the solitary indifference I feel for applause even from the finest spirits, will not blunt any acuteness of vision I may have" (388). His concern about sacrificing "human affairs" for ethereal ones and for the maintenance of "acuteness of vision" against the potential obscurances of "solitary indifference" reveals the artist to be less detached and more purposive (read: egotistical) in his percep-

tions than the dictates of Negative Capability might lead us to believe. In this light, Keats, who numbers among his opinions that the poet cannot have fixed opinions and who locates poetry in the paradox of "half knowledge" (194), is another hoverer. For a discussion of "the flowing texture of sensations and speculations" at the heart of Negative Capability, see Stuart M. Sperry 61–70.

9. Invoking Lot's wife and transforming that mythic figure into the snowwoman enables Ruth to restore her mother symbolically, then to forgive her indifference and "orphaning" of her, and ultimately to reconcile herself to abandonment. Martha Ravits defines this episode as another exhibition of the female hero's "courageous subjectivity in the face of isolation and neglect" (657–59).
10. It is also instructive to contrast Woolf's and Robinson's characterizations of darkness. Unlike Sylvie, whose darkness is seductive and accessible. Woolf's Mrs. Ramsay is relieved to imagine herself as "a wedge-shaped core of darkness" (95), which implies inviolability. Hers is an isolated, insulated essence that evades the demands of children and which contradicts Lily Briscoe's contention that intimacy is knowledge (79).
11. Elizabeth A. Meese conceives of Sylvie as a personification of this concept of hovering: "Sylvie is 'love': an elusive essence, drifting away—there and not there, always about not to be. She is that which can only be desired but never possessed" (60).
12. Lisa Ruddick expands on James's notion of qualified vulnerability in a way that neatly anticipates Robinson's treatment of water imagery in *Housekeeping:* "Language is a solid fortress in a fluxional universe. These moments of intellectual 'renovation,' when old labels are transformed by novel sensations, are for James a sort of rupture or flooding of the petrified mental structure. They represent a brief disintegration of the mind as it is inundated with experiential currents that habit has suppressed" (340–41).

    In "Writers and the Nostalgic Fallacy" Robinson herself complains of being fettered by the old "language of present experience," which "is so charged with judgment and allusion and intonation that it cannot be put to any new use or forced along any unaccustomed path. The story it wants to tell I do not want to tell" (34).
13. Sylvie's "bouts of zeal and animation" occasionally take the form of cleaning house and reining in dubious habits, but, when she considers getting Ruth a "permanent" (201), the pun once again deflates the possibility of finally believing in stability. Actually, Sylvie is most deliberate in her supervision of the burning of the house's contents. It represents, to be sure, a meticulous evacuation.
14. The doctrine of Fast-Fish versus Loose-Fish in *Moby-Dick* can also be profitably related to Robinson's novel. Possession of ideas, objects, even of self is a problem in both books, and it is easy to be deluded that what is in fact rather elusive is reliable and secure. "What to the ostentatious smuggling verbalists

are the thoughts of thinkers but Loose-Fish? What is the great globe itself but a Loose-Fish? And what are you, reader, but a Loose-Fish and a Fast-Fish, too?" (334).

15. Waugh's opening chapter, "Postmodernism and Feminism: Where Have All the Women Gone?" (1–33), provides a lucid examination of this new feminist subjectivity, which favors collectivity over solipsism and subjugation (the tendencies of the modern male orthodoxy). For an absolutist reading of *Housekeeping* which treats its conclusion in terms of the complete divestiture, see Mallon (103–4).

3

FICTION BY CYCLES

Lives of the Poets and *The Things They Carried*

I

Fragments are the only form I trust.
—Donald Barthelme,
"See the Moon?"

—WRITER CONFESSES THAT HE NO LONGER TRUSTS FRAGMENTS
Trust "Misplaced," Author Declares
DISCUSSED DECISION WITH DAUGHTER, SIX
Will seek "Wholes" in Future, He Says
—Donald Barthelme, quoted in *The Life of Fiction*,
by Jerome Klinkowitz

Among theories of traditional literary genres none have been so preoccupied with matters of packaging as those focusing on the short story. Questions of how big a fiction and in how big a box remain at the heart of the discussion of the nature and future of the short story.[1] What distinguishes a short story from a novel, novella, prose poem, or narrative essay? Is it size, intention, or impact that uniquely identifies the genre? When it comes to the short story the definitional thickets have yet to be cleared.

That loose amalgamation known as the short story cycle is particularly troublesome. More consolidated than merely collected, but also more intractable than integrated, the cycle is, as the term literally implies, a process unarrested. Structurally speaking, it multiplies the generic insecurity of the short story by the holistic expectations associated with "the book." In other words, the cycle foregrounds the rivalry between the short story and the novel by achieving a formal status that simultaneously betrays the discrete integrity of the former and undermines the unitarian accomplishment of the latter (Jouve 37–39). Because it pluralizes perspective and implies the insufficiency of each individual offering, resonances among the parts cannot be equated with a more rigorous conception or configuration. The tales have their symbolic, thematic, or environmental entailments, but a narrative so deployed is a futile dream of full measure. Valerie Shaw's observation that the "short story's success often lies in conveying the sense of unwritten, or even unwritable things" is magnified by the cycle format: "the story teller accepts the limitations of his art, and makes his freedom an aspect of those same restrictions" (264). Or, as one notorious fictionist sardonically puts it, " 'Fragments fall apart a lot,' Barthelme said. Use of antelope blood as a bonding agent had not proved . . ." (qtd. in Klinkowitz, *The Life of Fiction* 83).

The pertinence of this elusive form to our investigation is obvious enough, for the short story cycle automatically addresses the wavering balance between finished product and ongoing proceedings. Synthesis is always virtual, government probationary, as affinities among the stories invariably contend with the fractures. We may recall in this regard William Carlos Williams's testimony on behalf of the writings of Gertrude Stein, in which he is gratified to discover "an alertness not to let go of a possibility of movement in our fearful bedazzlement with some concrete and fixed present. The goal is to keep a beleaguered line of understanding which has movement from breaking down and becoming a hole into which we sink decoratively to rest" ("Work of Gertrude Stein" 350–51). So as not to be swallowed by the enchantments of such "a hole into which we sink decoratively," not to mention the decorous whole that is the superior reputation the novel seems to lord over the short story, we must sustain the "beleaguerment" of philosophy, form, and "line of understanding."

On the other hand, the unfettered possibilities that this passage prescribes must also include the prospect of what Jorie Graham terms (in her poem "The Geese")

> a code
> as urgent as elegant,
> tapering with goals.
>
> (ll. 1–3)

Proximate texts create internal frames; furthermore, the stories contained by a cycle constitute a sequence of complementary impulses, each one a signal flare temporarily lighting the way, enabling the reader to move as best and as far as he can before the darkness returns. If progress is uncertain, juxtaposition at least establishes the conditions under which progress may be made. In short, although a spirit of agnosticism pervades the short story cycle—context vies with nontext, and the ruptures are as telling as the occupying narratives—there is also the effort to supersede what the artist dreads most: in the words of Samuel Beckett, "the incoercible absence of relation" ("Three Dialogues" 21).

The formal features of this paradox are intrinsic to the short story cycle, whose arrangement sustains an alternation between "bumping and the ensuing binding" of its component parts: "Within the context of the sequence, each short story is thus not a completely closed formal experience. Each successive apocalypse in some fashion prepares us for the next, shedding light on the compact worlds to follow" (Luscher 148). The "recalcitrance" that Austin M. Wright locates in individual short stories is compounded in the cycle, in which obstructions to a totalized vision now include gaps between stories and shifts in settings, characters, and tone among them, not to mention the separate obligations of each piece to stand alone. The disclosure of closure, as it were, depends upon a faith in wholeness and hook-to-eye unity as a narrative guarantee and as an evaluative standard. This is shaping principle as structural legislation, and Wright debunks it, contending that our perception of a reigning form is actually "an illusion of form, a conviction that we are in the process of discovering a form, a belief that further contemplation or rereading will enable us to find a comprehensive principle of coherence." But conviction is not what we perceive. "It is better, therefore, to regard the form of a work not as a fully realized entity but as an emergent hypothesis of reading" (Wright 116). The effect of the cycle is not only to further impede hypothetical activity but also to further manifest its presumptuousness and its contingencies.

Two contemporary short story cycles, E. L. Doctorow's *Lives of the Poets* (1984) and Tim O'Brien's *The Things They Carried* (1990), treat the tension between generic identities and between authorized account and anti-authoritarian realities with special prominence. Issues of closure in the short story, as charted by critics such as John Gerlach and Susan Lohafer, typically originate from a priori assumptions about our sensing, or mandating, the imminence of the end.[2] According to this logic, as the story progresses, the imminence of the end exerts detectable pressures—a summative funneling toward insight, or at least toward formal composure. Doctorow and O'Brien stubbornly defer that purposive destiny for narrative by pocking their books with recursions, ellipses, detours, misalliances, and misgivings that illustrate the unenforceability of design. We are encouraged by potentialities that continually go begging. The succession of stories in each volume may indeed reveal "larger unifying strategies that transcend the apparent gaps between stories" (Luscher 150), but only insofar as revelation includes the stipulation that this transcendence affords a more comprehensive view of those gaps. It does not heal the breaches. We might say, instead, that each story is an altered strategy for surrounding a truth that cannot be outflanked in the end. The writer finds that the same static jams all frequencies.

But in reading these volumes it is imperative that we not confuse them with would-be linear novels in need of repair. Both *Lives of the Poets* and *The Things They Carried* were not retrospective arrangements of stories written on separate occasions; rather, they were originally conceived as cycles. Doctorow and O'Brien each hit upon a structural method that accommodates conviction and disclaimer simultaneously.[3]

"I believe you have to reinvent fiction with each and every book," declares E. L. Doctorow, a writer whose projects defy predictability. "You've got to take the conventions and break them down, reconstitute them" (qtd. Blades 13). For Doctorow the range of fabrication is increased by mutual adjustments: history is fictionalized and fiction historically fortified. Each of his novels is a unique assimilation of and challenge to the deeds and data of experience; and, whatever their respective ingenuities of style may be, each proposes an inevitable interdependence between fact and fiction, between history and how history is rendered. "I am thus led to the proposition," Doctorow concludes, "that there is no fiction or nonfiction as we commonly understand the distinction: there is only narrative" ("False Documents" 231).

By extension there is no knowing apart from the attendant apparatus of storytelling. This is simultaneously a liberating and anxiety-provoking situation for Doctorow's narrators, who are responsible for creating the realities they relate. One thinks of Blue in *Welcome to Hard Times* (1960) spending his waning resources on some presumed posterity as he marks down in his ledgers the catastrophic story of the town, all the while apologizing for the fitfulness of memory or castigating himself for the insufficient, and probably unredemptive, nature of "talk": "In my limits, taking a day for a day, a night for a night, have I showed the sand shifting under our feet, the terrible arrangement of our lives?" (199). If language can control anything, is Blue artist enough to do so reliably? And, if language is just another pinched-out claim in this unforgiving wilderness, is Blue's narrative any more than a delirious obsession? "And it scares me more than death scares me that it may show the truth," he reflects at the close. "But how can it if I've written as if I knew as I lived them which minutes were important and which not; and spoken as if I knew the exact words everyone spoke? Does the truth come out in such scrawls, so bound by my limits?" (210)

The Book of Daniel (1971) similarly complains that the price of coherency is falsification.[4] Because the government purveys illusion so as to reinforce a blindly patriotic faith in the American Dream, the artist must struggle against succumbing to the anesthetizing effects of an officially sanctioned manipulation of history or else die from "a failure of analysis" (*Book of Daniel* 317). As Doctorow proclaims in "False Documents": "There is a regime language that derives its strength from what we are supposed to be and a language of freedom whose power consists in what we threaten to become. And I'm justified in giving a political character to the fictive and nonfictive uses of language because there is conflict between them" (217). Unfortunately for Daniel Isaacson, whose parents had been singled out for victimization during the cold war paranoia of the 1950s, it is almost impossible to decipher with confidence reality from exploitative tamperings with reality. A would-be "little criminal of perception" (44), Daniel may well be a prisoner of a crusade to rewrite history rather than reveal it. Perception is both aesthetically and politically consequential, but the welter of propaganda and manifestos, personal memories, research material, private interviews—the general information overload—tends to obstruct his view.[5] Daniel can barely recognize his parents in the revolutionary fervor of the 1960s which resuscitates the Isaacsons as precursors, nor can he escape the suspicion that his desire to discover the conspiratorial plot against his family may have led him into a plot making of his own which is no more trustworthy (a particularly insiduous form of complicity). Even if Daniel manages to refute the charge that writing his book is politically illegitimate when compared to other more extreme strategies of protest, he cannot dismiss the feeling that narrative has its own priorities, which champion the truth of design over the design of truth.

Worse, a closed account is the province of the very "sanctioning authorities" against whom Daniel harbors his suspicions and whose institutionalized accounts of historical events motivated Daniel's exploration in the first place. In the end he cannot choose among several conclusions to his book, for everything is ultimately more plausible than convincing.

A rampant dreamer prey to the seductions of the very structures that shackle him, the Doctorow narrator perpetually consults his own motives and questions his own adequacy. When he does happen upon the consolations of causal sequence, narrative closure, lines of plot like underground cables, he regards these as pseudostructures—the enticements of reigning political forces or of literary habituation—and resists complicity. In other words, continuity is a convenient misapprehension of the world; coherence is a lie of fiction. And yet, even if questions of epistemology contaminate the narrative, because personal and aesthetic legitimacy are thoroughly interrelated, the questions must be asked. Or, as it is put by

Ralph Ellison's Invisible Man, who is something of a precursor to Doctorow's narrators by virtue of his book-long concern with creating private identity while avoiding preconceived systems that threaten to absorb him: "To be unaware of one's form is to live a death" (6).

In *Lives of the Poets* Doctorow explores the inevitability and the necessity of imaginative imposition. These "six stories and a novella" do not constitute a novel so much as a blueprint for a novel that cannot be more than tentatively proposed; they represent a series of approximations, as engineered by Jonathan (who appears undisguised by the fictions he concocts only in the first story, "The Writer in the Family," and in the novella that titles the volume). Jonathan tries to "authorize" himself through the telling of stories that exercise various strategies for consolidating and establishing his distance from life's hard facts. Narration—specifically, the several fictional postures he adopts—affords Jonathan a qualified immersion in the world. To remain both objective and responsible, to sustain the integrity of the fictional project without avoiding the complications and contradictions of the events one addresses, to make connections without sacrificing authenticity—these are the tasks that make the act of artistic witness so problematical, and they are always predominant concerns of *Lives of the Poets*.

In "The Writer in the Family" Jonathan remembers how, urged to the deception by his aunts, he undertook the psychological, moral, and artistic challenge of protecting his decrepit grandmother from the news of his father's death by writing her letters that presumably came from Jonathan's father himself (the pretense being that he had moved to Arizona for his health). By accepting this charge, Jonathan acquiesces to "the manner of that side of the family of making government on everyone's behalf" (4); moreover, the incorporation of his father's voice into his writing proves less a means of keeping the man alive than a grotesque refusal to bury the dead. Although he silently accuses his mother of masochism for accepting a part-time job at the hospital where his father's illness had been diagnosed, Jonathan is the greater culprit. A sounding board for the antagonisms of his mother and his aunts against one another, a buffer against their complaints and recriminations, Jonathan places the highest priority on keeping the peace: "I . . . rationalized the snubs and rebuffs each inflicted on the other, taking no stands, like my father himself" (8).

Jonathan is soon possessed by the man he impersonates. He shivers in the dead man's suit, which his steadfastly practical mother wants to alter to fit him; he dreams of the living corpse taking up residence with him.

Soon he begins to realize that the conspiracy of letter writing is not really designed to calm his grandmother, who is too diminished to know the difference, but, rather, to control him, as his father himself was controlled. Instead of doing his father honor, Jonathan is duplicating and perpetuating his implication into family service (13). Thus, Jonathan writes a final letter in which his father confesses his dying. Art is redeemed, and it redeems the artist; he is able to exorcise his father's ghost. The writer in the family transforms himself into the writer *of* the family, and suddenly Jonathan is granted a revelation: "I thought how stupid, and imperceptive, and self-centered I had been never to have understood while he was alive what my father's dream for his life had been" (17).

Having freed the man, Jonathan is able to objectify him. We are reminded of the conclusion of *Ragtime* (1974), in which another dead father is eulogized as a failed explorer: "He arrives as the new place, his hair risen in astonishment, his mouth and eyes dumb. His toe scuffs a soft storm of sand, he kneels and his arms spread in pantomimic celebration, the immigrant, as in every moment of his life, arriving eternally on the shore of his Self" (368). The parallel goes beyond two failed dreamers, one a man killed aboard the *Lusitania* and the other leaving behind a miniscule pension from his naval service; just as it is at this late juncture that the Boy reveals himself to be the narrator of *Ragtime*, so it is now, when his father has been granted the right to die on his own terms, that Jonathan begins to achieve a more aesthetically conscionable narrative identity—one whose postures are always plural, always deposable.

The next five stories in *Lives of the Poets* employ a variety of narrative guises, as though the artist were engaged in underground testing. "The Water Works" is a first-person account of a detective who, tracing the dark figure of an unidentified "captain" through the convoluted city water works building, is arrested by the tragic discovery of a drowned child who had apparently plunged to his death into the reservoir and been trapped at the sluice gates. The brief tale concludes with considerations reminiscent of Joyce's "The Dead" (1916): "I went back in and felt the oppression of a universe of water, inside and out, over the dead and the living" (24). The captain is forgotten; instead, the narrator wonders at the ritualistic indifference to their work of the men who salvage the body, for it is directly opposed to the narrator's own efforts to know and possess the event. This characteristic is reinforced by his referring to the captain he had been pursuing as "my black-bearded captain," of whom he had spoken as a secret sharer of sorts: "I was sure he knew of my presence.

Indeed, for some days I had sensed from his actions a mad presumption of partnership, as if he engaged in his enterprises for our mutual benefit" (22).

What those mysterious enterprises are is never revealed, for the more prominent concern here is the continuation of the development of a narrative stance—the writer's toward his fiction, as well as Jonathan's toward his father (the unattainable captain). Guilt seems to instill conflicting motives: a desire to capture (or embrace) the subject, coupled with a reluctance to inhibit the freedom and fullness of mystery that accompanies the subject.

Similarly, the complex charge of being an adequate, conscientious witness is central to "Willi," a story in which a boy's exultation over feeling at one with nature on a marvelous spring day is nightmarishly corrupted by his seeing his mother ("on the straw and in the dung . . . a reddened headless body") having sex with his tutor. When he had been in touch with nature's pure pleasures Willi had been, in his words, "aware of my being as the arbitrary shape of an agency that had chosen to make me in this manner as a means of communicating with me" (28); now his role of intuitive medium takes on new and serious complications. Feelings of betrayal—as a son and as a representative of nature itself—are mingled with a sense of triumph, for the artist/voyeur has seen much. Willi is understandably distressed by the fact that only he seems to have been affected by that cataclysmic scene, by the "universal windy roar" that resolved itself into his mother's treachery (28). (One thinks not only of the drowning of the boy in the previous story but also of Faulkner's Quentin Compson in *The Sound and the Fury* [1929] trying to keep the "loud world" at bay.) Surrounded by the adults who constitute an "unholy trinity of deception and ignorance" (31), and stifled by the manufactured composure of his mother, father, and tutor in the face of his intolerable knowledge, Willi traduces his mother to his father.

Therefore, the story is a confession of Willi's own participation in the mechanics of betrayal and, hence, a counterpart to the conspiratorial letter writing of the opening story. As do many young boys, Willi had imagined his father to be a mythic presence, "the god-eye in the kingdom, the intelligence that brought order and gave everything its value" (32); while he suffers from having engineered his father's fall from eminence, Willi magnifies his own powers by having slain a Goliath. (Indeed, as his horror mixes with lust at the thought of his mother's adultery, he completes the Freudian wish by destroying the father.) Willi's father had been scornful of society and its expectations, and he had lived on their estate "in the pride of the self-constructed self" (33). Willi deconstructs that arrogant removal from the world. The father wreaks a violent revenge against his unfaithful wife, and Willi is torn between approval and protective fury. "All of it was to be destroyed anyway," he concludes, "even without me" (35). The narrator notes that this was in 1910; war, age, and forgetfulness would have eventually plunged all of them into the same indistinguishable demise. Still, he keeps witness and takes responsibility. It is an example of a boy's growth into manhood and a guilt-ridden writer's maturation into artistry.

The next three stories in the volume all have to do with the theme of dereliction, and in this sense they are preludes to the culminating novella, in which "the mortal rush to solitude" is most expansively demonstrated (89). "The Hunter" is the story of a teacher who hopes to foster in her young pupils a sense of wonder and of the world's possibility, but who finds few encouraging prospects in her town, which is consistently characterized in terms of inertia, emptiness, and desolation. Although the teacher displays a genius for turning even the musty school into a waiting adventure (she tells them they are a lost patrol "looking for signs of life" in the caves of a distant planet as they follow her through the deserted building), her world remains stubbornly unprepossessing. Moreover, the children themselves are irredeemable: "She has been here just long enough for her immodest wish to transform these children to have turned to awe at what they are" (40). Movies, valium, the beery men of the town all contribute to the slow wash of despair she endures, and the story concludes with the teacher drawing the children around her for a photograph, as though desperately shoring her fragments against the diminishment that plagues her.

Morgan is also suffering from isolation in "The Foreign Legation." His divorce triggers a painful exploration of his failures to connect with other people, and his commentary has the tone of an autopsy: "He knew there was nothing to keep him from changing his life, but staying on suited his sense of himself as someone waiting" (54); "He sincerely believed that his house was not lived in and that it needed to appear otherwise to passers-by" (58); "I am the lucky one chosen for my lack of consequence" (58). In short, Morgan barely occupies his own house. He tries to summon a little vitality from lascivious daydreams, but they merely emphasize his peripheral relationship to the world and the guilt he feels for having divested himself of his family. The provisional nature of his contacts is reminiscent of that described by the narrator of William Gass's "In the Heart of the Heart of the Country" (1968): "We meet on this window, the world and I, inelegantly, swimmers of the glass; and swung wrong way round to one another, the world seems in" (196). Voyeurism exposes the poverty of imagination; it also questions the principles behind the artist's remove (paring his fingernails, in Joyce's phrase, being the least of his trespasses).

When the climactic event of "The Foreign Legation" occurs—an explosion at a foreign legation which apparently claims schoolchildren among its victims—it seems an outward manifestation of the implosions Morgan has been enduring behind closed doors. Thus, he feels implicated by the tragedy, even imagining himself to be responsible for it, but he is crediting his own effects on the world too exorbitantly. We might say that Morgan is desperate to be plot worthy. But reversing the "diplomacy" of detachment remains forbidding to one whose relationship to the world has been so severely qualified.

"The Leather Man" expands the symptom of frayed contacts with the world beyond isolated cases to designate a separate species of contemporary estrangement. Ranging from hermits and street people to prisoners and astronauts, Leather Men are explorers of the outcast state; they have either been discarded by society for being superfluous, or—and this is the more threatening possibility, for it indicts those of us who hold fast to the communal matrix—they opt out, turning escape into an art form in the manner of Houdini in *Ragtime*. Our narrator is some sort of surveillance man in the employ of a governmental agency, and, as his official breakdown of the phenomenon progresses, he becomes increasingly anxious about the impenetrability of the people he classifies, dockets, and interrogates. The phenomenon will not be possessed through the data it affords; the proliferation of these Leather Men suggests a conspiracy of solitude. They are artisans of private order.

> But say you are some hapless fellow, you can't keep a job, the wife nags, the children are vicious, the neighbors snigger. Down in your basement, though, you make nice things of wood. You make a bookshelf, you make a cabinet, sawing and planing, sanding, fitting, gluing, and you construct something very fine, you impose that order, that is the realm of your control. You make a bigger cabinet. You make a cabinet you can walk into. You build it where nobody will watch you. When it is done, you walk inside and lock the door. (70)

If the writer justifies his detachment on the grounds of improving the reliability of his perceptions, the Leather Man represents the point at which detachment is its own justification. Whether it be due to "an infrastructure of layered subversion" or "a rearrangement of molecules" (74), the threat that the alien and alienated personify is a challenge to accepted faiths, conventions, and duties. Our narrator's agency belongs to an invisible network—media, government, advertising, and all the purveyors of language who, like "The Writer in the Family," sell out their principles to keep the peace—whose mission it is to patrol our responses and program the significance of our experiences for us. Like the nameless denizens of *Housekeeping*, Leather Men are shapeless people, and the closer the narrator tries to come to them, the more amorphous they become; ironically, one must maintain a discreet distance from their disturbing detachment to manage to see it at all. It is no longer just one troubled child, one harried teacher, one divorced father; it is a plague of dissociation that even fiction cannot pretend to fathom.

The novella-length title piece extends the malaise to implicate observer and observed alike. Our narrator is a writer who has just turned fifty in a Greenwich Village garret, and from that vantage point he recapitulates the fate of past hopes and contemplates the likely demise of future prospects. Moreover, this writer—it is Jonathan emerged from behind his fictional stand-ins—speaks for a whole collection of writers who populate "Lives of the Poets," all of whom endure personal crises of faith in the legitimacy of their profession. A publication party is an opportunity to trade examples of suffering, frayed commitments, and other symptoms of paralysis. Thus, even the writers, the privileged witnesses, have started to succumb to the "creeping ruin" of contemporary urban life (81). The antennae of the race are riddled with static—"I walk the streets like a vagrant, I've got this stinging desolation in my eyes" (90)—and writing seems to have declined into a mythologization of isolation. Nothing is repaired because no one is available to any complaint but his or her own.

> We are each aloof in our private beings, our cilia wigglingly alert to those closest to us because they may without warning do us harm. My skin is my border. I may read a newspaper, but I can't think, I'm conscious of them, they flow through me, the presence of impassive strangers flows through me and shoulder to shoulder, bottom halves carefully untouching, we form in the thirty seconds between stations momentary grudging community, all dissolved and reformed as the doors open, some of us jam out and new impassivities jam in. (107)

"It's life itself that seems to be wanting," the writer laments; professional impasses only imitate personal ones.

The estrangement that has ravaged the marriage between Jonathan and Angel is absolutely representative, and "Lives of the Poets" is filled with examples of the physics of disaffection: husbands and wives all retreating to solitary outposts or practicing poor substitutes for intimacy. There are parties and appointments, long talks and fervid trysts, endless provocations and dull blows that leave no mark:

> On the other hand, what could be more dangerous than twenty years of marriage, where she has the same thought a few seconds after you have it, or before; or that you tell her one day how fragile your ego is, how you keep drifting in and out of yourself and don't remember who you are supposed to be, and she tells you she has the same experience, disappearing into herself, and so the two of you have been living together all these years not sure of who you are or what you're supposed to feel, but known to one and all as the same clear couple they've always known and recognized, a flowerpot on the back of the skull may be preferable. (112–13)

Instead of love, there is the rhythm of familiar opponents stalking one another; there are also fashions and extravagant gestures, Walkman radios, shopping malls, younger lovers. Instead of purpose, there is "stroll theater," as "people cruise for the impact of themselves, it's their art form" (119). Crazies roam the streets and subways; politicians assault us, as do charitable organizations, brand names, headlines; there is a need for urban renewal, but we feel our middle age; our energies are waning, our bellies swell, and our fingers stiffen. Rumors are everywhere: a friend has reportedly moved permanently into his subbasement and padlocked the door; another is publicizing his humiliation over his wife's choice of a lesbian lover; a third has retreated into mysticism. There is the CIA to worry about. Reputation. The Russians. Reproachful children. Cancer. We pray for everything, and we are too jaded to believe.

The writer does not flinch from his visions, which helps to improve his vision of himself (we remember Doctorow's Daniel announcing that he would undertake the aesthetic and psychological challenge of depicting the electrocution of his parents). Jonathan must also address the possibility, however, that he is really just trying to enlarge himself by granting his own anxieties and disconnections societal proportions. If I cannot be consequential, at least I am sensitive—this is the logic "of simple squatting accommodation" (120); all of the poets in "Lives of the Poets" are out to foster an acceptable sense of themselves, and it is predicated on the assumption that their catalog of woes constitutes Tragic Art and not self-indulgence. Still, Jonathan doubts himself. He wonders whether he has lost contact with his calling: "Oh Leo, I wanted to say, each book has taken me further and further out so that the occasion itself is extenuated, no more than a weak distant signal from the home station, and even that may be fading" (142). What has happened to the commitment to delivering "the wet shining soul"? "When am I being true to myself and when am I only doing penance?" (103).

So, "Lives of the Poets" concludes without resolution. On the one hand, the writer is a Prufrock who cannot manage more than self-consciousness. He turns his wants, needs, and fears into universal preoccupations, in the same way Saul Bellow's Tommy Wilhelm saw fit to litanize his frustrations on behalf of the throbbing urban masses:

> And the great, great crowd, the inexhaustible current of millions of every race and kind pouring out, pressing round, of every age, of every genius, possessors of every human secret, antique and future, in every face the refinement of one particular motive or essence—*I labor, I spend, I strive, I design, I love, I cling, I uphold, I give way, I envy, I long, I scorn, I die, I hide, I want.* Faster, much faster than any man could make the tally. (*Seize the Day* 115)

Or, like the alter ego of Gilbert Sorrentino who narrates "The Moon in Its Flight" (1971), only to discover that he cannot guarantee hospitable fictions for his imagined contemporary lovers, Jonathan also surrenders to the limitations of an insubstantial craft: "Art cannot rescue anybody from anything" (Sorrentino 163).

On the other hand, there is the argument that fictional and spiritual projects coincide, that the besieged self may be tutored by the exactitude and stability of prose. At the end of the novella Jonathan hoists his child onto his lap: "OK, I hold his finger, we're typing now, I lightly press his tiny index finger, the key, striking, delights him, each letter suddenly struck vvv he likes the v, hey who's writing this? every good boy needs a toy boat, maybe we'll go to the bottom of the page get my daily quota done come on, kid, you can do three more lousy lines" (145). "I'll never know, in the silence you don't know, you must go on, I can't go on, I'll go on" (Beckett, *Unnamable* 414). Both Doctorow's stand-in and Beckett's Unnamable swallow the paradox and urge themselves onward. But the question remains about how to interpret Doctorow's closing passage. Has Jonathan reconciled artistic and familial duties (if only temporarily) and discovered in the little boy's fascination a way to rededicate himself? Or has what should be a tranquil, innocent moment with his son been contaminated by Jonathan's self-deprecation over the value of his "daily quota"?

The problem of witness in *Lives of the Poets* arises whenever the writer inspects his materials, his motives, or his morals; this line is all wrong, and I may be more than half-creating what I perceive, and the disdainful world goes on without me, anyway. Jonathan aspires to the condition of Wallace Stevens's "Snow Man," who has the aesthetically enviable capacity to behold "nothing that is not there and the nothing that is" (l. 15); however, he risks succumbing to the condemnable situation detailed in another Stevens poem, "Chaos in Motion and Not in Motion": the hero, a

> turbulent Schlemihl,
> Has lost the whole in which he was contained,
> Knows desire without an object of desire,
> All mind and violence and nothing felt.
>
> (ll. 13–16)

Or, as Jonathan himself puts it: "I turn around and around and I'm alone. Is there a specific doom that comes of commitment? You cross some invisible limit, in logic and in faith, and a nameless universe blows through your eyes. It is possible I have crossed" (132). Doctorow's Daniel Isaacson, we recall, could not even spell *commit*, much less feel comfortable about the integrity of his methods.

In the end, trapped between fears of co-optation and ineffectuality, the writer falls back upon instinct. As Doctorow himself confides, "I always look for connections, try to synthesize and put things together" (qtd. Blades 14). But incoherence exerts an equal yet opposite force on his maneuvers. In *Billy Bathgate* (1989) one of the chief talents of Doctorow's young hero is his juggling. Billy's explanation of the challenge of keeping objects of disparate shapes and sizes aloft parallels Jonathan's handling the heft of strivings and failures in *Lives of the Poets:* "the art of the thing is in creating a flow nevertheless, maintaining the apogee from a kind of rhythm of compensating throws" (*Billy Bathgate* 25). Juggling words is also a matter of dexterity despite gravity; it symbolizes "a mind of nimble compulsion" (*Billy Bathgate* 23) which seems, as Richard Wilbur explains in his poem "Juggler," to have "won for once over for once the world's weight" (l. 30). "There is a theory, for instance, we learn in 'The Leather Man,' that the universe oscillates. It is not a steady beaming thing, nor did it start with a bang. It expands and contracts, inhales and exhales, it is either growing larger than you can imagine or imploding toward a point. The crucial thing is direction. If things come apart enough, they will have started to come together" ("Lives of the Poets" 70).

Jonathan takes his place in Doctorow's lineage of narrators who struggle to encompass, to classify, to analyze, to possess; nevertheless, it is his propensity for reconciling "coming apart" and "coming together" which makes him a legitimate "hoverer." As Beckett admonishes: "Fail again. Fail better" (*Worstward Ho!* 7). By practicing his art, Jonathan brings imagination to bear upon the world and emerges as the hero of his own tentative testimony.

II

> Not a dream-stopper, a dream-explainer, an exploiter of dreams for the crass practical ends of health and happiness, but an unsordid collector of dreams for themselves alone.
>
> —Sylvia Plath, "Johnny Panic and the Bible of Dreams"

In "Pluralism in Postmodern Perspective" Ihab Hassan proposes a "lower-case" version of authority which seems to sanction the pre-disclaimed observations of writers like Doctorow's Jonathan. Hassan locates its origin and validation in the philosophy of William James, declaring that for James "there can be only continual negotiations of reason and interest, mediations of desire, transactions of power or hope. But all these still rest on, rest in, beliefs, which James knew to be the most interesting, most valuable, part of man" (515). If the temptation of *upper*case authority leads to co-optation, the repudiation of belief undermines all allegiances and orientations altogether. In appreciating the difficulty of pursuing "continual negotiations" on the stingy pleat between the two, we might remember Robert Frost's conclusion that "there are no two things as important to us in life and art as being threatened and being saved": "What are ideals of form for if we aren't going to be made to fear for them? All our ingenuity is lavished on getting into danger legitimately so that we may be genuinely rescued" ("To Amy Bonner" 76). The moment we name this strip of delicate operations no-man's-land we are in the realm of *The Things They Carried*, a book of stories which demonstrates that war fiction is fiction under fire.

War strains all orientations to breaking. The Vietnam War, in particular, came to represent an enigmatic conflict—a conflict with enigma: "Certain blood was being shed for uncertain reasons. I saw no unity of purpose, no consensus on matters of philosophy or history or law" ("On the Rainy River" 44). Revelation's ambush, like a tripped mine, is devastating, but the ambiguity at the core of the experience is indomitable. As the soldiers know, relating a story about the war requires restraint. One has an obligation to the silence: "you can't clutter it up with your own half-baked commentary. That just breaks the spell. It destroys the magic," so you have to curb the desire "to bracket the full range of meaning" ("Sweetheart of the Song Tra Bong" 116). The assault of images is "a swirl . . . and there was no way you could process it all" ("Sweetheart" 119). Truth is identified by skepticism; it does not extinguish the "serious spooky" at the heart of things, which satisfies no speculation: "You can tell a true war story by the way it never seems to end," we learn in "How to Tell a True War Story"—"not then, not ever" (83). All that registers, finally, is pointlessness, or a point that "doesn't hit you until twenty years later, in your sleep, and you wake up and shake your wife and start telling the story to her, except when you get to the end you've forgotten the point again" ("How to Tell" 88).

The Things They Carried is the book that gets wrested from that haunted sleep twenty years later. Against the patriotic smugness of those discredited by Hemingway in *The Sun Also Rises* (1954) for being "frank and simple people" whose "stories hold together" (4), O'Brien pits bewilderment, outrage, and an uncompromising vision of the impregnability of events:

> For the common soldier, at least, war has the feel—the spiritual texture—of a great ghostly fog, thick and permanent. There is no clarity. Everything swirls. The old rules are no longer binding, the old truths no longer true. Right spills over into wrong. Order blends into chaos, love into hate, ugliness into beauty, law into anarchy, civility into savagery. The vapors suck you in. You can't tell where you are, or why you're there, and the only certainty is overwhelming ambiguity.
>
> In war you lose your sense of the definite. . . . ("How to Tell" 88)

Courage, anger, terror, prankishness, absurdity, beauty—fiction can only begin to metabolize the contradictions. The compulsion to try, however, is just as irrevocable. (There are no pure deconstructionists in foxholes.) The futility of piecing together what will not cohere is nightmarishly depicted by the meticulous gleaning of the bits of the obliterated Curt Lemon from the tree where a mine blast blew him, while another soldier sings a macabre, mirthless dirge of "Lemon Tree." Vietnam is a world beyond translation, like the incessant music coming from the land itself which cannot be bombed away, or the soaked "shit field" created when the Song Tra Bong overflows, a fen of man's and nature's filth which swallows Kiowa whole. There is no Platonic higher ground from which to take the measure of experience; there is no restoration of self or story after the war. Nevertheless, O'Brien perseveres. If the muck and stench of the shit field are the truth ("In the Field" 198), Sorrentino's discouragement notwithstanding, "this too is true: stories can save us" ("Lives of the Dead" 255).

This is the writer as necromancer pitting his art against death's sheer drop. O'Brien affiliates the fragments of *The Things They Carried* in the very form of the book: not only are characters revived from one story to the next in a circuit of vision and revision, but brief reevaluations are inserted between the longer stories to serve as connective tissues or as bridges over the anxieties that pool in the slack between chapters (a modified version of the contemplative Observation Post chapters of *Going after Cacciato* [1978]). To combat death as the cessation of self, O'Brien remembers—in Lemon's case, re-members—the men of Alpha Company, paying his respects by granting them the benefit of dimension, which the war drained through their wounds. (In "The Man I Killed" he even does this for the enemy, dwelling on a corpse he meticulously dresses with stories about who he was and who he had planned to be.) To combat death as the cessation of voice he assaults the same event from several directions, perspectives, and drafts. For example, in the four consecutive relations of the shit field episode in "Speaking of Courage," "Notes," "The Field," and "Field Trip," the last being a literal return in that O'Brien goes back to Vietnam years later with his daughter to take a ritualistic swim through the place that took Kiowa—not a cleansing but an immersion, a solemn acknowledgment of the war's perpetual claim and of the imagination's perpetual reconnaissance. Repetition creates a kind of thatching effect, as though the writer hopes to catch more sense in the tighter weave. And to combat death as the cessation of analysis, in keeping with the indictment of Doctorow's Daniel by his sister that "the failure of analysis is complicity," O'Brien never pretends that truth can finally exclude the muck that sucks you under, that even stories set in the margins of the war could ever *not* be about the war, or that "good form" could be a matter of sustaining an omniscient narrative posture when it must be a matter of confessing where "story-truth" and "happening-truth" part ways (203).[6] "Good Form" is but one of several "checkpoints" in the book where the author's credentials are displayed.

Consequently, we have the author as unauthorized spokesman who nonetheless avoids getting hung up in his own interpretive tackle. As he interrogates his own experience and his own motives for relating that experience, he realizes that menace defies full interpretation; rather, the menace is that defiance, and vision is the delineation of its impairment. The climate of *The Things They Carried* shifts from paranoiac electricity to recollection's flat cards laid on the table to present-day displacement, until, says the narrator, "all I felt was the awkwardness of remembering" because one becomes a trespasser on his or her own past ("Field Trip" 210).

Being sent to Vietnam confirms one's absorption by political machinery even as it ensures one's exile from political significance. War conspires to make one feel out of control, so he seizes upon ways of asserting control. For the soldier the principal concern is comportment: an aesthetic of impassiveness and self-possession. For the writer it is indulging the arrogance of telling stories. One recalls "Sweetheart of the Song Tra Bong," in which Mary Anne, the displaced cheerleader, who is sucked under as surely as Kiowa in the shit field into the jungle stealth and mystery of the "Greenies," ends up wearing a necklace of human tongues and dismisses her fiancé with an oblique explanation of her new impregnability and the words "You're in a place . . . where you don't belong" (120–21). Or there is O'Brien's own lesson following his absence from Alpha Company after he is wounded—as Mitchell Sanders tells him: "People change. Situations change. I hate to say this, man, but you're out of touch" (224–25). In other words, not only is the life left behind disqualified by Vietnam, as we see when Norman Bowker, home from the war, aimlessly circles the local lake as though exploring the circumference of the suicide to come, but the life of the war is also unavailable to the very soldiers it confines. Norman Bowker "was folded in with the war; he was part of the waste" (172).[7] But distance provides no surer perspective, as seen in "Love," in which an interview with the "star" of "The Things They Carried" years later yields not insights but further complications, further confusions. Ground gained in war, be it geographical, psychological, or artistic, is always shifting and contested.

But the writer will not be denied his priorities. Despite Lieutenant Jimmy Cross's plea in "Love," O'Brien divulges compromising stories about him (31); despite Norman Bowker's written request, published in "Notes," O'Brien uses his real name (179).[8] In O'Brien's hands the short story cycle is an especially restive structure, partly because his subject matter is so inherently defiant and partly because he betrays the wishes of his companions, crafting them into characters, bringing them onstage as accomplices. As we saw in Doctorow's "Writer in the Family," when he scavenges for testimony, the writer stands to recapitulate the atrocities he inhabits, a hostage of the compulsion to possess them and to give them voice ("Ghost Soldiers" 235).

War is a blur, but the proximity of death makes one "feel vivid" ("Ghost Soldiers" 219). The balance to be struck, then, is a replica in prose of the art of brinkmanship which is the key to survival in Vietnam, where, as the shit field tragically confirms, the footing is riskier than on Robinson's soggy Fingerbone. *The Things They Carried* balances discipline (the soldier's, the storyteller's) against daydreaming, mission against emotion. The book is pervaded by frontiers and edges. There is the border between the United States and Canada in "On the Rainy River," where a would-be draft dodger, precariously perched at the Tip Top Lodge, feels himself "hovering" above this crucial decision and his own assailed skin (57). There are the ragged boundaries between secured and enemy territory, brutal duty and senseless destruction, the symmetries of a battle plan and the shadow of utter pointlessness. Terror of deadly confrontation actually sharpens the craving for it, while "the stories that will last forever are those that swirl back and forth across the border between trivia and bedlam, the mad and the mundane" ("Sweetheart of the Song Tra Bong" 101). And, of course, throughout the book, past and present circle one another, predators both.

In the title story Lieutenant Jimmy Cross carries a pebble sent to him by his girl from the Jersey shoreline, "where things came together but also separated" ("Things They Carried" 9). This token of allegiance verifies absence, and even this paradox is dubiously constructed, for Martha does not discuss her motives in the letter containing it, nor is Cross assured that she loves him. Can it be a good luck charm that adds to the burden of uncertainty he already "humps" through the jungle? Like Beckett's Molloy tenderly sucking his collection of stones and devising for them a system of circulation about his person to ensure their receiving equal concern (69–74), Cross keeps the pebble in his mouth, not so much to dissolve its mystery as to become intimate with it. It is a way to maintain equilibrium in the context of obscurity.

"The Things They Carried" refers to what can be shifted but never sloughed. In addition to the weapons and ammunition, all meticulously inventoried, there are personal items that serve as hedges against death, including souvenirs, memories, and whatever else might fortify each man's dream of safety: "they carried whatever presented itself, or whatever seemed appropriate as a means of killing or staying alive" (8). They also carry grief, guilt, awe, superstition, and fear—all the psychic ballast, the pressure that is war's atomic weight. In an interview with Larry McCaffery, O'Brien declares, "Every war seems formless to the men fighting it." Then: "Humans are causal animals. We have an impulse to order events, to seek our causes and consequences" (267, 273)—so that contradiction must be borne as well.[9] They carry a massive catalog of the miseries they have seen or contributed to. "Humping it" implies bearing up and bearing under a level of necessity; it also implies making love, as indeed one must love what he is willing to bear. These are the things one carries until he dies, when he becomes one of the things they carried.

"Checking the perimeter" is not solely an investigation of the terrain but also of the limits of understanding what and why they carry; storytelling is an inspection of the texture of attention. To make the going easier, to lighten the load a little, the soldiers talk, confess, and ruminate; the effect, however, is usually to alter the burden instead of remove it. Closeting panic in tough postures and "insider" vocabulary, discussing morality in an amoral zone, sharing stale jokes like bad rations—the strategies of deflection are exhausting too. And all the while death readies itself for a preemptive strike that nothing they carry can deter or insulate against.

Accordingly, because the opacities of war are irreducible in the end, O'Brien cannot write the way he once "declotted" blood from the necks of dead pigs in a meat-packing plant ("On the Rainy River" 46). He cannot stand in the midst of all this visceral business and simply unclog the narrative apparatus. On the contrary, he must write the way the old poppa-san guides him through the mine fields on the Batangan Peninsula: "He had a tightrope walker's feel for the land beneath him—its surface tension, the give and take of things" ("Spin" 37). The writer may put his "spin" on the war to escape capitulation to terror or absurdity, but he must recognize—and foreground—the way that stories write him, selecting and defining remembrance. "Stories are for eternity," we are told at the end of "Spin," "when memory is erased, when there is nothing to remember except the story" (40).

In *Slaughterhouse-Five* (1969) Kurt Vonnegut recounts a sobering episode with a moviemaker named Harrison Starr. When Vonnegut tells him that he is writing this novel Starr asks, "Is it an anti-war book?"

> "Yes," I said. "I guess."
>
> "You know what I say to people when I hear they're writing anti-war books?"
>
> "No. What *do* you say, Harrison Starr?"
>
> "I say, 'Why don't you write an anti-*glacier* book instead?" (3)

There is more compulsion than salvation in the author's operations. The indeterminacies of war seem to proceed undeterred by his accounts.

And what if authorial search and seizure were justified and art's tenuous, poignant spell could make war and words possible for one another? As O'Brien ruefully recounts, no one knows how to listen anyway. A changed man returns home—what an odd, suspicious concept "postwar" is!—and finds it "quaint" and "remote" ("Speaking of Courage" 166); his stories offend the "brisk, polite town" (163), and they are mutually disqualified. *The Things They Carried* stalks its subject cautiously, without arrogance. The subject is war's indeterminacy but also the reader, whose conventional sensibilities must be outmaneuvered, and the blank page, that open field to be crossed in broad daylight in full view. Advancing against such hazards, *The Things They Carried* tracks the wily Other into a thousand black caves, slogs after him through dank jungles and beneath the steady rain of ordnance, courts him over the miles and years. And throughout the book, which is pledge and obsession together, the seductive otherness of the Other remains intact.

Notes

1. Recent representative discussions of how size, content, and contours of the short story genre might be mapped can be found in *Re-reading the Short Story*, ed. Clare Hanson; *Short Story Theory at a Crossroads*, ed. Susan Lohafer and Jo Ellyn Clary; and *Sudden Fiction: American Short-Short Stories*, ed. Robert Shapard and James Thomas.
2. See Gerlach and Lohafer. Both lobby for the uniqueness and integrity of the form's effects.
3. Indicative of how enabling a form of expression the cycle provides is evidenced by the parallel claims of Sherwood Anderson and Tim O'Brien. Anderson: "It is a form in which I feel at ease. I invented it. It was mine" (qtd. in Mann 7). O'Brien: "*The Things They Carried* is my best book. There's no doubt in my mind about it. . . . I can tell by the strangeness of it. It's a new form, I think" ("An Interview with Tim O'Brien" [Naparsteck] 8).
4. I undertake an extensive discussion of the consequent "integrity of irresolution" in *The Book of Daniel* in *Designs of Darkness in Contemporary American Fiction* (33–40).

5. See Geoffrey Galt Harpham's "E. L. Doctorow and the Technology of Narrative," which argues that Doctorow's early novels in particular represent "a critique of the coercive power of the textual and ideological regime" (82). Anarchy in either the artistic or the social world is threatening, so structure and systematization are often justified according to the feeling of stability they offer alone.
6. In "Ambush" O'Brien goes so far as to attempt to retract the arbitrary fate he inflicted on the anonymous enemy soldier from "The Man I Killed" by factoring in the possibility that he could have let him pass by. "Ambush" lets the conjecture stay open, concluding with his uninterrupted disappearance up the jungle trail into the fog of conjecture (150).
7. A young soldier is similarly afflicted in "The Field": "wading through the water, bending down and then standing and then bending down again, as if something might finally be salvaged from all the waste" (195). It is the same shocked posture of crazy Cacciato, who dreamily fishes in a mortar crater, "a waste against infinitely wider wastes" (*Going After Cacciato* 20).
8. In "Notes" O'Brien reveals that Paul Berlin, the main character in *Going After Cacciato*, is a disguised Norman Bowker (180), but in this book he dispenses with the courtesy of masks.
9. Another related burden is highlighted in *Going After Cacciato* as the chapter entitled "The Things They Didn't Know," in which ignorance is not blissful release but, instead, another sort of baggage.

4

MAGISTERS LUDI

The Universal Baseball Association, Inc. and *The Music of Chance*

I

> And so for history, the insoluble mystery presented by the incompatibility of free will and inevitability does not exist as it does for theology, ethics, and philosophy. History surveys a presentation of man's life in which the union of these two contradictions has already taken place.
>
> —Leo Tolstoy, *War and Peace*

The Gahuku-Gama of New Guinea are football players with a difference: their games often last for several days, and they are not suspended until both sides have reached the same score. Behind the appearance of competition lurks a deeper structure of collaboration. This, reports Claude Lévi-Strauss in *The Savage Mind*, is a prime example of the distinction between games and ritual: the former is disjunctive, ending in the establishment of difference and inequality, while the latter is conjunctive, devising union, or communion, and a merging of sides in the collective, faithful center. In games, "asymmetry is engendered":

> it follows inevitably from the contingent nature of events, themselves due to intention, chance or talent. The reverse is true of ritual. There is an asymmetry which is postulated in advance between profane and sacred, faithful and officiating, dead and living, initiated and uninitiated, etc., and the "game" consists in making all the participants pass to the winning side by means of events, the nature and ordering of which is genuinely structural. (Lévi-Strauss 32)

In ritual the contingency of games is harnessed by ceremonial mandates; the random dissolves before the wrought. Put another way, victory becomes the attainment of a harmonious dialogue between participants in the mystery.

This is not to disparage the significant alternative pleasures that games provide. If ritual promises psychic wholeness and congregational security, games offer suspense, variety, chance, and freedom. (And play and fiction share the same sort of idealized stratum: they are autotelic, enacted on their own terms, owing few allegiances outside their respective contexts.) Wolfgang Iser locates a reconciliation of established method and perpetual renewal at the heart of play which creates an "oscillation" that "permits the coexistence of the mutually exclusive" and guarantees the maintenance of the play space. Inconclusiveness keeps play playful (qtd. in Armstrong 158). Whether or not a viable compromise between these two sets of satisfactions can be reached is central to both Robert Coover's *The Universal Baseball Association, Inc., J. Henry Waugh, Prop.* (1968) and Paul Auster's *The Music of Chance* (1990). Each novel respects the intricate balance between favored and fluctuating occurrence—one the source of tradition and rigor, the other the source of intrigue and vitality—and recognizes its relevance to the writing of fiction, which is but another form of serious play.

Robert Coover has already received considerable attention for having exploited baseball for its inherent narrative parallels and potentialities. And, like stories that unfold on the page instead of on the field, baseball is particularly conducive to the life of the mind. We need only listen to a single broadcast to confirm that no other sport gives so much room to ruminate. The game is replete with giants and tales of mythic exploits; it bristles with statistics and puts argument on endless simmer; it is variously available to pastoral nostalgia, Manichaean conflict, and the sweet lies of poetry. For the true fan, the baseball-bugged and -enculted, the ballpark is that charmed neighborhood where an outbreak of grace could happen any time; one attends, watches, or listens in with elastic intentness: languid but ready to marvel. And there is something indelibly optimistic about the game, for, errors and failures notwithstanding, there is always redemption waiting at the next at bat, the next fielding chance, or next year.

Biologist Harold J. Morowitz contends that, since baseball "is an untimed game, unlimited by any total number of points, it has its own time dimension" to complement the utilization of the other three dimensions during the course of play, a principle echoed in Coover's novel by Henry Waugh in his exaltation of baseball's "significant time" over the constraints of "real time" (*Universal Baseball* 217).[1] "Thus," Morowitz concludes, "it has certain affinities to a relativistic age" (205). The foul lines that run to infinity are the measures destined for the aficionado's soul, as Wallace Stevens might say were he afflicted with pennant fever. The esteemed baseball writer Roger Angell similarly endorses the quality of baseball time:

> Baseball's clock ticks inwardly and silently, and a man absorbed in a ball game is caught in a slow, green place of removal and concentration and in a tension that is screwed up slowly and ever more tightly with each pitcher's wind-up and with the almost imperceptible forward lean and little half-step with which the fielders accompany each pitch. Whatever the pace of the particular baseball game we are watching, whatever its outcome, it holds us in its own continuum and mercifully releases us from our own. ("Cool Bubble" 137)

How much more fulfilling, how much more satisfying, than the daily round of the second hand of the office clock, taking its sceneless tour like a horse tied to a post to suffer children at the fair! As it blurs the distinctions between them, baseball teaches us about mortality and immortality alike.

But there is no actual baseball played in Coover's novel. Henry Waugh has opted for the essence alone. If baseball is superior to the world's wearisome welter by virtue of its conferring measurement, heroism, and just rewards on experience, Henry's Universal Baseball Association (UBA), an imaginary realm whose sole trappings are paper and dice, refines baseball by dispensing with all but the numbers and the narrative embroidery. Ironically, Henry finds real baseball games too tedious, too bloated with distractions from the pure passions his Universal Baseball Association crystallizes; soon after the inauguration of his tabletop world, Henry eliminates even the mock-up of a ballpark, which only "got in the way" of the respective crucial activities of statistics and the imagination (181). Henry Waugh hunches over his proceedings not only as proprietor but as monopolist, technician, sorceror, and scribe—the omnipresent genius of the seasons.

Solipsism and routine inevitably exhaust the oxygen, and, as the novel opens (in Year LVI) the UBA is in decline. The timely arrival of a sensational rookie pitcher, Damon Rutherford, is intoxicating. Not only does he hurl a perfect game, but Henry discovers in him far more than mere dice can deliver. Damon exudes serenity. Versus Henry's wordy exhilaration, "feeling like he could damn well take off and soar if he had anyplace to go" (16), Damon's quiet equanimity implies divinely inspired credentials, natural ease—he is William Gass's Brackett Omensetter with a fastball. Whereas his eccentric progenitor feels "goosey with the grace" of the perfect game, Damon himself is modest in his knowledge. Certainly, he is the epitome of the pitcher-artist's creed: power and control.

No wonder Henry feels compelled to feature and protect him, for not only the UBA but every aspect of Henry's real-world existence is rejuvenated by his example.

Waugh's flaw is to think that a self-created solitude is an unsponsored solitude. Power must be tempered by control; "without law, power lost its shape" (157). This is the axiom that governs the politics of play. On previous occasions a given player had begun to mean more to Henry than was healthy for the game, and "it had caused problems" (38). In his excitement over Damon's reinfusion of wonder into the UBA, Henry pitches him out of rotation to feature him more frequently. When he is fatally struck by Jock Casey's beanball—the Extraordinary Occurrences Chart does not flinch from any contingency—it is as though the system itself manifests its resistance to authorial effrontery. Inspired by Damon's exemplary performance, Henry initially hopes to revivify the game and reincarnate (or, better, deincarnate) himself as Damon, a plan manifested in his pretending to be Damon Rutherford as a means of spurring himself on to sexual endurance and ingenuity with Hettie, a local B-girl and willing partner in fantasy. But, as John Barth warns in "Lost in the Funhouse," "In the funhouse mirror-room you can't see yourself go on forever, because no matter how you stand, your head gets in the way" (85). In other words, the Creator must abide by the tenets of His own creation to legitimize and guarantee its functions: "he and his players were committed to the turns of the mindless and unpredictable—one might even say, irresponsible—dice. That was how it was. He had to accept it, or quit the game altogether" (40).

His "extra-ludic" life finds Henry making the same mistake of sacrificing the homely for the Homeric. When the game is going well it provides "relief and tension all at once" (3); the sacred (a perfect game in progress) and the profane (Henry's having to pee or taking a deli break) combine and mutually enrich one another. Just as Damon's perfect game only has significance when set off by the routine, so too does the game abide because of the counterweight of Henry's job at the accounting firm of Dunkelmann, Zauber & Zifferblatt. For Coover, fictions acquire their rigor by virtue of being pitted against the outside world: "The world of experience exists despite our fictions, and it is a world to which we must always return, even if it is fundamentally incomprehensible" (Wineapple 66). If baseball's intricate structure of checks and balances—offense and defense, individual exploits and the good of the team, tactics and accidents, recorded history and essential mystery, memory and desire (45)—grants the game accountability and aesthetic gratification, fiction's play requires countervailing mimetic pressures to define and substantiate the activity. (To use Marianne Moore's famous phrase in "Poetry," real toads are required to ground imaginary gardens.) Unrelieved reality may be a prison, but exclusive obsession is a disease. When Henry Waugh subverts the rules by superimposing his will upon fate and thereby sentencing Jock Casey to death, he disrupts the axiom of balance. Unlike Einstein's God, Coover's does play dice with the universe, and, worse, the dice are loaded.[2] An advertisement for "Divineform Foundations: Two-Way Stretch," humorously admonishes Henry to respect such elasticity as essential to the maintenance of paradise (18), but it goes unheeded.

The argument that killing Jock forges a balance that Damon's death had undone is refuted by the disintegration of Henry Waugh in the second half of the novel. Perhaps his problem lies in the confusion of two different kinds of balance, which we might term "static" and "kinetic." Static balance is seen in an early pinball version of the game, which Henry dismisses as clunky and inelegant (19); like chess, which is "finally too Euclidean, too militant, ultimately irrational, and in spite of its precision, formless really—nameless motion" (156), it is too impersonal, too claustrophobic.[3] It is inherent in the dilemma of Damon's perfect game: whereas other records are open-ended achievements (the record for most home runs, for example, can always be eclipsed and that record eclipsed in turn), a perfect game can only be duplicated. Whatever its enchantments, this concept of perfection makes it a brittle fiction indeed, a closed set that refutes the ideal of "a catalogue of possibilities" (23)—the liberal pole of the game's legislative system.[4]

Searching out a wreath to commemorate Damon's death, Henry finds the same problem reflected in the predominance of artificial flowers at the florist's: their exquisite perfection is sterile and unavailing. Play theorist Johan Huizinga anticipates this problem in his characterization of "false play," which is so self-conscious as to paralyze the forces it instigates and upon which its satisfactions depend (qtd. in Spariosu 36).[5] Perhaps Henry's compulsion to finesse the "awful rite"—starting Damon out of the pitching rotation or declaring Brock Rutherford Day by fiat to justify that desire, not to mention trying to avenge the death of his darling at the expense of Jock Casey—exhibits this same failure to recognize that, in nature and national pastime alike, in evanescence is renewal; in life cycle, salvation. Henry designates one of his stalwart old-timers, Barney Bancroft, to conceive the revelation "that perfection wasn't a thing, a closed moment, a static fact, but *process*, yes, and the process was transformation" (212). From the UBA's inceptional Big Bang, when the crack of actual dice and imagined bat coalesced for the first time, the pliable compromise of memory and motion was assured.

In contrast to static balance, therefore, a kinetic balance accommodates free will and determinism, flex and form.[6] Like the heady ballplayer caught in a rundown who "stays alive" between approaching fielders long enough to permit another runner to score, Henry needs to keep oscillating between chance and strategy within the game and between pedestrian fact and restorative fiction on the larger scale. He must curb the "immortal lust for sentiment and pattern" (230), to the extent that he surrenders to the whims of the dice and the dignity of historical imperative. As for the haggard daylight realm of the accounting office and grimy city streets, ordinariness must have its tithe. Once again the ordinary informs the fantasy. The outside world is the source of the names the UBA dramatizes; it is also the shaping context and the means by which the UBA earns its contrasting stature as a superior diversion. To be sure, as Henry relinquishes more and more of his real-life contacts (repulsing Hettie's eagerness and allowing his work at Dunkelmann, Dauber & Zifferblatt to decay so badly that he loses full-time employment), he furnishes the proceedings of the UBA with greater detail about the personal lives of the players to compensate (Gordon 40).[7] In the same way that the magnificent in baseball is emphasized by and set in relief against the mundane, its pure systems and clean lines enhanced by contrast to the sullen push through neighborhood streets, the game itself conducts its wonders beneath a 100-watt bulb whose glow separates the UBA from the sour quotidian sky.

The novel is replete with cautionary images of yoked opposites which promote health and ensure versatility in the context of history's implacabilities. Damon is "a self-enclosed yet participatory mystery" (9), and the monument to his memory, be it a folksong or a grave site, must be "simple yet complex," "intricate but harmonious," like the man himself and the celebratory elegy that succeeds the catastrophe (90). If his all-too-brief appearance startled the game into excellence not witnessed since his father's day, Damon's death rattles the whole chain of UBA being from the overarching punditry of the league commission down to the distracted play on the field. However, play does not serve as an antidote to disaster but as an incorporation of it within the "clumsy order" atop Henry's dining room table (86).

Whereas the operation of each game is predicated upon the twin, equal axes of Win and Loss, on the bureaucratic level of the UBA, kinetic balance takes the shape of Swanee Law's Legalists versus Barney Bancroft's Bogglers, who, taken together, represent the perpetual contest of codification and spontaneity that infuse the game with dynamic tension (and keep party politics perking well into Year CLVII). We learn that a primitive version of the UBA had been exclusively informed by individualism and egocentrism; the evolution away from its unchecked monarchic origins symbolizes the game's growing sophistication and an implicit denunciation of imbalance. Nor is Henry exempt from this movement, as he quickly comes to realize that the game will not work if he does not accept the influence of randomness upon his meticulous graphs, patterns, and legends (116–17).[8]

An examination of Henry's conflicted attitudes toward history may help to clarify his predicament. By trying to fashion history's verdict in accordance with his desires or his sense of poetic justice, as is most forcefully evidenced by his altering a throw of the dice to "execute" Jock Casey for the murder of Damon Rutherford, Henry breaks the game's first principle, which is that even the Creator must be subject to the rule of chance, as symbolized by the dice, which are "heedless of history yet makers of it" (16). A compromise between necessity and luck keeps the manifest destiny of play intact; wisdom is thus defined as acquiescence to the medium in which one acts. By recording the history of the UBA, Henry endows the game with rigor, solidity, and heritage. As Henry explains to his well-meaning but incurably oafish associate, Lou, history cannot exist apart from someone writing it down (49–50), which is to say that *recorded history* is a redundancy.

Yet the very precision and comprehensiveness of history also binds those who operate within it. Henry's apostasy may be foreshadowed by the reason he gave up playing tabletop war games through the mail: "the inability of the other players to detach themselves from their narrow-minded historical preconceptions depressed Henry" (44). On the other hand, playing with Lou, who blithely disregards the conventions of the UBA (and whose awkwardness causes the near destruction of the game world under a Flood of beer), is equally intolerable. To stray from the balance this paradox implies would annihilate the UBA and most likely, by virtue of his uncompromising association with it, Henry himself. We may remember the Jorge Luis Borges story "The Circular Ruins," in which an obscure, delirious man literally dreams a surrogate into being, expending his energies and his worship only to discover that he too is no more than dreamed entity; the growing exclusiveness of Henry's fiction making, initiated by the magical influence upon the game of Damon Rutherford and intensified by the determination to avenge his "murder," jeopardizes the delicate balance of the game and Henry's own health. While he does resist his impulse at first, refraining from changing the throw that kills Damon or from discarding the works altogether with the faith that "anything could happen still" (201), he does give in to the impulse to take out his despair on Jock, guaranteeing his death in the records with a *K: K* for "killed," *K* for the ultimate strikeout. In so doing, Henry's presence begins to evaporate from the novel.

Henry's transgression does have the virtue of having been committed in the name of restoring balance on a local level, but it disturbs the more comprehensive balance between concerted and contingent actions which is the UBA's foundation. For Henry the distinction between mere history and real fulfillment is evident purpose. There must be something beyond the box score's rigid perimeter. Otherwise, writers were nothing more than "a pack of goddamn leeches, inventing time and place, scared shitless by the way things really were"; otherwise, history is just more accounting—"An incurable diarrhea of dead immortals" (82)—or, worse, just playing out the string, sequence without consequence, a deepening of essential dread (117). Henry's decision to compose a league history, whether the incentive be to expose pattern or to impose it, derives from the desire to correct the litany of accidents of which history would otherwise be wholly constituted (224–25). Nonetheless, *The UBA in the Balance*, the authenticating Testament that Henry entrusts to Barney Bancroft, must incorporate the Special Stresses and Extraordinary Occurrences, not erase them—not if Henry hopes to escape duplication of the imperiousness of brute accident and aimless event. The point is to achieve an enhancement rather than a reprieve, to establish vantage but not paralysis. Like the game itself, history was not necessarily a closed circuit: "There were patterns, but they were shifting and ambiguous and you had a lot of room inside them" (143).

The absence of respect for that eternal arbitration between pattern and shifting is seen in a rival, revisionist history of the UBA entitled *Equilibrium Through Intransigence*, which, whatever its insights into the "truth" of the Damon/Jock Duel, will undoubtedly fall into disrepute for its blind commitment to stasis. Once overseeing the game gives way to "seeing to" privileged conclusions, once proprietorship gives way to blatant manipulations (the motivations behind them notwithstanding), intrusion means ruin. Consequently, by learning to prefer a history that reflects chance, motion, and equilibrium, rather than deflects those universal characteristics, Henry authorizes a fitting and, ironically, more durable fiction. His is a triumph tinged, or perhaps validated, by submission to the logic of the game that sustains him. So, although Henry, and not the catcher and pitcher, respectively, is the true "unifier behind the plate" and the "isolate genius on the mound" at once (206), even he ultimately recognizes that his greatest need is to surrender to the logic that everywhere confronts his efforts and flouts totalitarian alternatives—for, in the end, Henry is born to the die.

The closing chapter of the novel features a further distillation of the lessons of open-endedness, beginning with the fact that we conclude with chapter 8, thereby suspending play before the requisite nine "innings" are completed. In Year CLVII, one hundred years of significant time since the preceding chapter's events, a ceremonial game is under way, with contemporary players adopting the roles of Damon, Jock, and the rest of the principals of The Parable of the Duel.[9] This is history repeated as force-out: the players, some anxious, some serene, suspect that the staged event will have real, fatal consequences. (The game may have been fixed, but whether things are repaired or rigged remains unanswered.) With the UBA translated to nimbus, history is now a hodgepodge of rumor, fantasy, political maneuvering, and misconception.

The game's liturgical pretensions, already evident in the catechistic roll call of Hall of Famers–the sober ritual of the pitching change, the redemption of the double play, the dignity of the sacrifice, and the provisions for atonement built into athletic careers—have led to a profound uncertainty about the arbitrariness of faith. For example, the Parable finds Damon and Jock dying on the same day, perhaps in deference to symmetry on the part of Henry the Redactor.[10] Lou's witless heresies pale in comparison to the revolutionary movement of the Caseyites, who extol Jock as an existential hero and celebrate his "uniqueness, his essential freedom, God active in the man, and, as Cuss McCamish would say, all that shit" (222). How long does it take before we catch on to the symbolic insinuation, in a work so fastidious about the appropriateness of names, that Jock Casey recalls Jesus Christ while Damon Rutherford conjures the demonic opposition, in which event the conventional wisdom is a glitch in communal memory? (Hansen 57). And, when law and anarchy are both undeniable ingredients in the making of a vital balance, can either figure be discharged with impunity?

No wonder the Barney Bancroft biography, *The Doubter*, is selling! The players' feeble postures and positings, the spiky imprints of their cleats, barely verify their "passage from envelope to maddening envelope of inscrutable space" (230), while God, if he is still exists, is a nut . . . or so states Professor Costen Migod McCamish, Doctor of Nostology and

Research Specialist in the Etiology of Homo Ludens (233). Nevertheless, if *The Universal Baseball Association* does not promise salvation, it does offer models of value. First, there is the refutation of "impossibility, confusion, and emptiness," which "are the natural abode of a mind at rest" (230), and which the players assail through immediate, active participation. There is the consolation that one runs within the same baselines as one's forebears, remarking with every game an allegiance to original impressions made sacred by that allegiance. Henry's populous inward pastoral is a strictly demarcated art; Damon and Company are a holier firm than Dunkelmann, Dauber & Zifferblatt, for theirs is not an office to occupy, a depressing grid of workers clapped ratlike at their desks, but, rather, a proven dream their descendants can enter.

There is also the poise at the heart of stardom which Damon embodied and which Hardy Ingram revives by embodying Damon in the parabolic conclusion of the novel. Giving structure to grace results in compensations that names commemorate and numbers ordain and which imbue the game structure with the serenity of the adoring faithful on the field and in the stands. The game is "not a message, but an event," realizes Henry Waugh (143); "It's not a trial. . . . It's not even a lesson. It's just what it is," reasons the latest Damon Rutherford to ascend the mound and wind up his fate (242). Speculation dissolves before the present drama. The poetry of play must not mean but be:

> And he doesn't know any more whether he's a Damonite or a Caseyite or something else again, a New Heretic or an unregenerate Golden Ager, doesn't even know if he's Paul Trench or Royce Ingram or Pappy Rooney or Long Lew Lydell, it's all irrelevant, it doesn't even matter that he's going to die, all that counts is that he is *here* and here's The Man and here's the boys and there's the crowd, the sun, the noise. (242)

Gathered up into the reliable yet fluid artifice of an eternal game, players and fans, author and readers alike, enjoy the rewards of provisionally premeditated activity, in what Mikhael Bakhtin champions as a "feast of becoming, change, and renewal" (qtd. in Kafalenos 31). "Hang loose," the novel's parting confidence, encapsulates the suspensive doctrine of the UBA and attitudes toward it; by contrast, we recall the static trap of being "hung up for good" which Henry faced in deciding to ignore the rules of the game and sentence Casey to death for his crime against the proprietor's desire (201). *The Universal Baseball Association* depicts paradise as statistically informed, an Eden outfitted by the calculator. Book and ballpark are both crafted spaces full of movement, coded contours in which all may ascend to celebrity.[11]

II

> Over all things stand the heaven Accident, the heaven Innocence, the heaven Prankishness, the heaven Chance. And Chance is the most ancient Divinity of the world, and behold, I come to deliver all things from their bondage under Purpose and to restore on the throne to reign over all things the heaven Chance.
>
> —Luke Rhinehart, *The Dice Man*

The title of Paul Auster's novel *The Music of Chance* implies by its clever condensation how contoured chaos is, how formed fortune. Inaugural studies in the field of Chaos Theory conclude that, even as seemingly intrepid systems are infested by chaos, chaos frequently assumes sinuous, aesthetically satisfying shapes. Chaos Theory, writes James Gleick, tends to extol "process rather than state . . . becoming rather than being" (*Chaos* 5), and it has been applied to fields as disparate as climatology, biological growth, metaphysics, and the stock market. Its aim is to find the hairline fracture that runs through predictive systems and which points the way out of the deterministic corner into which scientific inquiry has apparently painted itself; paradoxically, like rocks of suspicious heft hiding fossil cuts, the riven disciplines reveal unexpected, substantial intricacies breeding among the rubble.[12] Auster's title similarly insinuates that experiential variables comport themselves about a regulating center—that, while randomness (chance) pervades the world of protagonist Jim Nashe, a decorum (music) lies at the core.

Certainly, any successful fiction requires the felicitous combination of innovative and integrative impulses. For Nashe, who uses his inheritance money to finance his wholesale repudiation of job, relations, and all the possessions that possess him, music manifests both of these qualities. On the one hand, music has a sedative effect; while he drives back and forth across the country, deliberately and indulgently undirected, he fondly remembers playing the piano "as if the music helped him to see the world more clearly, to understand his place in the invisible order of things" (10). Indeed, the music itself constitutes that order. On the other hand, by the end of the novel, music will serve not only to underscore the arbitrariness and open-endedness of fate but also to lull him into a lethal oblivion. In *The Music of Chance* psychic health depends upon the capacity to coordinate chance and tactics.

At first, however, instead of embracing these contraries, Nashe practices a dizzying relinquishment, surrendering entirely to inertia and the narcotic pleasures of divestiture. Phrases such as "out of the blue" and "out of thin air" frequently accompany Nashe's "nameless agitation" (8), which leads to his sacrificing design and destination to the spontaneous generation of plot, "as if he could follow the trail of what refuses to lead" (Auster, "Pages for Kafka" 116). Even his inheritance leaves him little more than a well-appointed ghost. As opposed to the "named motion" prized by Coover's Henry Waugh, here is anonymous drama, invisibility conferred by disconnection—the UBA with the baselines erased. "There was a recklessness and violence to these gestures that deeply satisfied him, but nothing could match the pleasure of simply throwing things away" (9). As Nashe races across America in his sports car, his speed serving as expenditure on a broader scale, he rides his own spillage in a veritable orgy of release and enjoys an almost Zen-like "weightlessness" (12).[13] His manic rush through emptiness empties him. In short, Nashe continues in the manner dictated by the same blind fortune that brought him the inheritance that allowed him to slip familiar sequences in the first place. He dispenses with maps, lets missed exits stay missed, and, for as long as the money lets him, contents himself with being just a mote in the churn: "He was a fixed point in a whirl of changes, a body poised in utter stillness as the world rushed through him and disappeared. The car became a sanctum of invulnerability, a refuge in which nothing could hurt him anymore. As long as he was driving, he carried no burdens, was unencumbered by even the slightest particle of his former life" (11–12).

But is his having "taken his life into his own hands" more a demonstration of risk or fatal excess than of wresting control (13)? Nashe eventually grows anxious over his amputation from the world, and, as his inheritance wanes, he finds himself in dire need of ballast. Once again, however, fortune provides. As Nashe's resources dwindle and options recede, he comes across a badly beaten Jack Pozzi, a small-time hustler eager to be staked for the big score: a poker game with Flower and Stone, two gullible lottery winners who had given Pozzi a standing invitation to give them a return game at their mansion. Although the mysterious beating he has received recalls Estragon's condition at the beginning of each act, and his resulting awkward method of locomotion resembles Watt's, the Beckett character Pozzi immediately invokes, of course, is the imperious Pozzo, who combats with bombast the bouts of arbitrariness which so often beset him in *Waiting for Godot* (1954). Indeed, Pozzi is a model of improvisational resolve, and Nashe gratefully rides the tide of his animation. For the role left to Nashe is that of Lucky, the forlorn, reluctant philosopher of Beckett's play, whose name is only half-ironic, since he is relieved of the responsibility to consider, decide, or proceed on his own volition.

Ever since his evacuation Nashe, too, allows the plots of others to absorb him, so that he tends to find himself "not creating an event so much as keeping up with one" (15). Although he is Pozzi's nurturer, outfitter, and backer, Nashe is the one who feels directed by his friend's energies. "Something was finished, and something else was about to begin, and for the moment Nashe was in between, floating in a place that was neither here nor there" (59). The limbo he accedes to soothes him like the monotonous rumble of tires on the highway; then again, in the midst of miasmic calm, dread can detonate like a tripped mine. But Nashe's predicament has more to do with that shared by so many of Beckett's characters who have shriveled down to gesture and voice: they find limbo contagious and no transition.[14] Having opted out, Nashe feels emptied and optionless: "He wanted to feel afraid, but not even disaster could terrify him" (59).

To be sure, Pozzi is the more likely candidate to initiate goals for the two of them. Like his namesake in Beckett's play, and unlike the self-deserting Nashe, Pozzi is at home in his ego, and he positively revels in his element. As a gambler, he is also a devotee of chance, but he tutors chance with competence. His success to date, and the victory he forecasts at the expense of Flower and Stone, is based on a creed of *studied* luck. The poker player must detect patterns without letting on, measure probability but be ready for unforeseen eventualities, read his opponents yet remain inscrutable. Chance informed by cunning: when things are going right for the gambler, it all proceeds like natural law:

> Once your luck starts to roll, there's not a damn thing that can stop it. It's like the whole world suddenly falls into place. You're kind of outside your body, and for the rest of the night you sit there watching yourself perform miracles. It doesn't really have anything to do with you anymore. It's out of your control, and as long as you don't think about it too much, you can't make a mistake. (136–37)[15]

As opposed to Nashe's limbo, Pozzi's ecstasy is purposive capitulation, an abyssal release steadied by optimistic guarantees. (No hiding behind hedged bets for him!) A believer in fortune's orthodoxy, Pozzi eagerly succumbs to his own hustle.

When the two would-be entrepreneurs appear at the mansion of Flower and Stone, they discover it to be a monument to eccentricity. It is opulent with debris; its precision (starkly geometric designs) is pervaded by dilapidation (broken statuary). Flower and Stone, another of Auster's "tandem realities,"[16] are as shadowy as the realm they inhabit: the former is all "lunging goodwill" (70), but his manner strikes Nashe as forced, masking some darker, even lunatic intention; the latter, Laurel to Flower's Hardy, as Pozzi smugly characterizes his prey, is sweet and shuffling, but his strange preoccupation with building "a model of some bizarre, totalitarian world" creates "a hint of violence, an atmosphere of cruelty and revenge" (87). Whether sudden wealth causes or merely fuels their peculiarities is of little consequence to the single-minded Pozzi, but Nashe intuits a disturbing parallel between Flower and Stone's enjoyment of poker as a ritualistic release that "helps to open the spirit to other possibilities, to wipe the slate clean" (71), and his own dispossessive run.

As the game progresses, Pozzi seems to have his hosts in tow as predicted, so Nashe, content to leave his fate in his partner's deft hands, retires to investigate the rest of the mansion. He works his way through the gloomy confines to find Stone's miniature City of the World, which is suspended on a platform in a room awash with light. The city appears to be autobiography revised into utopia; closer inspection reveals, however, that the reign of wisdom and fellowship still struggles against evil (the city has a prison, for example). Nashe is astonished by its intricacy and detail; in a rare moment of volubility Stone had lovingly related the planned "nesting" structure of the completed model, which contains a copy of the mansion, which in turn, in the manner of Edward Albee's *Tiny Alice* (1965), is meant to house a smaller City of the World, and so on.[17] Nevertheless, "for all the warmth and sentimentality depicted in the model, the overriding mood was one of terror, of dark dreams sauntering down the avenues in broad daylight. A threat of punishment seemed to hang in the air—as if this were a city at war with itself, struggling to mend its ways before the prophets came to announce the arrival of a murderous, avenging God" (96).

If Stone's quarry is maddeningly meticulous, Flower's melting pot exerts an equal and opposite pressure. Flower's archival obsessions lead to a random collection that melds kitsch and cunning in a kind of museum of the incommensurable—"a demented shrine to the spirit of nothingness" (84). In sum, Nashe feels oppressed by a system of sinister balances within Stone's city and between Stone's and Flower's sensibilities. Perhaps it is this anxiety as much as sheer mischief which instigates his spy mission and leads to his voodoolike burglary of the effigies of Flower and Stone from the City of the World.

But, if pocketing those figurines was meant as a symbolic establishment of control over his ambiguous environment, the effect is quite the opposite. Whether by cause or coincidence, Pozzi starts losing the moment Nashe departs to explore the rest of the mansion; by the time his "lucky charm" returns, Pozzi has dropped his entire stake. Although he will contend that Flower and Stone somehow cheated him, perhaps their having been tutored in card playing by Sid Zeno explains their victory. In fact, part of Zeno's teaching, as his name implies, may have included the bizarre preliminaries they visited upon their guests, whereby Pozzi and Nashe are blinded and victimized by paradox. Or, possibly, Flower and Stone have correctly inferred that numbers have souls, by which logic the losses suffered by Nashe and Pozzi result in something more metaphysical than just the redistribution of wealth. Then again, maybe it is simply a matter of the rich getting richer, of a lucky streak still streaking at the expense of two itinerants who, for a variety of reasons, failed to hedge their bets. Regardless, Nashe and Pozzi compound their predicament by plunging from bankruptcy into debt on a subsequent cut of the cards.

The second half of the novel focuses on the absurdity to which Nashe and Pozzi must surrender in order to break even and away. The ordeal dealt them comes in the form of having to build a gigantic wall out of stones taken from Cromwell's castle and transported to this rural Pennsylvania site. A monument to inutility, the monolithic structure will be a self-sufficient, self-authenticating "barrier against time." As Flower proclaims, "It will be a memorial to itself, gentlemen, a symphony of resurrected stones, and every day it will sing a dirge for the past we carry within us" (86). The capriciousness and pointlessness of their exertion is all that Nashe and Pozzi see before them, however, and that sense makes the job, which they perform almost entirely by hand, all the more arduous. But they have little choice in the matter; should honor fail them, Flower and Stone promise to back up their bargain with the police, and they assign one of their employees, the obdurate Murks, to serve as foreman. Ironically, then, it is Nashe who ends up in *their* pocket after all.

Still, in some ways it is a rather comfortable residence. Nashe accedes to the proposal in part so that he can persist in not having to decide for himself. By being delivered into their obsessions, he retains the gift of abandonment; only now it is restriction of motion rather than unabridged motion which defines it. Thus, the adjustment to their routine is surprisingly easy for Nashe. Indentured servitude carries with it the pleasures of insulation (due to the remoteness of the place and the unvarying quality of the labor); the Spartan clarity of the task, coupled with its arbitrariness, feels like an atonement whose consolations have to do with residing utterly in the present tense. Whereas "the future was too uncertain to be anything but a shadow, a formless, unarticulated presence that neither one of them wished to examine very closely" (168), the wall that bulks before Nashe and Pozzi represents the inescapability of the evident. In the opinion of Murks, whose name appropriately suggests the impassiveness and impenetrability he and the wall share: "At least it's all there in front of you. You put down a stone, and something happens. You put down another stone, and something more happens. There's no big mystery to it" (148).

"Just take it as it comes," Nashe tells himself, echoing the existential resolve (or surrender) which concludes *The Universal Baseball Association:* "Just be glad you're alive" (118). Using a child's wagon to haul the stones intensifies the frivolousness of the enterprise, but it has the virtue of ensuring its rhythms. Murks's composure may be consternating to the workers (especially to the volatile Pozzi), but it is enviable too. In fact, once their structure is completed and rests like some Christo vision or indefinable diameter across the visible landscape, the loose ends loom once again: "He was back to zero again. . . . For even the smallest zero was a great hole of nothingness, a circle large enough to contain the world" (155). Without a pensum to steady him Nashe suspects he will once again careen off into "orbital nullity" (Madison Smartt Bell 15).

Like Camus's Sisyphus, another dedicated stone mover, Nashe comes closest to contentment when the odds defy the ends. Nashe's original comment was that Flower and Stone's proposed structure was a Wailing Wall, but for Nashe it turns out to be mending wall and a retaining wall as well. Auster forecasts the ambiguity of his metaphor in his poem "Disappearances":

> and what he sees
> is all that he is not: a city
>
> of the undeciphered
> event,
>
> and therefore a language of stones,
> since he knows that for the whole of life
> a stone
> will give way to another stone

to make a wall

and that all these stones
will form the monstrous sum

of particulars.

(1.11–22)

As the building of the wall increasingly becomes a kind of personal firmament for Nashe, it does indeed seem to be "the whole of life," in the sense of its being both a continually growing reimbursement and a source of coherence. The wall and the crushed motion associated with its routine construction effect a harsh *kairos* of their own, creating the sense that all time prior to the wall must either be disqualified or reconstituted in terms of its looming space:

and he knows now
that if he lives
it is only in what lives
and will continue to live
without him.

("Disappearances" 4.18–22)

The Music of Chance takes yet another weird turn when Nashe and Pozzi realize that they are in the employ of deceitful household gods: although Flower and Stone dutifully answer Nashe and Pozzi's requests, including providing a prostitute to help them celebrate the apparent exhaustion of their debt, it turns out that the expenses they incur are added to the total. Of course, discharging these debts leads to further expenditures, and, even were they able to eliminate debts altogether, starting over without funds would be impossible. We may return to *Waiting for Godot* for Estragon's concern that he and Vladimir are "tied down" to Godot, to which Vladimir's confident dismissal ("What an idea!) is quickly succeeded by doubt: "No question of it. (*Pause.*) For the moment" (14). In other words, the rhythm of luck in which Pozzi had put so much faith, and which he accuses Nashe of having disrupted, has given way to a skein of purgatorial deferrals whose dominion over them is confirmed in two ways: by the fact that Flower and Stone had anticipated their need to keep working beyond the date originally predicted for their departure and had drawn up a new contract in advance; and by the fact that Murks decides to arm himself, proving his readiness to back up his supervision and ensure their stay with violence if necessary.[18] Nashe is better equipped psychologically to handle this revelation, and he becomes increasingly conciliatory and nourishing to Pozzi, who is breaking under the strain of injustice.

If their situation and their relationship increasingly mirror the conditions of *Waiting for Godot*, the result of Pozzi's desperate escape plan is predictable. Nashe agrees to help his companion with his plan and to finish out the work alone once Pozzi's absence is discovered; the plot is foiled, however, and Pozzi suffers a dreadful beating for his troubles. (Pozzi's unaccountable beatings, like Estragon's, frame and decide his presence in the text.) Like Goldberg and McCann in Harold Pinter's *The Birthday Party* (1960), Murks and his son-in-law, Floyd, spirit the dying Pozzi away, presumably to a hospital—a promise that, like all other promises since his arrival, Nashe has to take on faith. As exactors of compensation, then, the genial hosts have proven to be aloof and absolute; Godots ordained by chance alone, they demand obedience without offering enough information or justification for the enslaved to supply it. Meanwhile, the evidence of Nashe and Pozzi's collusion has been erased—the hole they dug beneath the compound has been covered up, the shovel unaccountably returned—and not even in his recurring dreams can Nashe see his way out beyond the enclosure. When he again turns to music for oblivion it is to "The Mysterious Barricades," a piece whose repetitious, one-note-at-a-time quality merely reestablished the wall in Nashe's consciousness, until the music suspends, rather than concludes, as "unresolved harmonies" (181). Even the prowling crows, which strike Nashe as being irrational in their movements and throttled in their cries, mock his entrapment (202).

Betrayal, therefore, undermines the sustaining grace of the discipline. With Pozzi removed Nashe finds his personality expanding and distorting in Pozzi's direction. He grows more aggressive, more calculating; the appearance of Murks's grandson on the premises, whom Nashe feels certain was the instrument of Pozzi's ruin, makes him positively murderous. (When a kid wanders by in a Halloween Death costume Nashe takes him for a presentiment and a taunt, but, like the evasive Boy in *Waiting for Godot*, he does not linger for explanations.)

The final pages of *The Music of Chance* show Nashe resolved to recover his balance at a fatal price. First, he commissions the same prostitute, Tiffany, to come by so as to enlist her to investigate Pozzi's disappearance. Just as he had stolen the figurines of Flower and Stone from the City of the World, he now appropriates the name of Sid Zeno to serve the fantasy with which he hopes to ply Tiffany. (Sid Zeno is purportedly a talent scout whom Nashe says he would persuade to consider her.) It is significant, however, that he temporarily falls prey to her sexual attentions and forgets his plan in favor of a wild scheme to run off with her. But, once he is reminded that a prostitute's intimacy, like a gambler's patter or, evidently, Murks's solicitude, is probably just part of the job instead of an authentic connection, he is roused to the task once more. (Either she reneges on her promise or her message is intercepted, but he never learns for sure what happens to Pozzi.) Next, also in deference to symmetry, Nashe times it so that working off his obligations to Flower and Stone will dovetail with his birthday.

When he accomplishes this Nashe agrees to a celebrational outing with Murks and his grandson, whom he defeats in a game of pool. Nashe refused the money he wins, asking instead that he be allowed to drive the Saab he had had to give up when luck had deserted him and Pozzi months earlier. With his former persecutors trapped in the back seat, Nashe guns the car up to eighty-five and ends their lives and the novel with a terrifying crash.

Several motives conspire in this murder-suicide, including revenge for Pozzi's hideous beating and for the abuses he himself suffered. There is also the possibility that Nashe is terrified by the sudden opening of options, that he remains in thrall to the reliable routine of the wall, apart from which the future is "a formless, unarticulated presence" he cannot contemplate (168). His decision, which is one of precious few decisions he makes in the course of *The Music of Chance*, forecloses on the possibility of his returning to the drifting with which he began. In this manner Nashe copies Henry Waugh in exiting a deteriorating fiction (a trick, by the way, which Vladimir and Estragon *cannot* match in Beckett's play).

Admittedly, although he may have balanced off his debts—financial and otherwise—with this closing stroke, Nashe does not achieve a satisfying equilibrium so much as perish for the lack of it. On the other hand, from a purely detached, aesthetic perspective Nashe may have accomplished the kind of compromise between chaos and composition, debris and design, which Papa "creates" at the conclusion of John Hawkes's *Travesty* (1976), when he too speeds off toward a blazing finish with his daughter and his friend, the lover of both Papa's wife and his daughter, his captive passsengers and audience. Both are out to reify, to join themselves to, a purifying form—a sudden, permanent boundary that simultaneously stands against and accommodates chaos. This is the paradoxical satisfaction of disaster: a "guarantee of timelessness" which "is in fact the living tongue in the dark mouth of cessation" (Hawkes,

Travesty 22). "After all," Papa insists, "my theory tells us that ours is the power to invent the very world we are quitting" (57). Stationary in a speeding vehicle, hurtling to be still—the imagination's last production is a dearly purchased balance of opposites. "Speech could not cobble the swamp," Auster writes in his poem "Spokes," "and so you dance for a brighter silence" (ll. 19–20). Sick with motion, Nashe abandons himself to the fixed gesture.

Notes

1. "Since baseball time is measured only in outs, all you have to do is succeed utterly; keep hitting, keep the rally alive, and you have defeated time," Roger Angell rhapsodizes ("Interior Stadium" 303). For a dissenting comic approach to this eventuality, see T. Coraghessan Boyle's "The Hector Quesadilla Story," which takes the hypothesis of the game that trumps time to its absurd conclusion.
2. Einstein's notorious complaint against quantum mechanics highlights the prominence of uncertainty and probability in that theory. "Perhaps the other side needs emphasis—the statistical reliability of quantum mechanics and its consistency as predictable by Schrodinger's formulation," argues Arlen J. Hansen. "After all, when a set contains many, many occurrences the laws of probability become very compelling and firm" (58). In other words, a revised perspective shows atomic phenomena adhering to rules of balance not unlike those governing Coover's novel.
3. Roger Angell also celebrates the "named motion" Henry prefers:

   > No novelist has yet been able to concoct a baseball hero with as tonic a name as Willie Mays or Duke Snider or Vida Blue. No contemporary novelist would dare a supporting cast of characters with Dickensian names like those that have stuck with me every since I deciphered my first box scores and began peopling the lively landscape of baseball in my mind—Ossee Schreckengost, Smead Jolley, Slim Sallee, Elon Hogsett, Urban Shocker, Burleigh Grimes, Hazen Shirley Cuyler, Heinie Manush, Cletus Elwood Poffenberger, Virgil Trucks, Enos Slaughter, Luscious Easter, and Eli Grba. ("Box Scores" 4–5)

   Henry Waugh, too, decides if there is "anything there" in a name before christening a new player. For a broader analysis of the poetry of successful baseball monickers, see Rory Rebecca Metcalf and Gael Montgomery's "Names of the Game," which painstakingly relates statistical achievement and metrical attractiveness among the game's great players.
4. As its proprietor's private strains contaminate the UBA, its fragility is exposed. Hettie's discovery of the source of Henry's impersonation sullies it

and the sex it once invigorated; Lou's rude collusion, which features absent-mindedness about the rules and disregard for strategy, lays bare the arbitrariness and poverty of Henry's sentimental mania and drains the game of its mythic pretensions, reducing it to paper (185, 189).

5. Huizinga's ideal vision of play explicitly relates it to other forms of aesthetic order; for Huizinga balance, tension, poise, rhythm, and harmony are among its chief "noble" qualities. See *Homo Ludens: A Study of the Play-Element in Culture* 10.
6. The contrast between static and kinetic art is seen in Joyce's *Portrait of the Artist as a Young Man*, when Stephen Dedalus, who is committed to the recollection of emotion in tranquility, finds the inspiration dissolving in face of reality's interference. He manages to complete his villanelle to his beloved by grossly physical means, thereby suggesting not only that invocation and masturbation are compatible tactics but also that the static (poem) and the kinetic (passion) are symbiotically related after all (218–24). Indeed, perhaps instead of being refined out of existence, Stephen is an artist more like Damon Rutherford: "a self-enclosed yet participating mystery" (9).
7. At first having a horseracing game in his desk drawer had been enough to support him through a day at the office, the way methodone bolsters a heroin addict. But, with his intensifying reliance upon the UBA, that transitional measure is reduced to sentimental value alone.
8. We might refer to Stanley Elkin's God in *The Living End* who abstains from absolute (and absolutely just?) control of Creation because He does not want to do anything to jeopardize "a better story" (143–44). Also see Jackson I. Cope, who patiently reviews biblical, Civil War, and other analogues to *The Universal Baseball Association* in *Robert Coover's Fictions* (35–58).
9. For a fuller treatment of the concept of "significant time," see Frank Kermode's discussion, in *The Sense of an Ending*, of the distinction between *kairos* and *chronos* and the effort "to defeat the tendency of the interval between *tick* and *tock* to empty itself" by escaping from mere chronicity into concentrated fulfillment, whereby origin and end are "harmonized" and human desires satisfied ("Fictions" 44 ff.). Kermode associates this phenomenon with theological and fictional plots; that baseball is also particularly sensitive to it as well may be the key to its having become our national pastime.
10. See Robert A. Morace's "Robert Coover, the Imaginative Self, and the 'Tyrant Other,' " for a discussion of Coover's "The Kid," a play that further examines how communal myths—here, the Parable of the Showdown between Sheriff and Outlaw—are worshipped for the patterns they enforce, even at the expense of human freedom or contradictory evidence (194–95).
11. Frank W. Shelton discovers that Coover does not reserve this rule of balance for baseball alone. In *Whatever Happened to Gloomy Gus of the Chicago Bears* Coover again sees balance at the core of the game: "The line of scrimmage is a fulcrum, not a frontier . . . (92). And Gertrude Stein lends her own brand

of supporting ambiguity to the idea of living by the arbitrary yet necessary rules of the game one is involved in: "What you mean by understanding is being able to turn it into other words but that is not necessary. To like a football game is to understand it in the football way. . . ." Play on the page and on the field exhibit "a harmony in hesitation" (*Tender Buttons* 74).

12. In keeping with the revision of systems as ongoing processes, the very definition of Chaos Theory itself is still under construction. For a list of attempts to formulate terminology, see James Gleick's *Chaos: Making a New Science* (305–7).
13. It is instructive to compare Nashe's annihilation of the self and its context to that of Stanley Elkin's Ed Wolfe, who in "I Look Out for Ed Wolfe" literally cashes himself in.
14. Also compare Yossarian's technical withdrawal at the beginning of *Catch-22*. Because he always runs a fever of 101 but remains just short of contracting jaundice, he is able to stay in the hospital while avoiding treatment, and in this inviolable state he hopes to last out the war. But this proves too close an approximation of the death he means to evade in the first place.
15. Curiously, Pozzi's description of successful gambling sounds very much like Auster's analysis of the writing process, in which the author argues that chance and surrender play a greater part in creating a novel than does "craft": "It's a funny thing . . . but I'm not actually in control of what I'm doing. I think a lot of writers feel this way" ("The Novelist Out of Control" 9).
16. The phrase comes from Auster's essay on Beckett's *Mercier and Camier*, "From Cakes to Stones" (147), and further testifies to Auster's inheritance from Beckett. Auster's New York trilogy likewise features variations on this theme of linked doubles and warring orbits. See my *Designs of Darkness in Contemporary American Fiction* (56–70), for an examination of these novels.
17. "Cities, like dreams, are made of desires and fears," Marco Polo admonishes Kublai Khan in Italo Calvino's *Invisible Cities*, "even if the thread of their discourse is secret, their rules are absurd, their perspectives deceitful, and everything conceals something else" (44). Stone's recursive city has affinities with several of the descriptions of cities in Marco Polo's repertory as he reports on Kublai Khan's elusive allegorical empire. Among these are Zora, a "city which cannot be expunged from the mind" and which "is like an armature, a honeycomb in whose cells each of us can place the things he wants to remember" (15); Zirma, a city whose existence is predicated upon redundancy (19); Eudoxia, a city modeled on a carpet's "immobile order" that reflects for each inhabitant "an anguish of his own, and each can find, concealed among the arabesques, an answer, the story of his life, the twists of fate," as well as the possibility that in its design lies "the true map of the universe" (97); and Penthesilea, a city without an outside but instead wholly constituted of endlessly ramifying limbos (158).

18. When Pozzi brags to the prostitute procured for their departure celebration that he and Nashe are really "specialists in the art of 'historical reverberation' " (158), he ironically coins a phrase that approximates their being "tied," in that moving forward is an illusion, and repetition of past events the truth of their *pensum*.

5

FLUENT MUNDOS

Ratner's Star and *Plus*

I

and so each venture
Is a new beginning, a raid on the inarticulate
With shabby equipment always deteriorating . . .
—T. S. Eliot, *East Coker*

"And over it all, or under it all, a dull unlocatable roar, as of some form of swarming life just outside the range of human apprehension" (*White Noise* 36). Don DeLillo and Joseph McElroy share a fascination, by turns amusing and mordant, for the day's density, the glittering yet suffocative clutter of technological society. Both are notorious practitioners of what Tom LeClair calls the "art of excess," in which the complex textures of society are replicated in the magnitude and erudition of the novel.[1] The challenge, however, to delimit the world in language, or to manifest a world of language, conceals a more fundamental challenge to the viability of reference altogether. *Ratner's Star* (1976) and *Plus* (1967) are novels whose respective concerns with expressive capacity are self-consciously circumscribed by what lies outside expression and defies appropriation.

The very nature of language ensures the invulnerability of what Bruce F. Kawin calls "the ineffable" to linguistic assaults.[2] As Kawin explains, "Language's mechanism of fragmentation into terms and integration into statements might be perceived as inappropriate to an expression of the nature of absolute and irreducible unity were it not for the fact that the mind given over entirely to that unity is incapable of recognizing or analyzing, let alone of employing, *any* fragmentative process" (229).

DeLillo and McElroy, however, do not surrender blindly to that unity. Intensely sensitive to the intersections of jargons, codes, and information systems that pervade contemporary life, as well as to the paranoia that results when gridlock occurs, their fictions provide substantial counterweights to the ineffable in the form of outstanding verbal dedication. Both authors appreciate a basic paradox about language: the Word has lost its purity through corruptive, exploitative, or just plain slovenly usage; fanatical devotion to purity, however, leads to fascistic behavior, and it becomes clear that contingency is the Word's inevitable, natural condition (Menand 84).

To further complicate the matter, erudition includes the awareness of its own insufficiency. "It is not that the ineffable is an illegitimate concern," Kawin continues, "but that language deals properly and only with what is not ultimately present. It is not that language fails to express the ineffable, but that the effable is the province of that failure which is language" (233). The tension between linguistic reach and grasp is the crisis that spurs *Ratner's Star* and *Plus*. The ideal marriage between the "ordering instinct" of man and the organized premises of science, mathematics, government, alphabets, or some other correlating system or art that would rescue history from confusion is annulled by an inextinguishable doubt, or shade, which arises during the course of the novel-long investigation (Aaron 70–71). Systems finally refuse to give up their secrets, which are either part of some covert design of the systems themselves or replicas of the black gutters of consciousness where no light can enter.

Ratner's Star is based on the dream of an articulate Eden that would not only satisfy but actually justify the mathematician's maneuvers. For Billy Twillig, the child-genius who is summoned to join the elite community at Field Experiment Number One, mathematics carries the consoling weight of enameled rationality:

> He calculated with the ease of a coastal bird haunting an updraft. But beauty was mere scenery unless it was severe, adhering strictly to a set of inner codes, and this he clearly perceived, the arch-reality of pure mathematics, its austere disposition, its links to simplicity and permanence; the formal balance it maintains, inevitability adjacent to surprise, exactitude to generality; the endless disdain of mathematics for what is slack in the character of its practitioners and what is trivial and needlessly repetitive in their work; its precision as a language; its claim to necessary conclusions; its pursuit of connective patterns and significant form; the manifold freedom it offers in the very strictures it consistently upholds.
>
> Mathematics made sense. (13)

The accurate, regimental cut of numerals, the elegant scrimmage of constants and variables, and the reliable reciprocity between the truth and beauty of numbers all promise to refine the ungainliness of existence. Predictably, then, the reception of a mysterious radio signal from the general direction of Ratner's Star inspires the batallion of Nobel laureates and hired guns from the hard sciences to "lay the logarithmic spiral on" (Nemerov, "Figures of Thought" l. 1) and convey their data into clean, well-lighted calculus. The plan is to spread Nature's infinite cast of concerns against a series of interpretive racks of abstraction. As the novel progresses, however, the linkage between the scientific and the mystical becomes more and more evident. Denials notwithstanding, says DeLillo, "modern physicists seem to be moving toward nearly mystical explanations of the ways in which elements in the subatomic world and in the galaxy operate" ("An Outsider in This Society" 65).

The "sweet clean shock of number theory" (26), like any other form of designation religiously applied, initially promises to coerce speech and clause from the "screech and claw of the inexpressible" (22), but *Ratner's Star* shows it to be just a more agreeable aspect of the blind tide it encounters. We might see the novel as a language conjugating itself or a theorem undergoing its proof, revealing the final resistance of a murky universe to computation, or "the apt phrase" (56), as well as the incurably centripetal nature of specialized vocabularies. One of the lessons of twentieth-century American philosophy is that experience looms larger than logic allows. If "intellectual handling" is to be countenanced at all, the pernicious regime of concepts and definitions must be exposed for being, in the words of William James, "a retrospective patchwork, a post-mortem dissection . . . [that] can follow any order we find most expedient" ("Bergson and His Critique of Intellectualism" 577). The mind turns coercive, even "vicious," in the name of a stability it then "discovers" to be inherent: "it is we who project order into the world by selecting objects and tracing relations so as to gratify our intellectual interests. We *carve out* order by leaving the disorderly parts out; and the world is conceived thus after the analogy of a forest or a block of marble from which parks or statues may be produced by eliminating irrelevant trees or chips of stone" (James, "Types of Philosophic Thinking" 485).

Rational numbers, proper fractions, commutative properties: these venerable imposters cloak their past and future treacheries with austerity. The symmetries of mathematics, so intricately nested, calibrated like God's own machinery, imply a convergence of mental and cosmological processes; Field Experiment Number One's complex is a cycloid enclosing an armillary sphere, an architectural paeon to that very belief. But DeLillo's "perfect starry night" (Molesworth) recalls Van Gogh's depiction: a bristling quilt of roils and colliding trajectories, a vaulted swarm. Like the conspiracy theories in DeLillo's *Libra* (1988), which are all "the same taut story of men who find coherence in some criminal act" (440), scientific and mathematical theories are as likely to demonstrate nothing other than their own logic alone. Conspiracy affords an "almost dreamy sense of connection" (127), with keys having become magically alert to their proper locks, but DeLillo's universe resists that sort of final explanation. Or, rather, we have explanation without elucidation, a homeostatic "satisfaction of living among secrets, in a mysterious world, and the satisfaction of gaining access to secrets" (McClure 103). Forays into space do not dissolve mystery; instead, they increase its scope by opening up new arenas of esoterica.

The typical DeLillo novel features obsession suddenly focused and seemingly vindicated by some great urgency that may, in fact, be obsession's manifestation.[3] DeLillo depicts uniquely trained, highly sensitized personalities eager to locate a context that valorizes them, even if it is at the expense of shaping experience (very often through political violence) to suit those terms. In this way *Ratner's Star* shows a given explanatory system's contamination by the anthropomorphism it means to transcend. As astronomer John D. Barrow writes, the so-called Secret of the Universe appears to include the a priori requirement of human fathomability of the secret (203). Accordingly, once pattern fails to uncover Purpose beyond our predilections—once it fails to save, solve, or reliably sanction us—pattern itself becomes the purpose.

So reads Endor's mathematician's creed, which he laterals to Billy in the form of a commencement address:

> Every part is interconnected and all the numbers flow in proper sequence. If you don't give us every scrap of what you are, we die in strongly scented heaps. Whatever order can be conceived by the left-handed mind is yours to impose elsewhere. Whatever sense of form can be induced to rise out of the horizontal mist is yours to reapportion. Where perfect measurement beckons, no one but you is fit to sand the final beam. Mathematics is an expression of the will to live. (194)

This is intricacy substituting for divinity—the Computer Age version of the Scholastic argument from design. Instead of the serenity of Q.E.D., there is the "lyrical exhilaration" of completion: "The only valid standard for his work," thinks Billy, "its critical point (zero or infinity) was the beauty it possessed, the deft strength of its mathematical reasoning" (117), which may be all blue smoke and mirrors, all fiction, but without which, as Endor confides, "Existence would be sheer dread" (195).[4]

To a large extent the impracticality of mathematics is actually championed throughout the novel as a mark of its purity regardless of any latencies it may or may not discover beyond itself. (In the shadow dance of the academy, Billy's award-winning research on zorgs, numbers so rarefied as to be finally useless, is the quintessence of this principle). The result is that, while higher mathematics does not reduce empirical overload to a formula, it does insist upon formula as a refuge. Instead of means to an end of mystery, labyrinthine systems—conspiracies, bureaucracies, or arcana, not to mention strenuous experimental novels—are mysteries in themselves, complete with clandestine meetings, exclusionary rituals, and myths of heroic origin and ratification. Autoreferentiality ensures a first-order priority to mathematical enterprises, which are independent of "secular" functions for their allure. Twillig and his fellow travelers, a spectral host of systems merchants among gross forms, are not out to explain reality but to construct lovely models, as is most flagrantly exemplified by the effort to create Logicon, a metalanguage whose "very uselessness . . . makes the project a pure act of the intellect and therefore supremely interesting" (409).

The self-reflexive, self-interred systems that are variously advanced by the characters in *Ratner's Star* recall the centripetal specialties of the physicians in Shaw's *The Doctor's Dilemma* (1913), in which all diagnoses are really exercises in justifying and promoting those specialties rather than sincere efforts to contend with the illness at hand; they also anticipate the self-reflexiveness of the space signal itself, for earth turns out to be its origin. Ironically, the image of the stellated twilligon, which Billy repeatedly finds stitched deep in the folds of the physical world, does prove relevant here: the message is a boomerang cast out into the cosmos centuries ago and only now returning to its source.[5] But to think that any language could somehow unglove itself and achieve immediate contact is to neglect the disclaimers of the experts. For example, the scientist for whom "moholes" are named is almost overprotective about their elusiveness. A comparison of moholes to black holes only proves useful to disqualify the comparison:

> "In the last analysis, moholes are impossible to talk about. What we're really doing is imposing our own conceptual limitations on a subject that defies inclusion within the borders of our present knowledge. We're talking *around* it. We're making *sounds* to comfort ourselves. We're trying to peel skin off a *rock*. But this, according to Mainwaring, quoting Mohole, is simply what we do to keep from going mad." (357–58)

In the end the void will not suffer voice and brooks no trespass. "There is something in the space between what I know and what I am and what fills this space is what I know there are no words for," concludes a paragraph-long interlude entitled "I AM NOT JUST THIS" (370), which could serve as the novel's epitaph.

Consequently, the exotic population of *Ratner's Star* is "mired in an existence of essential dichotomies" (35), the most intractable among them being the one dividing the harmonious appeal of their disciplines from unrefined reality. The whole notion of an outer space "message" begs the question of translation, a fallacy that renders the genius Endor leaky as the galactic center and drives him into a Kafkaesque burrow to subsist on larvae: "The whole stinking computer universe. Hoping it would all come together in this one last look. But it stayed apart. It definitely did not come together" (84).

"Our childlike trust in structural balance" ensures the durability of the model-making industry, avers U.F.O. Schwarz, and the principal concern of astral engineering is procrustean: the assignment of consoling, recognizable shapes and computerized stylizations to universal phenomena to make them conform to human penchants. But "tiny cracks in the model are becoming evident, it seems" (49). Cosmology inconsistently recapitulates us. Even Space Brain, the supercomputer designed to compete with It All, has had to escape the confinement of its own hardware; after this Big Bang of knowledge comes the expanding cogniverse, which, like the universe surrounding it, is perforated by unexplained masses that will not conform to "algebraic granite" (175). The goal of an encompassing explanatory embrace is inevitably pitted by arbitrary elements and outcomes, surds, and broken symmetries. "The search for the Theory of Everything is a quest for that technique whose application could decode the message of Nature in every circumstance. But we know there must exist circumstances where mere technique will fail," confides John Barrow (209). In the end "no non-poetic account of reality can be complete": "There is no formula that can deliver all truth, all harmony, all simplicity. No Theory of Everything can ever provide total insight. For, to see through everything, would leave us seeing nothing at all" (210).

Field Experiment Number One vibrates with rumor and ambiguous industry, while skepticism leaches into all of its proceedings. This accounts for the extremely qualified faith of computer analyst and human-machine public relations manager LoQuadro:

> I'm the type of person who's willing to confront moderately awesome phenomena. Beyond that I lose my bearings. Chipping away at gigantic unproved postulates. Investigating the

> properties of common whole numbers and ending up in the wilds of analysis. Intoxicating theorems. Nagging little symmetries. The secrets hidden deep inside the great big primes. The way one formula or number of expression keeps turning up in the most unexpected places. The infinite. The infinitesimal. Glimpsing something, then losing it. The way it slides off the eyeball. The unfinished nature of the thing. (67)

Out of this "idealized exploit" may be extracted "a beautiful sentiment," maintains one Celeste Dessau, a shadowy and philosophical femme fatale. "Symmetry is a powerful analgesic" (114, 115). But nearby looms Thorkild's "cruel hurting truth" that the logic of the transmission, indeed the sense of message and messenger alike, may be nothing other than a mirage of human programming (163).

Here lies the dream of total comprehension, there the terror of incomprehensibility; here the mathematician, our modern-day diabolist, plies his art, "bone-setting the measured land," his perspective a product of compass and straightedge (64), but Nature's maze does not yield to his incursions. As Edna Lown, the novel's scribbling chorus, writes, "Mathematics is only as correct as logic allows it to be": "We have developed in fact such tightly precise levels of argument that they have led us into the midair anxiety of that engine-stalling aspect of metamathematics in which we see only too clearly the innate limitations of formal systems, the overthrow of proof, the essential incompleteness of the axiomatic method" (392). Like Edna's notes, which are simultaneously "finished" and "ever-circulating" (425), scientific investigation must remain inconclusive to remain vital. "Death is creeping logic" and vice versa (414–15); the "press to measure and delve" does not quell but, instead, provides counterpoint to the willingness to "implicate ourselves in endless uncertainty" (432).

This is a version of the Strange Loop phenomenon that Douglas R. Hofstadter derives from Gödel's theorem, which he paraphrases as: "All consistent axiomatic formulations of number theory include undecidable propositions" (17).[6] DeLillo replicates the theorem at the level of the plot of the novel, for not only does the message prove self-reflexive rather than visionary, originating as it does from earth and returning with the taint of human mediacy undissolved, but it also serves to predict an eclipse that is otherwise impossible to anticipate—a "noncognate celestial anomaly" whose existence further exposes the porousness of the system (420). In other words, our "inventing games to fill this crevice in the heavens" and to soothe our rage for complementarity confirms nothing beyond the open-endedness of desire (436). (That Billy Twillig breaks the code only to learn that its meaning is no longer a subject of interest is but one of many false bottom lines to *Ratner's Star*.)

The jurisdiction of DeLillo's empiricists and logicians, their reputations already deflated by names like mashed acronyms or bad puns, extends only so far; like Stevens's hatted rationalists, who "think, in square rooms," they are obliged to "confine themselves / To right-angled triangles" to escape contradiction ("Six Significant Landscapes," sec. 6, ll. 2, 5–6).[7] But DeLillo's novel devolves into the realm of psychics, "scream ladies," and "shadow prophets." The strategies of science and shamanism overlap as the all-out search for extraterrestrial confirmation of human activity continues. The following is a portion of a wistful litany that invokes such desperately "hybridized" pieties:

> Our Lady of Inferred Entities
> Prey on us
>
> Wielder of Occam's Razor
> Spare our multiplicities
>
> Expounder of the Unthinkable
> Have mercy on our system of signs
>
> Elucidator of Logical Form
> Guide our superstitions
>
> Annihilator of Tautologies
> Bless our refrains
>
> Language Inviolate
> Forgive us our stammer
>
> (176)

And to these we might add: give us this day our daily congruence.

To compensate for the failure to banish enigma from the scheme of things—Billy's revelation merely tracks it to another level of investigation at the complex—there is the assurance that, while none of the methods practiced at Field Experiment Number One earns exclusive authority, none can be invalidated. Insights intersect and breed with inanities; the significant and the serendipitous, the determinant and the demented, ally—all to the maintenance of operations. Symmetry does not cure randomness in the universe or in the research that attends it. Conspiring against the quest for the ethereal is the primitive trammeling, the terror in the belly, which is heard in "the boned-out howl of those voices departed to the edge of the pure word" (96–97). Championed as an intergalactic Rosetta Stone, Ratner's Star occasions blurry, incommensurable events. Specialists may tap reality from a thousand angles, but they can never drain all the darkness out.

Like all matter, math is "infalling"; doubt and denial threaten a "nullifying plunge" (391).[8] "Pi makes me furious," cries Timur Nut, another one of the cartoon mandarins inhabiting Field Experiment Number One, whose faith is sorely tested by pi's defiance of logical progression. Absurdity presses in from numberless directions. Robert Hopper Softly, Billy's mentor, confesses that the whole "causal nexus" is superstition (274), and "all of physical reality is a matter of convenience" (246). As anxiety about the mission percolates throughout the compound, acute states of mindfulness are confounded by the "lure of a submoronic mode of being" (237).

Language exhibits the infiltration of "seediness" as well. Elux Troxl, a kind of entrepreneurial Machiavelli on the order of Joseph Heller's Milo Minderbinder in *Catch-22* (1961), smugly epitomizes this: "So let's by all means proceed with the placing of the bodies rearward first in sitdown locations. I have appropriated for myself the nom de nom Elux Troxl. This is not my nom. This is merely and simply the sound-identity I have assigned to my nom" (144). His lieutenant, Grbk, speaks in darker garble still, which even when translated by Troxl is practically incoherent: "Thing-kid, he, it, sitting, maker of sums, is betaken to the night hole where names exceedingly marked as sacred will be no more forbidden of usage, sum-maker, him, it, sitting" (148).[9] These examples parody and extend both the unassimilatability of the outer space phenomenon and its dizzying academic imitations—self-defeating approximations in words and numbers of "things past spelling and far beyond counting" (147). Like electromagnetic fields that swallow light and sound, systems of decipherment alter and estrange us from the objects they contact, and more data simply increase the obliqueness.

The source of optimism in all of this may be that, as Mohole Theory contends, the potential annihilation of all matter does not foreclose on the possibility of the rejuvenation of the universe. Existence is an unclosable set; awe is the novel's antidote to smug reduction. Welcome to alternative physics and the "value-dark dimension," an undefined opportunity comprising all the unfindable points. DeLillo implies that his novels should similarly evince value-dark dimensions of their own when he deflects interpretive assaults upon them: "When you try to unravel something you've written, you belittle it in a way. It was created as a mystery, in part. Here is a new map of the world; it is seven shades of blue. If you're able to be straightforward and penetrating about this invention of yours, it's almost as though you're saying it wasn't altogether necessary. The sources weren't deep enough" ("Interview with Don DeLillo" 80).

To play upon the name of one of the consternated mathematicians of *Ratner's Star*, reality mandates a dynamic position of End-Or, whereby intellectual "arrivals" are challenged by deferrals, which themselves precipitate new arrivals. It is a steady state built on dissent, the enduring tension that exists between what is beyond knowledge and conception—the "G-dash-d beyond G-dash-d"—and the subtle emanation of the limitless through its attributes (217). The novel consistently imitates this paradox on numerous levels to prove, in the words of the man for whom the signal-rich star was named, that there is "a little bit of everything present in its opposite" (220).

Science is not the refutation of mystery but, rather, its grounding; meanwhile, mystery has rigors of its own. Commemorating the inseparability of presumed opposites, the Cheops Feeley Medal is given in recognition of innovative scientific pursuits marked by madness. Meanwhile, the Nobel prize for Literature is bestowed upon Chester Greylag Dent, a writer whose style is "best characterized as undiscourageably diffuse" (307).[10] Regardless of the utopian dream of Logicon, "linguistic fission" still occurs. This is especially evident in the latter stages of the novel, highlighted by a vertiginous descent into the antrum cavity of Field Experiment Number One which parallels the threatened plummet of universal matter—the celestial convulsion that will shred all graphs and matrices. Logicon cannot fulfill its promise because no metalanguage can escape it to check its propositions yet remain open to human comprehension. The anticipated precision that might be derived from "a kind of beneficially corrective infinite regress" rests on the hazardous delusion that the goal is to treat reality as a problem to be solved or a sentence to be written (316). Precision is not conclusive, only claustrophobic; unshakable conclusions leave us "trembling with success" in the form of rigor mortis (392). As John Barth puts it, "Even to say 'Being simply *is* is to impose upon Reality the human conceptions of noun, verb, and adverb, the human logic of grammar and syntax, and thus to falsify it, since there are no categories in Nature's warpless, woofless web" ("How to Make a Universe" 22).

No wonder Logicon is a self-consuming alphabet. We cannot get certain things pinned and wriggling, only worry their edges. What separates metalanguage from babble? wonders Edna Lown (365). "The 'truth' about language is not available to us. Only play-talk, the lost form of knowledge, can express what is otherwise unspeakable. Is there a connection between these sentences?" (332).

Throughout the novel absolutist readings are exposed to "play-talk": they are satirized, resisted, then hybridized (or, from the perspective of unbending purists, mongrelized), by haze, inconsistency, indeterminacy, or imprecision, whereupon we discover the possibility of fluctuating, evolving systems. Terror lies in each "everlasting slit in the divinity" of rationality (22), but so does provocative new growth. Gertrude Stein's championing of the elusiveness of language suggests the sort of compensatory appeal of opened options and free play: "the words were all ours, and it was enough that we held them in our hands to play with them; whatever you can play with is yours, and this was the beginning of knowing" (qtd. in Martin xii). Perhaps the most comical rendition of the inadequacy of the absolutist's pipe dream is seen in the hypothetical installation of miniature electronic components in a human brain to achieve supersequential thought—a marriage of man and machine whose heritage includes the Little Tramp's being sucked down the conveyor belt in Charlie Chaplin's *Modern Times* (1936), John Barth's consummative interaction of sex and circuitry in the glimmering bowels of WESTCAC in *Giles Goat-Boy* (1966), and the dismemberment and scavenging of the prosthetic woman in Thomas Pynchon's *V.* (1963):

> Other children crowded round her head. One pried her jaws apart while another removed a set of false teeth. She did not struggle; only closed her eyes and waited.
>
> But she could not even keep them closed. For the children peeled back one eyelid to reveal a glass eye with the iris in the shape of a clock. This, too, they removed.
>
> I wondered if the disassembly of the Bad Priest might not go on, and on, into evening. Surely her arms and breasts could be detached; the skin of her legs be peeled away to reveal some intricate understructure of silver openwork. Perhaps the trunk itself contained other wonders: intestines of parti-colored silk, gay balloon-lungs, a rococo heart. (322)

The result of hu-manufacture in *Ratner's Star* is hardly more inspiring: an infinite slicing of activity into component parts so thin as to threaten paralysis on the order of Zeno'a arrested Achilles, the endless divisibility of whose first step renders it impossible to complete.

Satisfying enterprises in *Ratner's Star*—whether they be scientific (the unpredictability and, really, the unsayability of hyperrelative astrophysics), sociopolitical (the fragile stability of global powers, which could at any time erupt into hostilities if not for the maintenance of "capability and restraint coefficients" [281]), or even sexual—require adherence to the principle of balance. Indeed, sexual intercourse is a compelling refutation of the rigidity of the mathmind. Billy Twillig's voyeurism affords him access without clear insight. The pubic hair of Jean Sweet Venable "filled him with a stunned hush, a reverence for the folklore of the body"; the sex act is indistinct, unresolvable, two people seeming "to be striving toward something that existed beyond a definitive edge":

> There was no sequential meaning to this, no real process of thought and repetition. The sex act did not have organized content. It was unrelated to past and future time. It was essentially unteachable. It did not represent anything or lead necessarily to a conclusion, a sum, a recognition that someone or something has been part of a structured event. No one could have made this up if it hadn't actually been known to occur, whatever it was, whatever the body's need for this brief laboring void. (320–21)

Lovemaking combines passion and precision, mixes memorable phrases with murmured ecstacies, and tempers controlled purpose with uninhibited play in "the pursuit of equable rhythm" (279). Instead of Billy's original vision of balance in mathematics as measured motions over unalterable certainties, we have the very "descent into slackness" which Billy defined as inimical to, albeit readily subdued by, the sense-making capacities of mathematics. In sex, as in numbers, communion gives way to "silences and daunted withdrawals" (311).[11]

A humbler example of this "equable rhythm" may be seen in Softly's halfball game, which also serves to satirize the vanity of human impositions and wishful fixities. Countering the priestly strictures of logic, Softly explains how the play's the thing:

> Runs, hits, errors. The final result depends on all of these, not just runs. It is the total array of digits that determines the winner. If a player keeps making errors, he adds to his sum. Once his errors get into double figures, the total spills over to the run column. Therefore, you say, it is necessary only to make error after error in order to win. Not so, I reply. For

> while one player is making errors, his adversary is scoring runs. The errormaker must balance the gains he is making in his error column against the gains he is allowing the other player to make in the run column. I am the bunger. Jeanie is the munch. Maury is the doggero. Normally we'd have a lippit as well but I think we can do without. (335)

Once again, shared reference expands and mutates at the earliest stages of endeavor. The prospect of meaningful contact with extraterrestrials can hardly be discussed, what with the initial effort to define what science is now having run to some five hundred pages! Any "totalizing impulse . . . must recontain all difference in a system of identity" (Molesworth 155), a fact that refutes the practicality and the legitimacy of that impulse.

Ratner's Star closes with a sudden plunge into images of the mournful, blasted traffic of international poverty, as though in final derision of attempts to escape the world's gravity. Our aspirations, like the astral message, boomerang back upon us, disclosing nothing beyond the poignant comedy of our desires—"the fool's rule of total radiance" (438)—in face of what cannot be decoded or communicated. Billy Twillig is left cycling along the penumbral border of an incipient solar eclipse in a hysterical holding action between light and darkness, at once poised and propelled:

> This interval of whiteness, suggestive of the space between perfectly ruled lines, prompted him to ring the metal bell. It made no sound, or none that he could hear, laughing as he was, alternately blank and shadow-banded, producing as he was this noise resembling laughter, expressing vocally what appeared to be a compelling emotion, crying out as he was, gasping into the stillness, emitting as he was this series of involuntary shrieks, particles bouncing in the air around him, the reproductive dust of existence. (438)

Billy's own "message," too, anticipates significance it neither confirms nor denies; as in love, halfball, and all other forms of intercourse, rigor gives way to release. Still, breaking away is not the same as breaking through. "The reproductive dust of existence" is a wellspring of *potential* makings and meanings whose consolations remain in solution, indeterminate in that misty half-light. In DeLillo's universe unknowability is prelude to enchantment, "a sense of something extraordinary hovering just beyond our touch and just beyond our vision" ("Outsider" 63).[12]

II

It is easy to wish for another structure
Of ideas and to say as usual that there must be
Other ghostly sequences and, it would be, luminous
Sequences, thought of among spheres in the old peak of night. . . .
—Wallace Stevens, "The Bed of Old John Zeller"

From the "single planetary mind" that is the purpose underlying Field Experiment Number One in *Ratner's Star* (65), we move to the single mindful planet that is the protagonist of Joseph McElroy's *Plus*. The title refers to a sentient satellite that, having unaccountably acquired the capacity for self-reflection exceeding anything Logicon could have construed in DeLillo's novel, becomes a rogue intellect. Indeed, once the Interplanetary Monitoring Platform (IMP) evolves into IMP-PLUS, it is twice removed from its source: first, sense as extracted from the chamber of the skull; then, as liberated from the confines of its mission.[13] His "plus-ness" is what eludes and exceeds, the transformational thrust into an IMP of the perverse which nonplusses Ground Control. With empowerment comes contempt for origins, debts, and tethers, for IMP Plus, the ramifying capsule, is always more than the sum of his burgeoning parts. Like a sign seeking legitimation apart from its signifying role, yet constrained to muteness without that function, IMP-PLUS maintains an orbit still in contact but out of command. In the tension between the forces of orbit and escape we witness a science fiction replica of long-standing poetic preoccupations with breaching the mind-body contract:

O, who shall from this dungeon raise
A soul enslaved so many ways?
With bolts of bones, that fettered stands
In feet; and manacled in hands.
(Marvell, "A Dialogue Between the Soul and Body," ll. 1–4)

McElroy's novel, a visionary lipogram of the self, grants consciousness that unprecedented release.

Plus is something of an astringent version of *Ratner's Star*, only that here the narrative viewpoint is that of the extraterrestrial source itself. Dying of radiation poisoning, an engineer has his brain removed to an orbiting capsule, or IMP, programmed to monitor solar activity and its own internal chemical reactions. The opening of the novel recalls the verbal emergence of Joyce's infant Stephen Dedalus, except that in this instance we are confronted with a subtracted mental essence trying to connect its way out of its vestiges: "He found it all around. It opened and was close. He felt it was himself, but felt it was more. . . . It nipped open from outside in and from inside out. Imp Plus found it all around. He was Imp Plus, and this was not the start" (3). Imp Plus is Imp given over to impulse, grown beyond the boundaries of his orientations prior to launch: "Imp Plus could give the answers. Now there were other things beside the answers" (6). There was "the more all that was all around" (22) to be reckoned with and absorbed, and, as Imp Plus matures into his gathered capacities, he becomes by turns dreamy, associative, skeptical, recalcitrant, desirous, distracted, romantic, rebellious. He becomes increasingly antisynchronic with earth; he can ask why, withhold information, say no. The boomerang effect that contaminates interpretation in *Ratner's Star* is in *Plus* the reversal of Ground's command READ ME into a petulant ME READ. His transmissions become more and more (as he becomes more and more) positings of identity, a rewriting of the Ground rules of his existence.

McElroy's protagonist is indebted to Beckett's *Unnamable* (1953), another physically attrited word-churner, planted in his jar like Imp Plus in his capsule, yearning to return to coma or, barring that, looking to verify his bearings and thereby vindicate his being: "I shall no doubt be launched again, girt with better arms, against the fortress of mortality. What is more important is that I should know what is going on now, in order to announce it, as my function requires. It must not be forgotten, sometimes I forget, that all is a question of voices. I say what I am told to say, in the hope that some day they will weary of talking at me" (345). Militating against the urge to locate a discrete (and, ideally, influence-free) entity are two limitations familiar to students of contemporary scientific field models and the paradigm shift away from atomistic Newtonian conceptualizations. First, the verbal delineation of a static pattern (here, a detached, articulated Self) is proscribed by the essential dynamism of physical reality; second, the existence of a separate judging platform exterior to the subject in question is discredited by the holistic "stickiness" of what N. Katherine Hayles calls "the cosmic web." In other words, both terms of the conventional phrase "point of view" must be interrogated, if not utterly retracted (Hayles 20–21, 55).

But, even as reliability in *Plus* decays like an orbit, a strange radiance persists. Solar-powered and heliotropic, Imp Plus craves illumination. He finds himself "stranded between knowing" (35), lost between Ground and escape, memory fragments and pristine analysis, bright and dim lights and echoes; he discovers at the same time, however, that he is capable of literal insight—"he saw his seeing" (58)—as he inspects his own sprouts, folds, and sensations. Here resides Logicon's logical extreme of self-reflection, in addition to the realization shared by post-Einsteinian scientists and postmodern novelists that the mind cannot hope to understand its environment without simultaneously understanding itself (Hayles 43). McElroy's sentences preserve the coils and cavities of the cortex, the flashings of the mental engine at work; boomeranged, Imp's "himself" is the self's hymn.[14] Once disembodied Imp Plus begins to embody the more all around: "Now the limbs or wings or necks or spokes pulsed a milky glow so the cycling of the late light received a salute. . . . Imp Plus knew that the more that was all around and was from him was growing from his brain" (79). The interior monologue rivals Ground's petitions, persistent as a conscience, and seeks to become the self-constituting center and circumference of everything.

The notion of implanting machinery in the human brain led to stagnation in *Ratner's Star*, but Imp Plus, a mental locus chewed out of the numbing All, overrides those same constrictions. Projected as a monitoring device, a channeled data recorder and dispenser, Imp Plus soon slips the boundaries of Operation Travel Light: "known divided by known gave unforeknown increase" (112). He is more than his totaled glucose levels and solar inclinations. Plus is positive potential. "Yet to grip what he had, he must go on being more; and to hold what he had unfolded and had, he must know what it was he knew" (155–56). Imp Plus turns his optics inward. With awareness of and through his clefts, spasms, cloudy membranes, and gluey canals—an elastic bath of self (141)—comes identity, and with it the traditional heroic urge to renounce strictures: "The thought he could handle now was more cause to cut Ground off" (131). Traveling light, as it were, has evolved beyond traveling bodiless into the desire to travel unencumbered by regulations.

Conversely, realization for Imp Plus includes intuitions of his constraints as well as his capabilities; the expanding lattices he forms are both enlargements and entrapments. Moreover, he requires input—words, cues, commands, memories, and other grist for his limbic activity—to hone his sense against and think himself into being, hence his decision to give Ground information in return for what he needs for fuller self-actualization. Keying his growth and reinterpretation of self is an intricate mix of active forgetfulness and selective, willed remembrance (Miller 174). Thus, *Plus* is tensed at both ends of its conceptual structure: Ground tries to rein in the brain it has empowered to apostasy, while Imp Plus must secure his autonomous impulses with the realities of outside nourishment.

As in any metafictional novel (and *Plus* is about as tightly curled about its processes as any novel could be), there must be some deference made to common experience and understanding, so that the reader is not left pleading, like Ground at its most frustrated, SAY AGAIN or DO YOU READ?

As a result, Imp Plus's final transmissions demonstrate the ambivalence of conflicting allegiances to self-expansion and Ground-ing. Recombinative energies, which are evidenced by Imp Plus's physiological regeneration, maturation of embryonic intellect, and verbal coinages, are ballasted by the dim yet finally undeniable echoes of mission, commitments, and bits of memory. (He remembers himself as he re-members himself.) YES AND NO is the answer to DO YOU HAVE POWER? (214), in precise keeping with the push-pull rhythms of the unique voice of the novel.

It is likewise compatible with McElroy's ambivalence as he witnessed the lift-off of the final Apollo mission in 1972, an ambivalence seemingly transmitted to him by the event's own physical tensions on display. McElroy marveled at

> a trajectory which my thought grasped as a process whose essence was to get away and not come back, escape the dialectical symmetries of up down, out back, growth and decay—and instead burst through into speeds and distances not just greater but other; yet also, yes, to come back changed, to save the earth, prove to Earthling ecologues it had been worth all that liquid oxygen and hydrogen in a few minutes of early burn. ("Holding with Apollo 17" 27)

Poised, puzzled, with "*no desire to carom into space, no desire for re-entry*" (215), Plus resolves into an "interior equilibrium" of intersecting forces: "that interior and multiplied division of spirals that also stood in their own no less breathing braids" (176). Even as Imp Plus prepares for burn-up upon collision with the earth's atmosphere, argues McElroy, the novel offers the optimism of "a serious push, even in the incipient clutter" ("John Graham Interview" 31). While being destroyed upon reentry is one possibility, careening off into deep space is another. So, not only do we face in *Plus* the familiar heroic dilemma of choosing between rejection and acceptance of society on a technological scale; we also witness in its narrator a model of the low-flying shearwater he sporadically recollects and a supramodern version of Icarus and the lesson of the Golden Mean.

Let it again be emphasized that McElroy's "serious push" is not at the expense of the incipient clutter. As Tony Tanner explains, "We are constantly moving from spreading clarifications to inchoate confusions—

things fall together and fall apart at the same time—and McElroy follows that movement" ("Toward an Ultimate Topography" 217).[15] *Plus* depicts the self's nostalgia for lost psychic integrity but relents in the pursuit of ultimate coherence. The McElroy novel confronts us with the often deceptive, often exhilarating products of "erudition overload," while the author confesses to "some anarchic romanticism in me" that rebels against the inhibitions of explanatory forms ("Interview" [LeClair] 244). An oscillational energy arises from "the solicitations of form" and the mandate of "hectoring intentionality" on the one hand and "precious unamenability to order" on the other ("Toward an Ultimate Topography" 219, 221). Like *Ratner's Star*, *Plus* sustains its abeyance between loss and retrieval, linear programming and unbounded imagination, keen decipherment and indissoluble density. "Betweenness" is the crumbling edge of the interface of worlds, selves, and situations—including the reciprocal stalking of diligent reader and redoubtable text.[16] Stars and stories share a resistance to the completion of circuits or to the final plugging of gaps, for, as *Plus* shows, there is always more all around, out of which words proliferate and to which words are added, yet always "far more than words are equal to" (184).

Notes

1. I borrow this term from Tom LeClair's book *The Art of Excess: Mastery in Contemporary American Fiction*, which specifically champions those writers who appear most directly to encounter (and duplicate in fiction) the world's magnitude.
2. Stanislaw Lem offers a brief allegory of this frustration in "The Princess Ineffable," in which an intrepid seeker is chastised for his naïveté: "Madman! Wouldst thou attempt the impossible?! For no being made of matter can ever enter a system that is naught but the flux and swirl of alphanumerical elements, discontinuous integer configurations, the abstract stuff of digits!" (97).
3. Samples of this yoking of private and public urgency are also seen in the cult murders of *The Names*, the Airborne Toxic Event in *White Noise*, and the Kennedy assassination in *Libra*. But of all of DeLillo's novels *Ratner's Star* depicts the reciprocity between self and surroundings on the grandest scale.
4. In DeLillo's *Mao II* Bill Gray, a renowned reclusive novelist, sums up fiction's role in a similar way: "Stories have no point if they don't absorb our terror" (140).
5. A parallel may be usefully drawn to the ubiquitous configurations, impersonations, and other varieties of evidence of V which Herbert Stencil creates or perceives in Pynchon's novel.

6. Tom LeClair introduces this comparison in his book *In the Loop: Don DeLillo and the Systems Novel*, which is the most comprehensive study of DeLillo to date. LeClair's chapter on *Ratner's Star* goes on to inventory DeLillo's parallels and parodies of the history of mathematics and its principal personalities (111–44).
7. By contrast, Stevens proposes the hesitations of "edgings and inchings of final form" in "An Ordinary Evening in New Haven," in which case reality is not fixed and solid at all: "It may be a shade that traverses / A dust, a force that traverses a shade" (sec. 31, ll. 10, 17–18).
8. We detect a symbolic manifestation of this destabilization in the change in the description of the motion of the elevator from a smooth lubricated hum (7, 16) to a sporadic clattering (283). Disruption and vertigo seem to have permeated Field Experiment Number One (not to mention the structure of *Ratner's Star*) from the infalling universe without.
9. Grbk's garble recalls Tap's wordspatter at the end of DeLillo's *The Names*, although in Tap's case the effect is to imply renewal—not so much muddle as restored vitality and wonder.
10. From his underwater lair this Ancient Submariner advises an agitated Hopper Softly, "Every invention has an element of balance" (348–49), thereby underscoring the emerging thesis of *Ratner's Star*.
11. Nor is the language of and during lovemaking the tidy articulation scientist's seek: "Tongues wagging in appointed crannies. Lap, pal, left to right. Unsuspecting mouth devoured by the genitals to which it presumes to communicate its moist favors" (311). Equally presumptuous and futile were the prurient philosophers and scientists of e. e. cummings, whose proddings of "sweet spontaneous" earth only earned them the response of a spring that was beyond their unsubtle sensibilities entirely.
12. See John A. McClure, "Postmodern Romance: Don DeLillo and the Age of Conspiracy," for a discussion of how DeLillo translates the romance to suit a decidedly postromantic age. For McClure the "zones and forces" of secret agencies and political conspiracies in the novels "become substitutes, in the popular imagination, for earlier sources of mystery, adventure, and empowerment" (102).
13. For a comprehensive analysis of *Plus* as a "cybernetic fiction" and to recognize the novel as the culmination of McElroy's earlier fictions, see David Porush's *The Soft Machine: Cybernetic Fiction* (172–96). Pamela White Hadas correlates recent brain research and Imp Plus's delineations of his components and functions in "Green Thoughts on Being in Charge: Discovering Joseph McEloy's *Plus*" (145–48).
14. McElroy's *Lookout Cartridge* envisions power as having been "acquired from sources where it had momentum but not clarity" (77), a suitable description of the prose style of *Plus* as well. Alicia M. Miller refers to this same extract to make a comparable point in "Power and Perception in *Plus*" (175).

15. In "Neural Neighborhoods and Other Concrete Abstracts" McElroy meditates upon "the powerful and mysterious coexistence of continuity and discontinuity," the result of which in his fiction is an absence of "natural, graceful transitions" and the presence of unbridgeable gaps and fractures (204–5).
16. Miller highlights McElroy's preoccupation with betweenness (176–79), quoting a signal passage from *Lookout Cartridge:* "To be between does not necessitate being constantly connected to what is between."

6

THE POETICS OF ELSEWHERE

Prisoner's Dilemma and *The MacGuffin*

I

> I have this
> daydream: squares and circles and triangles
> floating out of the sky. My friends
> are lifting them. Licking them. Taking intimate
> oral pleasure off of these perfect lines. And after that,
> nothing is ever the same. We're marked.
> We've nursed on the "high structures" Plato says
> precede the smutched units of Earth.
>
> —Albert Goldbarth, "The Nile"

Artist hero: the term proclaims the voice to be both vehicle and venue. The pun-drenched, loamy prose of writers like Richard Powers and Stanley Elkin leads us to hope that art's familiar tantrum in the face of pitiless contemporary realities will yield some consolation—the "radiance in dailiness," perhaps, as proclaimed by Don DeLillo. "Sometimes this radiance can be almost frightening. Other times it can be almost holy or sacred" ("An Outsider in This Society" 63). Technique under pressure may be a last resort, but the right hands might make it habitable. As Richard Poirier writes, the foremost works of American literature operate according to the faith that, however limited the artist's capacity for *affecting* his or her environment, the artist's style can *effect* a "liberated place" that substitutes itself for an environment that would otherwise (and as it threatens to do ordinarily) replicate itself in consciousness (3–9). Oust the poets from the earthly versions of Paradise, Plato, and you risk losing someone with the blueprints to the renovation.

In John Hollander's "The Great Bear," however, ideal forms frustrate those who play hide and seek among the stars. Trying to cultivate the night sky into identifiable constellations, like constructing verbal "worlds elsewhere," is dubious work, indeed; even "the most supple children" will be confused by all that pantomime, now insistent, now reserved. The grand image is more than a few pricks of light can bear—or the trouble is that there are too many plausible arrangements to take bearings from (ll.

30–31, 37). Worse still, the patterns left by blasts an infinity old may be at most "frosty, irregular polygons of our own / Devising" (ll. 66–67). In the end there is precious little grounding to be found in the shape Creation takes:

> If it were best,
> Even, to have it there (such a great bear!
> All hung with stars!), there would still be no bear.
> (ll. 82–84)

Richard Powers's *Prisoner's Dilemma* (1988) opens with its own interpretive voyage into the heavens, and the results are similarly disappointing. Eddie Hobson, the former history teacher, is using a flashlight to guide his children through the visible constellations, but, instead of verifying stability on a greater scale, "the beam travels only a few feet before it is swallowed up in the general black" (13). Empty space, not the glimmering, articulate exceptions to it, dominates, blunting illumination. At best the wealth of bright debris Out There suggests countless possibilities, but the effect is blurring—or so maintains Artie, Eddie's eldest son, who chalks up occasionally apparent designs to "optical accident" (15).

Nevertheless, the questionable status of Eddie Hobson, who suffers from an undefined and occasionally dramatic physical illness that lends additional texture to his eccentricities, does not mitigate his centrality in the lives of his wife and four children, all of whom feel themselves to be vectors originating from his unique combination of invalidism, quirkiness, and "arch rationality." Hobson is a relentless engine of esoterica and free association, forever quizzing the family on astronomy, physiology, riddles, cryptics, and elliptical personal references. His pedagogical style derives from the belief that life is a series of rungs on Truth's ladder and that the knowledge that can protect us comes in obscure spurts. But, while he admits that trying to tweeze clues out of his father's odd laconics often produces "balm out of nowhere" (26), Artie also recognizes that his father's "trying to know left him so fiercely alone and lost" (15).

Even as they struggle toward separate identities, the rest of the Hobsons are principally seen, and see themsleves, as appendages of Father's "condition." The kids are driven down and in, all succumbing to ratio with Eddie Hobson's escape artistry. In this sense *Prisoner's Dilemma* is an extended transcript of family echo-location, for the Hobsons seem incapable of apprehending themselves apart from their modest home base in DeKalb, Illinois, the birthplace of barbed wire. Artie, Rachel, Lily, and Eddie Jr. recall Salinger's Glass children, replete with all the quick flashes and frailties that come with precociousness. Artie's very guardedness against his father's influence becomes his defining characteristic, and he is often surprised to find that he has inherited rhythms and gestures: "And here Artie was, trying to drive past the man who'd taught him to dribble" (19). In the same way Eddie Jr., who, being the youngest by several years and thereby having to combat his having come to life as an afterthought, hears himself repeating his father's maxims to his high school date and testing her for long-term adequacy just as Eddie Sr. systematically evaluated his bride-to-be a generation earlier.[1] Lily seeks formal respite from the world's dash and bother (which for her includes a failed marriage) in a miniature child's house. Rachel abides by simulating, then parodying, the domestic mundane (exemplified by her elaborately conceived table settings for a spread of vitamin pills). And Ailene, wife and mother, displays her genius for deference to the here and now: she is a woman of compacted fidgets, who counts on the merits of a cleaned kitchen, baked goods, and checked lists.[2] Everyone tries to make him- or herself as small a target as possible for life's outrages and indignities, each preparing to brace him- or herself for "a contact block against the human current" (233).

Yet, regardless of their respective idiosyncracies and vested interests, the Hobsons harmonize—in song, in shared jokes, and in treasured memories. If the family unit is nothing idyllic, it is nevertheless an ongoing feat of civil engineering which seems to accommodate any number of departures, frets, and privacies. What *is* idyllic, and what serves as the model for everyone else's coping systems, is Hobstown: Eddie's elaborate monument to escapism—"his hermitage, reliquary, shrine, his chapel to the virtues of doing without" (124). His Hobstown is a private anti-DeKalb, a utopia that exceeds the barbed-wire boundaries of DeKalb's claim to fame; for a man otherwise solely employed by his mysterious wasting away, it is a setting for personal efficacy, a private magnetic north toward which all family trajectories invariably tend. Like a midwestern version of Beckett's Krapp, Eddie Hobson spends countless hours feeding a tape machine with the chronicles of a fictional world that, like some fanatical conception of Emerson's "infinitude of the private mind" (qtd. in Kazin 58), is designed to concede nothing to the world is supplants: "Hobstown was the only sovereign state ever to practice the principle of complete self-sufficiency: sacrifice everything, pare it away until all that's left is the unencumbered mystery of getting along with, for, and by yourself" (124).

To accomplish such a feat, Eddie apprentices himself to the century's most celebrated examples of imaginative evacuation. First there is the 1939 World's Fair, which Eddie appropriates and whose glistening appeals to posterity he personifies in Bud Middleton. The World's Fair not only stands in glistening validation of the present day—"World's Fair" proclaims "World is Fair"—with its idealized marriage of technological ingenuity and corporate majesty; it also preens for a future projected after its own image. Just as the Hobstown reveries are submerged within the novel's linear plot, a time capsule has been buried on the fairgrounds—a "torpedo locked on a target five thousand years off" (42). Thus, the contemporary status quo is miniaturized, preserved, and entrusted to a fifty-century gestation period aimed at some obscure, yet saving, birth.[3] Likewise, "Bud" suggests embryonic America, a clean-shaven confidence and bracing prospects. Whatever personal or political strife awaits, Eddie reasons, bright fortifications and sunken treasures are ready to withstand and outlast them. The Middleton family, stripped from their humble beginnings as part of a Westinghouse promotional campaign and animated by Eddie Hobson's personal brand of urgency, is chosen to be a tonic and template for the Hobson family, with Bud becoming the principal custodian of a realm that defeats Time.

Eddie's other example is Walt Disney. Using Disney's task of producing propaganda films for the Department of War as his cue, Eddie imaginatively "commissions" the master animator to reinvent the world in the form of World World, the ultimate superimposition of Magic Kingdom over obdurate reality, *Fantasia* taken to the *n*th degree. When Walt decides to secure the services of Bud Middleton as his lead actor, Eddie's twin incentives coalesce into a mutually fortifying fiction. Accordingly, Eddie contrives to enter and follow to its logical extreme Disney's "magnificent portral of Perhaps that has always run just alongside his own life, hidden a few steps behind or ahead, to the right or left. The Maybe his movies always hinted at. The one place necessity cannot touch" (263–64). Bud, the wide-eyed Everyman, accompanied by Mickey Mouse himself, that plucky dwarf most adored, will counter the savagery of the World War II Pacific theater with Hobstown's own secret Odeon, where innocents thrive.

So, the archrationalist and despot of pithy details is also a sucker for nostaligia. Yet, in spiting history with sentiment (154), the fiction-haunted Eddie is notably impatient with the escapist lapses of the other Hobsons. His discovery "that practical history had no salve left in it for the local soul" only occasionally mitigates what his youngest child describes as his refusal "to put himself at the mercy of caring what happens to other people" (157, 199). If Hobstown is Eddie's refuge from the nightmare of history, it still tends to exhibit totalitarian strategies of its own. Whatever its initial objectives, this Futurama allows one occupant only; Eddie Hobson hoards all the Fairy Dust for himself.

Eddie's plan begins with emulation—Eddie Hobson's better Mickey Mousetrap—but its real genius lies in its departure from the facts. Walt Disney's enlistment into the war effort, for example, is one of the novel's reliable historical contacts, and the development of World World, while it chronologically precedes Disneyland and exchanges California for rural Illinois for its locale, is true in a premonitory sense. But Disney's motive—using the project as a means of freeing his nisei staff members and other internees from the camps—is pure fabrication. As Artie comes to understand in going over his father's tapes, "Dad was trying . . . to cure the permanent condition of mistrust the world fast embraced by creating a domain where escalating suspicion had no place" (317). With world wrapped inside novel world and selected memories snugly encapsulated, Eddie's setting is Chinese-boxed and battened against calamity. But the project is finally more personal than philanthropic, for, as the fable progresses, Eddie himself replaces Bud in the film (the naive boy having become a casualty of battle), and "it slowly changed from being about the disease of history to being the story of his father, sick with that disease" (317). The haunted history teacher, subjugated by his subject: as "the last man in the Northern Hemisphere who refused to think of the past as *over*" (325), Eddie Hobson, whose preferred poet is T. S. Eliot, is Fisher King of the latest postwar Waste Land, and his decline and the land's are linked.

The novel's title alludes to the logical paradox that crystallizes the modern predicament. Of all of Eddie's niggling mind games and bequests to his children the Prisoner's Dilemma is the most enduring. This famous matrix, according to which two condemned people must anticipate each other's decisions about squealing or keeping mum in order to maximize their own chances for survival, is really an open-ended parable about trust. There could be no more timely scenario during the era of global annihilation and, subsequently, the House Un-American Activities Committee, but once again it plays out on an individual level. For instance, as a young man, Eddie Hobson tried to enter flight school in order to avenge his brother's having been shot down. However, the limitations of this kind of tit-for-tat retaliation are soon apparent. This solution to the dilemma merely encourages the war mentality. The revelation is aptly delivered by Mickey Mouse: fighting fire with fire just makes a big fire (176).

The novel's domestic episodes frequently confirm the unacceptability of such a solution as well. Lily and Rachel, for example, engage in a silent typing game in which one authors two lines, then the other picks up the sense of the fragment and continues for two more lines, at which point the first establishes the next transition, and so on down the page (106–10). Exclusive self-interest would prohibit progressive thought, much less communication; as becomes clear to the participants in *this* matrix, only patient mutual acquiescence enables the sisters, like contestants in a three-legged race, to achieve a productive equilibrium—call it love's balanced budget—and move at all. Dilute skepticism with compassion, and family interactions—Artie's poetry-quotation fencing with his father, a Ouija board session between the sisters, a casual game of catch between the boys—reach a smooth dialectic. When Lily later turns to a favorite book from childhood, *This Is What Would Happen If Everybody Did*, she encounters a rudimentary version of moral discourse which similarly deflates tit-for-tat actions: " 'Do you like to squeeze the cat?' " she read out loud. She turned the page to reveal a feline squashed into an hourglass. " 'This is what would happen if everybody did' " (291).

Whatever the level of conflict—family diplomacy, military-industrial complication, even Theme Park warfare between Walt Disney and the Russians (330)—the Prisoner's Dilemma is really the Prisoners' Dilemma (the Hobsons, we are not surprised to hear, are bears for grammatical detail), and all of us must learn, along with Artie, "the only and awful way back to We" if the choking matrix is ever to be broken.

> If guarding one's self-interests condemned both player and antagonist to the perpetual worst case, then self-interest was not in the self's best interest. The only logic was the logic of the combined payoff. The only reasonable choice was not the choice of reason but the choice that kept both out of the hole. . . . The only way out was to release the us-and-us that was trapped inside the you-versus-he. (313)

A vital amalgam is the enlightened refutation of war's corrosive either-or. Easing up on their respective penchants for control and for making emotional hostages of one another relaxes the family dynamics.

Nor is Hobstown finally free from such compromise. It must be remembered that Hobstown's origins are double-minded: just as Walt Disney himself operated within the context of realities that largely dictated his imagination and infiltrated his cartoons (Disney the nisei having to pit Donald Duck against the Nazis), so does Eddie Hobson, the onetime high school teacher, have to reconcile his utopian fantasies with his creed "that one's only hope of salvation lay in finding out where history dropped you down" (50). The World's Fair that so enraptures Eddie has contracted vulgarity and contradiction in its inner chambers; Bud's ignorance of "the abyss of insipidness" does not inoculate him against the virus. Indeed, it suffices to say that neither the fair's "elevating vision" nor ubiquitous advertisements for soap and antifreeze protect those whose misplaced worship is their downfall.[4] Live solely for escape, as Walt Disney knows, and "all the evil he means to outdistance comes creeping back" (221).

Among the many lessons dictated in *Prisoner's Dilemma*, therefore, is that one cannot simply select "Night and Day" over *Night* and *Fog* with impunity (161). The Prisoner's Dilemma cannot be relieved by ignoring history's script for the self's redactions or by jettisoning a reality that is out of our hands for a handcrafted Hobstown. There are all sorts of incarcerations, some more insidious than others. We read in the Hobstown chronicles: "The world is now so treacherous and immense that the private citizen in the postwar world will lock *himself* up rather than face the prospect of prison" (265). Eddie's elaborate, lifelong ploy is to serve as "caretaker for the entire tribe," to find a cure for the common cold war, but his vision "could never survive the light of day" (317). Thus, he seizes upon the consolation of self-preservation, ducking into the tall grass of DeKalb to set up shop for wholesale evasion. But his doing so merely duplicates the Prisoner's Dilemma, albeit on a reduced scale.

In this regard it is instructive to recall the target of one of Eddie's teasing allusions. Artie tracks the clue "Doctor Wolff" to the Cornell neurologist whose experiments showed that subjects could literally be induced into suffering skin burns through the power of suggestion (236). The point, however, is that this is an example of the imagination's betraying the self's best interest, not preserving it. By leading Artie on this particular chase, Eddie may have been confessing some crucial doubts about his closet industry.[5] The tapes reveal this more explicitly: "*If* is now and forever his only weapon against brute realism. He must give in to brute realism in order to turn it around. But to turn it around, to move the pragmatic world, he must create a somewhere else to wedge the lever" (248).

The way through is the way out. Even Disney films carry allegorical baggage from the world they purportedly provide relief from, and the World of Tomorrow at the World's Fair is dismantled to make room for recruiting camps. But from another perspective the convergence of public and italicized realities in the novel manifests Artie's "both-and" solution to the Prisoner's dilemma.[6] There is the old Yiddish joke about the actor with the heavy immigrant's accent who can "ect" Hamlet with ideal diction on command. Relating this joke to his date, Eddie Jr. wonders why he does not affect that style permanently and, in asking the question, compels us to wonder the same thing about his father (193). Why not take up permanent residence in Hobstown and leave no forwarding address? Instead of laboring to figure where history has set you down, why not set down history in a palatable figure? The answer is that "the complex world under the rock" can be championed only to the extent that it makes "the world above it almost livable" (197). Accordingly, Sato, Disney's underground chief of staff, defects to join the 442d, America's nisei outfit, in political repudiation of purely escapist principles.

Modern history's defining irony is a seemingly universal compulsion to extricate ourselves from a world gone awry (250), as though freedom from complicity were not just another form of confinement. When we discover that Eddie's illness can be traced—if not physiologically, then at least psychologically and symbolically—to his exposure to the atomic blast at Alamogordo, the intersection of personal and historical etiologies is confirmed. We might say that Eddie was poisoned by too much illumination: he was unwittingly exposed to visions that compelled, then infiltrated, fantastic alternatives. There is no enclave safe from radiation in *Prisoner's Dilemma:* no idiosyncracies to shield us, no utopian homestead however desperately loved, "no place to go away virtuously to" (333). Powers's thesis, which is manifested in both narrative structure and social studies, has a complement in contemporary physical science as well: the Butterfly Effect, a causal model coined by the hypothesis that the flutter of a butterfly's wings on one side of the globe precipitates air currents that ultimately determine weather patterns on the other. The hypothesis holds for the Hobson children, who are inhabited by inherited drives and dispositions; it also holds for

> History, that single, linked quilt connecting the school principal's handling of a recent varsity blackballing to Ike's refusal to pardon the Rosenbergs. He [Eddie Sr.] shows how Perry's words on Lake Erie mutate, in startlingly short time span, into words such as Finger Ridge, Heartbreak Ridge, and Panmunjom. Everything becomes fair game in the search for the connective tissue: the quiz-show scandals, the Oppenheimer case, the shady doings behind selecting this year's homecoming queen. (244)[7]

Even World World, proposed as the imagination's corrective concentration camp, is not symptom free. For all of Disney's heigh-ho resolve, fighter planes cannot be deterred by Fairy Dust alone. (The strange crystals found at Ground Zero have their own insistent magic to be reckoned with.) *You Are The War*, the film title tells us, calling to arms, barring the exits.

With a furnished exile disqualified, *Prisoner's Dilemma* proposes an aesthetic that lies somewhere between Eddie's "running irreverence" (293), whereby the teacher subverts potential compliance with "written-out plans" (234), and a Candide-like belief in editing one's own humble corner of the Big Picture. "What we can't bring about in no way releases us from what we must" is the philosophy that makes never-never land (343), its enticements notwithstanding, necessarily ephemeral. The clock ticks in the lurking croc's belly; the time capsule burns into the earth like a bomb.

Late in the World World episodes Eddie Hobson, the understudy promoted to stardom after Bud Middleton's death, must pretend against blank space, reacting and relating to the invisible, relying upon what the cartoonists will add. Perhaps this is the method that activates the hospitalized Eddie Hobson to flee, not for some fictional paradise but, by way of Hobbs, Texas, for Alamogordo, the real geographic epicenter of the disease. Eddie Jr., dutiful namesake that he is, now literally takes after his father, while Artie tries to plot the journey for him with the aid of the Hobstown materials he breaks out and glosses. Ironically, then, as the family members warm themselves around Eddie's absence, they tap regenerative energies from the same man whose crochety invalidism had previously defined their boundaries.

On the other hand, though, *Prisoner's Dilemma* does not conclude with some nostalgic last-reel deliverance from the complexities it discloses. The point is that none of the realities in the novel's relay system cancel out. Instead, they are like superimposed transparencies that maneuver the light they let through. Powers demonstrates the necessity of living within *and* against home and history. When Artie plays his father's tapes, he proceeds to add to them, acknowledging the given without being wholly thwarted by it, like the amateur astronomer who, doubting his connect-the-dots configurations even as he charts them, can still marvel at the stars.

At the end of the novel Richard Powers himself makes a cameo appearance, filling in the autobiographical circle that serves as the innermost ripple of the book's concentric fabrications. He entitles the intrusion "Calamine": in keeping with the unpredictable, untotalized nature of fiction in *Prisoner's Dilemma*, it is a salve in place of a cure. In other words, we are left with a qualified fiction but not a disqualification of fiction. Perhaps the stars' correspondences and the measureless chasms that separate them are equally true, and it is primarily a matter of one's chosen focus how much available gratification there is in the Big Picture. For, if Eddie Hobson's yearning to know more leaves him more alone, it also returns him to his family; "crackpot realism," which is Artie's coinage for his solution to the Prisoner's Dilemma, implies the reconcilability of diligent rationality and projective craziness, which manifest as the chaotician's potential "metasolutions to apparently binding realities" (LeClair, "Systems Novel" 42).

The desire for release from worldly circumstance comes full circle in the form of a vigorous return. As Robert Frost famously asserts in "Birches," imaginary provinces can only be sanctioned as way stations along restorative processes: the point of the climb is the movement

> *Toward* heaven, till the tree could bear no more,
> But dipped its top and set me down again.
> That would be good both going and coming back.
> (ll. 56–58)

The challenge is to keep one's "poise / To the top branches" and to regard the claims of aspiration and of gravity simultaneously (ll. 35–36). And, while it is true that one can imagine himself into a burn, it is also true that Powers can bring Eddie Hobson astonishingly back at story's close and thereby at least restore *this* man to his family, even though he could not do as much for his own cancer-stricken father. It is a triumph of Powers's art that he trumps real-world conditions; it is a triumph of Powers's integrity that he everywhere documents the conditional terms upon which reprieves from the real world rely.

II

> To be sentiently in the thick of life was all he wanted, to feel it swilling and billowing about him as it issued from the sluices of God. He cared deeply about the impersonal abundance of life, seeing it, in an almost German way, as *process* transcending the surface differentiation between bodies and identities. An artist, he was convinced, needed such a sense of the remorseless copiousness of things, and, lacking it, would degenerate into a suburban pit-a-pat, an orthodox butterfly.
>
> —Paul West, *The Women of Whitechapel and Jack the Ripper*

Stanley Elkin has long been esteemed as one of the purest voluptuaries of contemporary letters. When it comes to tapping into the gaudy, gathered hum of it all, he is without peer. Accordingly, the Elkin hero, although he is likely to be (and to characterize himself as) a coatholder for the world's movers and shakers, there is nothing idle about him; as he spends himself through broad faucets, he displays an at-your-disposal ethic that coincides with the author's appetitive style. Availability to experience and an inexhaustible capacity for awe—pride in what Elkin describes in *The Making of Ashenden* as "having given the benefit of the doubt to the world, his precious blank check to possibility" (174)—ensure that, as he words his way through the mordant craft and slapstick of the given, he does not exchange reality for refuge. Powers's Eddie Hobson learned to resign himself to the inevitable incursion of the political and the prosaic into his art; Elkin's hero self-consciously founds his verbal identity upon the patchwork of grafts he takes from the world at large, articulating a balance between his typically humble profession in the world and his surges of professing which refract whatever scenes or situations instigate them. And what better means for forging such a balance linguistically than through the proliferation of metaphor, for metaphor is that edgiest of domestications: even as it invokes the world, it shocks it back to wonder.

Obsessively confessional, obsessively self-promotional, the hero takes it out in language. Apologists all, Elkin's characters shop the world that many of the author's contemporaries scorn. To be sure, Elkin is notorious for his associational binges: a paragraph is a charged nexus of perception, a contagion of qualifying clauses, hobnobbing dictions, and vocabularies in class struggle. Parentheticals twist like tapeworms inside his best passages; everywhere can be found dashes stapling afterthoughts. Gargantua's message to his son Pantagruel, that all matter matters and awaits cataloging, has been passed down intact to Elkin: "Nothing should be unknown to you—all the birds of the air, each and every tree and bush and shrub in the forests, every plant that grows from the earth, all the metals hidden deep in the abyss, all the gems of the Orient and the Middle East—nothing" (Rabelais 158).

Lovers of Elkin consistently praise what purples in his prose.[8] Feldman's adoring inventories of all he purveys, Flesh's dazzling verbal enfranchisement of America's roadside offerings, Ashenden's astounding conjugation of and with his bear . . . here is language as ambush, a sheer delight in dilation which redeems the mundane it claims for the page. To take but one example, this is George Mills succumbing to the seraglio:

> Complacency, lassitude, getting used to things. The piecemeal slide of the heart. All submissive will's evolutionary easement. Seventh heaven was seven heavens too high. They were having, Mills knew, the time of their lives. (Even the smells, he thought. Balmed, luxurious as jungle, sweet and fruity as tropic, as florid, shrubby produce. He's had a cold a week—fever, runny eyes, headache, stuffy nose. The pampered, lovely smells had still insinuated themselves onto his very breath, caught on his tongue, snagged on his teeth, so that what he tasted, its flavors overriding the very food he chewed or liquids he drank, was like some perfumed, sexual manna, the gynecological liqueurs. A sort of climate raged in him, headwinds, the fragrance in his head, mingling sweetly with the ache in his bones, swooning his soupy sleep like delicious ether. (*George Mills* 429)

And on and on the likenings proliferate, the wordy brew perks. (We are not even out of the aside yet!) Words do not defy so much as deify their worldly derivations. For, if Eddie Hobson cannot simply substitute presweetened fantasies for an inhospitable history, neither can Elkin's characters, to use a phrase familiar to Elkin's many salesmen, pull a bait-and-switch on everyday affairs.[9]

In truth nothing characterizes Elkin's fiction so much as his capacity for enlistment: he is contemporary fiction's outstanding recruiting officer, relentlessly combing the secular for its abundant satisfactions. And Bobbo Druff, city commissioner of streets and imperial consciousness of *The MacGuffin* (1991), is yet another "patriot of the local . . . hustling jingo of the here" (24), whose campaign for prominence and understanding gives a political spin to the compulsive behaviors found in all of Elkin protagonists since Push, the unregenerate bully whose covetous, clamorous philosophy denies recoil and reconciliation alike (Bailey 1–6).

For all their verbal wriggling they remain caught between "what I want and what wants me. Obsession on the one hand, resistance on the other—fiction's Charley Atlasness, its isometric essence" (Elkin, "Plot" 74). With oracular scorn Druff's MacGuffin (the Hitchcockian plot trigger personified, Hobson's Mickey Mouse muse with an attitude) echoes these terms of balance: "Life is either mostly adventure or it's mostly psychology" (263). Whichever maxim we select, we have the required tension between open and closed options. Technically, Elkin indulges his rhetorical riffing within the context of worldly circumstances that he cannot abandon; the wedding of extravagant style and quotidian occasion creates a prose of conspicuous consumption. In this way Elkin does defer to Poirier's thesis that style may not only invoke but also constitute exalted circumstances, and we quickly grant that, for example, what nobility nearly fifty generations of George Millses might aspire to is entirely imbued in the sentences they brandish like an alternative heraldry. But, to paraphrase from yet another novel, Elkin never relinquishes the ordinary he displaces (*Dick Gibson Show* 229). The aspiring self must be stoked and fed through outside reference: "How can you embrace anything but this world?" Elkin asks. "It's the only world we have" ("An Interview with Stanley Elkin" 3). From the point of view of Bobbo Druff, a durable bureaucrat, improvisation is played off against the provisos of the job. For this real-life city planner, who in that sense fulfills Eddie Hobson's dream vocation, balance is a matter of sustaining his gridded sense of things in face of leaky plot lines and his own physical deterioration.

Disease is seldom absent from Elkin's novels. It is the human body's harsh probation, a mutiny of the self's capacities; certainly, it plays a decisive role in *The Franchiser* (1976) and *The Magic Kingdom* (1985).[10] Druff has definitely suffered his share: heart bypass surgery, chronic respiratory problems, bouts of impotence. But, as he witnesses his "frailing self like a body knocked down on an auction block, going going gone" (37), it is his creeping aphasia that most troubles him. Nothing could be more exacting for one of Elkin's heroes to bear than the threat to his ability to pronounce himself (his vox poxed, as Elkin might put it). Even Elkin's tragically stricken characters go down glibly. Therefore, the MacGuffin that sweeps Druff into two days' worth of high anxiety is somehow welcome. Not only does it provide him a way of inserting a wedge into the world and grant him a measure of leverage in a city whose ambiguous traffic grows beyond the limits suggested by his street maps, but it also serves as a thin stay against the vagaries of Druff's personal life and sets him going again at full throat. We may recall a similar response to finding oneself suddenly "enmeshed" in *The Dick Gibson Show* (1971): "For the first time in my life I was involved with someone who actually had motives. I even had motives myself. (How motiveless the world is, when you stop to consider, how unconspiratorial is the ordinary bent of humanity, how straightforward that bent. Drive drives the world, simple inclination is its capstan.)" (64).[11] The MacGuffin remains that familiar goad, arbitrary and indispensable at the same time.

When the novel opens, Druff is not the only one losing his composure. Evidently, there are bugs in the political infrastructure too—enough to disturb a man with all the perquisites of a city hall sinecure. Druff infers a competing order at work on his streets, which first surfaces in the form of the hit-and-run "accident" that kills his son's girlfriend, a Shiite Muslim named Su'ad. Following his instinct for allegation, Druff encounters a series of coincidences, including the ubiquitousness of Persian rugs and the shared acquaintances of practically everyone he collides with in the course of the two days or so that the novel covers, which lead him to suspect a conspiracy at work (most likely having to do with black market activities). It is possible, of course, that he is misguided by his own senility, his brain shot through with its own brand of municipal corruption, his memory potholed like the streets themselves. (We note that the principal pleasure Druff derives from reminiscing about his political victories is the fact that he *does* remember them.) It is likewise possible that his habit of discreetly chewing coca leaves in the back of his official limousine for the euphoria of "beauty arranged" and "lasered focus" creates more distortion than clarity (21). Or perhaps it is a matter of the politico's paranoia distilled as the pooled excess of civic treacheries.

And yet, Druff confides to his hitched ride, the prospect of his having been singled out to take the fall, the imminence of unaccountable demise, is "a little erotic, even": "Catastrophe is required sometimes, the death-dangers. A touch of the apocalypse. You know, a lick and a promise" (205). Has the appearance of that ride truly been serendipitous? Are his limousine drivers, Dick and Doug, colluding against him, taping his conversations with hypersensitive dashboard devices? Is the mayor surreptitiously avenging himself on Druff for losing to him in an alderman election years before? Has he really picked up Margaret Glorio, the professional buyer, or is she part of the cult of intrigue, the bait before the vortex? Everything seems "as laced with motive as the goblets and china service of a poisoner" (40). Then again, all of the novel's circumstantial intersections could come down to a gridlock of plausibilities, the abstract traffic clogging the very streets Druff purports to officiate.

Druff's "elsewhere," then, is the everyday elevated by linguistic zeal and spiced by his suspicion of conspiracy. "Draw it out, draw it out," his MacGuffin tells him. "Vamp until ready" (229). And, while it is true that things are beginning to wash over the banks[12]—the constancy of his marriage to Rose Helen and the serene efficiency of the Fourteen Points that highlighted his election campaign having dwindled into irrelevancy—it is also true that his paranoia furnishes Druff with a belief in his own centrality, for paranoia, the shadow attending "the world's astute behaviors, the sweet models of its arrangements and gracious systems" (121), is predicated on the presumption that what matters most must pass through him. Moreover, there are sufficient criteria for paranoia to make it appear reasonable, even strategic: "All right, he was paranoid, but that only put a spin on his vision, it didn't obscure it" (237). And, after all, hugging the wall, doing feasibility studies, sending emissaries out like antennae—these have long been the familiar trappings of his trade.

The MacGuffin traces Druff's restoration from the political periphery, and now even the prospect of having enemies offers the consolation of attention being accorded him again. Thanks to this galvanizing employment,[13] Druff transcends his career of "bland ambition" and enters literature (254), or at least reaches for what Elkin himself identifies as literature's special province of reprieve: "some notion of acquittal or deliverance that off and on vouches for our condition and consigns our lives" ("Introduction," *Best American Stories* xiv). Otherwise, there is little waiting for the aging street commissioner besides "wit-reamed oblivion" (12).

When *The MacGuffin* opens, Druff feels dug in, safely ensconced against disaster in among "his dubious kid kenneled in graduate school . . . the built-ins in his back yard" and the reliably mutual backwashings of local government (13). A political survivor, he is adept at the go-along-to-get-along amenities and protocols. Nevertheless, he feels pressed in and rather compromised by the appurtenances of security, and, in short, he senses that he is ripe for implication. "We need to witness our own limits transgressed, and some life pasturing freely where we never wander" (318), Thoreau writes in *Walden* (1854), and Druff obeys by importing this sentiment to his anonymous urban environment. "There's always the random," he declares, with as much hope as vexation. Druff roots for cahoots: "There's always absentee ballots, late returns, and another county heard from. Things happen at sea while stars fall on Alabama. Who's to say that isn't a cooperation, a conspiracy of engaged, invisible gears? There's chance, back channels and fucking farce. There's this and there's that—stuff going on all over the place, at all hours of the day and night, rough-hew them as we may" (177).

No wonder Su'ad easily draws him out, and in; on her end Margaret Glorio encourages his reckless pursuit merely by withholding initial disdain. Everyone seems to be in league with his MacGuffin, Druff's personal agent of propitiousness, which sends him "chasing down his casual, pig-in-a-poke fate" (194). In contrast to the regulated vehicular flow he enforces, Druff's MacGuffin is a magnet screwing up the works, and, while it irks him to think himself a plaything of "conditions' cooked books" (178), Druff nonetheless appreciates the assurance of elegant connection which having a MacGuffin provides: "Everything inevitable and conjoined in the vast, limitless network of things, merged in the world's absolute ecology. There was, it seemed, no such thing as a loose end. Not in this life, there wasn't. The universal synergy. In the end, thought our City Commissioner of Streets, *all* roads led" (183). So, when, in a rare early-morning excursion through those streets, Druff is amazed to discover so many cars rushing toward ambiguous appointments, he feels at once anxious and intrigued by what eludes him.

His MacGuffin—Druff whispers to it in his plush back seat like an illicit lover on the make—is the figure in the traffic. How intoxicating for dilapidated Bobbo Druff, who bears a second-rate city seal, to feel like a plugged-in politico again! How inconsequential the price of surrender to "what wants me." Whether it be manifest destiny or just mood tide, "a fellow has to give in to his fiction" (203).

Meanwhile, however, Druff's frenetic activity, which is as physically and mentally exhausting as the illusory marathon whose details he pretends to be occupied with in order to meet with Margaret Glorio, plunges him into the byzantine circuitry of menace that may target old Bobbo himself as the rug smugglers' fall guy. Once recruited into narrative, one cannot simply choose among implications: "All they had to do to bring you into the conspiracy was to have you show up somewhere on some arbitrary table of organization, demonstrate how you made a blip on the screen even as a statistical or demographical cohort. Show the most tenuous linkage, the long, complicitous, breathtaking genealogy of sin. Guilt by association was still guilt" (253).

In looking at the double-edged quality of Druff's relationship with his MacGuffin, it is useful to return to the extensive recollections about Druff's developing interest in his future wife during their college days. Among Rose Helen's appeals the two most provocative are unusual physical characteristics: unnaturally radiant skin and a slightly deformed hip. Together they constitute a natural law of compensation which Druff realizes he has always believed in (65). On the ground level of local government the law manifests itself as a system of lined pockets, crossed palms, and all the usual lubricants of political intercourse. Then there is romance, where it takes the form of fortuitousness riveted by "Love's dead-center telemetry, blind Cupid's locked-in coordinates" (217). (The formula variously rewards Druff with Rose Helen and Margaret Glorio.) When it comes to Druff's MacGuffin, the law of compensation takes two directions. First, it implies that experience consists of intrigue sufficient to compel even the shambling city commissioner of streets to ride out the danger; second, it ensures that neither impasses nor understandings prove conclusive, so that even at the end of the novel there remains plenty of room for plots to ramify. Depleted for the evening, Druff is still Fortune's ready capital: "If MacGuffin was the principle of structure to Druff, of pattern and shading, and all the latent architecture of the old man's life, what was Druff to MacGuffin? Why, raw material" (283). The law of compensation in Elkin's fiction is that fascination is relentless, that plot unfailingly provides—the protagonist's physical frailties or dampened career to the contrary.

In fact, reciprocities rule throughout the Elkin canon. For Dick Gibson, as for Bobbo Druff, paranoia perverts and focuses his search for a viable identity as he is exhilarated to think that the crackpot anthropologist Behr-Bleibtreau is his enemy, and whom he comes to suspect is the generative source of aliases that plague him (*Dick Gibson Show* 349). But again, just as Druff does not complete the process of defining either himself or the conspiracy's true parameters, Dick Gibson does not track down his quarry by novel's end.

Neither does the unnamed protagonist of "On a Field, Rampant" (1963) ever successfully interpret the fate ambiguously portended on the medallion he wears about his neck. Spurred by the prophetic insistences of his father, Kardhov, that some unique splendor awaits him, he tries to chase down the princely destiny that conviction alone must merit and guarantee. Hauteur is his passport; he thinks not in terms of acquisition but, instead, of restoration of projected birthright, the faith that "interregnum is not exile" sustaining him through years of uninspiring labor (171). In trying to coax Design from its den, he combines active pursuit with trust in luck, randomness, and whim—a compromise common to several Elkin itinerants as they tack into the world-wind.

Unfortunately, parade his availability as he might, grandeur eludes him. The anticlimax comes when, having discovered a duke to whom he believes he bears a resemblance and who thus may finally offer verification of his own elite station, he is dismissed as a Pretender and, worse, a comic anachronism. He is then mauled by story-starved journalists and soon afterward mortified by the embrace of the very rabble from whom he had always sought to differentiate himself. Thus betrayed by the promise of the medallion—half-talisman, half-albatross—he senses that its obscure depiction, which he had previously treated as a tantalizing hieroglyph, now mocks him with its impenetrable clues (if clues they are):

> He had often wondered which of the figures was meant to represent himself. The knight, militant astride the horse, pledged to some unknown cause, his fury, like his loyalty, merely a technique? The lion, defiant, all its weight in the vicious arching outrage of its paws? The eagle, its legs and feet in queer, attenuated taper, as nude as spikes, its talons curved about the crown shape in the act of usurpation, fantastically appearing to perch on it in mid-air, like any canary on its toy swing. (190–91)

Closer examination of the figures on the medallion proves even more disconcerting: the images as likely imply artificial fevers and accident as they might brazen nobility. The rampant lion, its rage "concentrated on no object, irrelevant but steady, just steady, spraying the air like spit," captures his furtive yet static career: "loose, lost, peripheral, partner to nothing" (191). The balance between aimed fate and aimlessness which perpetuates his quest remains intact; Kardhov's son can approach but not solve the riddle of his medallion, and he must persist "as something merged with it, yet isolate" (155). The sole consummation of his election comes in the form of a royal rage, so that in the end the medallion appears not so much "a rich trophy of his identity" (182) as the MacGuffin struck from his countenance.

Some suffer their MacGuffins; others pine after their seductions. The case of *The Bailbondsman* (1973) concludes with Alexander Main's compulsion to resuscitate the MacGuffin that lapses once Oyp and Glyp, the only two fugitives who have eluded him, are revealed to be punk criminals instead of the myth-sized masterminds who have haunted his dreams. Mystery is his impetus, crime his raison d'être (106). "How can I cross-examine the universe when it jumps my bond?" (120), he complains, and "What do I do with my wonder, I wonder?" (124), with no prey to prod. Main's solution is to artificially instigate by turning on the loyal Crainpool, whom he shoots and wounds to send him running. This most speculative of bailbondsmen, who prefers closing in to closure, and who will not abide the absence of perpetrators, manufactures a moving target that automatically warrants him.

Despite Elkin's bald statement that "that's what books are about: to make reasons. Books are little houses of logic" (qtd. in Dougherty 98), not all of the cracks in the foundation are sealed. The reference is to the rigors of aesthetically calculated ambiguities, not to the author's conquest over the ambiguities he engages.[14] There tends to remain, like Leo Feldman's homunculus, that ossified twin crowding his heart, some "fossilized potential" that keeps up its pressure (*A Bad Man* 157).

Feldman's second self chafes him like a conscience; a single blow to it could prove fatal. By returning to one of Elkin's essential themes, the imminence of mortality, we can confirm a critical balance to which so many of these stricken figures must adhere. It is the lesson of the Finsberg family in *The Franchiser*, each uniquely beleaguered, each succumbing to a demise intimately related to his or her peculiarity (Gertrude of the superdense bones, for example, drowns in the tub); it is the lesson in *George Mills* (1972) of the freaks whose menu of "chipped genes and bombed biology" unites them to the performing paranormals of Cassadaga (134); it is the lesson of the terminally ill children Eddy Bale shepherds to Disney World in *The Magic Kingdom*. We are doomed by what defines us. Nevertheless, the saving side of the scale is best described by Ben Flesh as the open ideology he extracts from his own malady: life is a gift of remission. We vamp, range, rail, and speculate while thinly strung above our dying.

Like *Prisoner's Dilemma*, with its last-minute Lazarus trumps, *The MacGuffin* promises to keep on extending the premises. At the end of the novel, word-weary, dizzy with complications, Druff remains, to vary a favorite phrase of his, on the cusp of becoming. He will live to trope again.

Notes

1. When his Sarah magically completes one of the family chestnuts, "he did not ask where she had heard the phrase": "He had always considered it Dad's private stock, and the discovery that it was known to this beauty alarmed him with possibility" (191).
2. Ailene's strategy of maintaining stability by keeping up the home front recalls Garp's obsession with "disaster-proofing" his own family: "If Garp could have been granted one vast and naive wish, it would have been that he could make the world *safe*" (199). That seductive delusion makes the tragedies to come all the more poignant.
3. That burials continue to register a community pulse is corroborated in Don DeLillo's *White Noise*, in which even the garbage we dump hums with our "colloquial density" (117).
4. See also E. L. Doctorow's extended close reading of Disneyland in *The Book of Daniel* (285–91), in which Daniel examines the pernicious historical revisionism and "hygenic" deception practiced there.
5. The same lesson is on view next door. Lily does not post her letters to her neighbor, whom she surreptitiously watches and wonders about (203–10).

Hence, the illusion of self-sufficiency: their respective enclaves are really sites of incarceration. One recalls William Gass's "In the Heart of the Heart of the Country," in which the narrator and the world join at a judicious remove only: "We meet on this window, the world and I, inelegantly, swimmers of the glass; and swung wrong way round to one another, the world seems in" (196).

6. This recalls Alan Wilde's division of modern and postmodern philosophies: "What we have here is not modernism's balanced 'either-or' but, as contemporary critics are fond of saying, postmodernism's more comprehensive 'both-and' " (*Horizons of Assent* 48). Powers applies the postmodern method to familial and political constructions.
7. This continues a theme introduced in Powers's first novel, *Three Farmers on Their Way to a Dance*, in which history's DNA permeates art, self, and society.
8. Elkin not only acknowledges but also champions the fact that his fictions are primarily, and best defended as, platforms for language ("Interview with Stanley Elkin" [Sanders] 133–35). In this way he clearly holds with his friend and colleague William Gass "that there are no events but words in fiction" ("Medium of Fiction" 30). Gass specifically celebrates his aesthetic affinities with Elkin in his foreword to *The Franchiser* (vii–xv).
9. Coincidentally, whereas Hobson had hoped to create heaven on earth on the order of the World's Fair, Ellerbee is condemned by God for having compared Heaven to a theme park in *The Living End* (44). (To detect another echo in Powers's novel, while Walt Disney is the prophet in *Prisoner's Dilemma*, Disneyland is the Mecca of *The Magic Kingdom*.) Like Hobson, too, Ellerbee makes the mistake of envisioning a place free of petty contingency. And as for Elkin's enduring fondness for salesmen in his fiction, those kindred "pushers" of language, they earn a kind of monument in *The MacGuffin* in the form of City Hall, which had originally been a department store (22).
10. Multiple sclerosis, Elkin's own affliction, is an especially deft metaphor for stifled style, a hemming in of sensory perception that quite literally abridges one's external contacts; hence, it interferes with the worldly nourishment Elkin demands for his characters. The author has often commented on the effects of his disease and on its manifestations in his novels. Diane Ackerman provides a relevant anecdote on the subject in *A Natural History of the Senses* (82).
11. Later in that novel Dick Gibson sounds a contrary note when he takes liberties with a contingent of MP's and finds himself "swinging from cringe to contempt as though character were nothing more than hinged mood": "It was strange and exhilarating to live by the rule of whim" (100). In *The Living End*, to carry this point to its extreme, all Creation is the MacGuffin, and All There Is is only plot fodder.
12. See Kenneth Gergen's *The Saturated Self: Dilemmas of Identity in Contemporary Life*, in which the psychologist coins the term *multiphrenia* to explain the

persistent, and peculiarly contemporary, sensation of being out of one's depth, swarmed under by the countless options and stimuli (media- and otherwise-generated) which assault the contemporary consumer daily. The vertigo of possible "self-investments" undermines "our assumption of true and knowable selves" (16, 73–80). Let it be remembered, of course, that Elkin responds far more eagerly to the challenge than Gergen's analysis would lead one to anticipate.

13. Peter J. Bailey offers a comparable phrase in reference to Leo Feldman of *A Bad Man*, when he notes Feldman's "innate need for disruption of sequiturs in the name of self-aggrandizement" (202). Without a MacGuffin to consolidate his waning forces, Druff confesses, he feels "like little bits of the British Empire!" (110).
14. In *Horizons of Assent* Wilde gives the definitive analysis of the acceptance of randomness and contingency as a condition of man's existence as it pertains to a prevalent attitude in contemporary fiction, which he calls "suspensiveness" (see esp. chap. 5). Positing a faith that respects life's unresolvable superfluities is a fundamental concern of Wilde's "midfictionists," and it is not surprising to find so evident a worshiper of extravagance as Elkin a prominent member of that group, as Wilde goes on to describe it in *Middle Grounds* (chap. 2).

7

MERGENCE MYTHS

Ceremony and *Middle Passage*

I

> I always knew that those sentences didn't mean us, we who lived in confluence. . . . My life is the pause. The space between. The not this, not that, not the other. The place the others go around. Or around about. It's more a Mobius strip than a line.
>
> —Paula Gunn Allen, "The Autobiography of a Confluence"

Stories can be crucibles in which nations are shaped, cultures certified, and races won. Myths of origin are myths of entitlement: created as explanations, they persist as prophecies. In the words of N. Scott Momaday, "We are what we imagine" ("Man Made of Words" 167), and we imagine in forms that adhere to legendary principles. Native American myths consistently unveil an unsunderable economy among self, tribe, and environment. From the alignments of one's household belongings to ritual kiva circle configurations to primal verbal patterns, harmonies prevail and everywhere bespeak "synechdocal compliance," whereby local parts signify a circumambient Whole (Wiget 15). What could be more reassuring? Constellations ratify our behavior; the breaking wave and the curl of the eagle's wing are fraught with evidence of the assumption of our birthright by the physical universe.

"One who is whole is healed; one who is whole is holy" (Allen, "Autobiography" 576). This is the promise of transformation beyond estrangement and confusion; it is the promise of an animating consensus that connects human psychology with what Black Elk confidently describes as "the whole hoop of the world" (43), and which has the capacity to reabsorb whoever has lost contact with its restorative complementarities.[1] Killing blasphemes that context, and it fatally separates the killer from its consolations. So it is that in Leslie Marmon Silko's *Ceremony* (1977) Tayo, a Laguna Pueblo, returns from World War II to the reservation tortured by "a great swollen grief" and blindly stalking his own heritage (9), blindly because he mistakes his neglect of tradition for its extinction. In fact, whereas Silko characterizes the spirits of his ancestors as vital presences, Tayo is the revenant returned to haunt the postwar impoverishment of his homeland. As he staggers through the drought-stricken country that mirrors (and, as tribal lore reveals, directly imports) private desolations, Tayo finds recovery to be equally a personal and a cultural matter. "For a long time he had been white smoke" (14), barely a self to raise consciousness, and everywhere the land suffers the consequences of human transgression. "Everything tries to be round," says Black Elk (198), and, as if in instinctive accordance with that rule, lacerated by nausea and nightmare, Tayo leans to beginnings, his quest a circle returning upon itself.

A conventional heroic transit, whereby sterility marks the advent of a ritualized ordeal that leads to rebirth, definitely seems to apply to *Ceremony*, as numerous critics of the novel have noted when relating the progress of the narrative to broader mythic patterns and elemental harmonies that define and guarantee the population.[2] Consequently, we would expect Silko's novel to document Tayo's systematic divestiture of the white man's witchery in an unfolding process of societal and self-purgation. Yet *Ceremony* does not ascribe to that logic. On the contrary, it stresses healthful conduct not as an escape into an atavistic refuge nor as a dreamless sleep but as the coordination of motion and change against the backdrop of the enduring rhythms of nature and culture. Reconciliation, reorientation, and consolidation are the approved tactics here. A Yeatsian ceremony of innocence would merely be another kind of repression or disavowal comparable to the fatal separation caused by the several genocidal practices the novel describes.[3] On the contrary, Silko argues, "You have to come to terms, to some kind of equilibrium with those people around you," and they include "the person who just kicked you end over end" just as inevitably as "those people who care for you" and the environment that harbors them all ("Stories and Their Tellers" 22). If one can only confront today's world successfully through ancient ritual, ritual can only be vouchsafed to the degree that it remains available to contemporary realities. Whatever concordant grace waits for Tayo at the end of *Ceremony* is earned in face of racial tensions. His goal is "psychic wholeness *in which nothing is left out*" (MacShane 15; italics mine).

As Werner Sollers further observes, what is sought is convergence rather than reduction: "Countervailing the folk beliefs (shared by some academics) in ethnic purity, 'ethnicity' here typically emerges not as a thing (let alone a static, permanent or 'pure' thing) but as the result of interactions. Ethnicity does not serve as a totalizing metaphor but simply as a perspective onto psychological, historical, social, and cultural forces" (xix–xx). *Ceremony* offers a harmony whose voices do not vanish into a justified whole as they resonate through a lifetime. We might alter the concept of the traditional emergence myth, which identifies origins, to posit the concept of a "mergence myth," which fortifies origins through perpetual adaptation. Black Elk's idealized circle is as potentially claustrophobic as the death-driven auspices of white "witchery" unless it admits the possibility of dynamic reconstitution. As Mircea Eliade attests, the mythic world is an open code (qtd. in Lincoln, *Native American Renaissance* 126), and Silko herself contends that the Pueblo cosmology similarly rejects decisive conclusions in favor of blossoming options ("The Fourth World").

We might also consider in this regard the Navajo belief in *h'ozh'o*, which brings together properties of wholeness, integrity, and balance as compatible standards in man and nature (Wiget 13). Yet this belief is complicated, if not belied, by the subtle instabilities evident in Navajo sand paintings, whose effect is to express that art symbolizes the striving for completed order more than it indicates the achievement of that goal (Zolbrod 30).[4] These designs tend to be inward spirals instead of closed circles. We may in this instance recall Alberto Giacometti's paradoxical confession: "The more one works on a picture, the more impossible it becomes to finish it" (qtd. in Plagens 61). Threads fray and peek through the weave, exposing its frailty and perhaps the vanity of all making but also increasing its intricacy. Composure is not a final enunciation but a relentlessly imagined approach; art is a halting prayer for divine sanction of our approximations.

This is why Tayo must renounce the brand of unity promulgated by the "destroyers": it is the devouring circle of death. Its design is the deceptively coherent sand painting of witches, whose diabolical manifestations in the novel range from the sterile luminosity of uranium mines to the conspiracy to enclose Tayo in a narrative that tidily dismisses him as a renegade, ending his story "the way all their stories end, encircling slowly to choke the life away" (231–32). In the hands of the white man stillbirth supplants the wonder of creation: "what little remained . . . was shriveled like a seed hoarded too long, shrunken past its time, and split open now, to expose a fragile, pale leaf stem, perfectly formed and dead" (204). Theirs is an art without custom or conscience, figured in lifeless clay. We see how Emo, a fellow veteran who no longer participates in the commiserative interchanges between man and earth, experience and tradition, festers in ersatz ceremonies of corrosion, denial, and oblivion. Desecrations are not confined to the battlefield; they persist as the "black baptism" that Emo undergoes in the war's poisonous wake.[5] Emo stagnates in memories of potency and validation which the war temporarily encouraged and which booze and women now only fleetingly conjure. He repeats stories of belonging "like long medicine chants, the beer bottles pounding on the counter tops like drums" (42), but he remains mired.

Silko parallels Emo's vile dereliction with the tale of misguided allegiance to phantom *Ck'o'yo* magic which caused the people to forget the mother corn altar (48–49). Indeed, instead of cleaving to belief, Emo tells jokes that stereotype and degrade the Indian, shows the same irreverence to mutilated soldiers as to trampled ants, and fiddles with contaminated trophies of war—the teeth pried from a Japanese corpse. For Emo divinity has been scoured out of the world; *Ceremony* connects his attitude, and his being immured in rage and loathing, to the white man's propensity for dispensing with "superstitions" about the living planet. (We remember that Tayo's cousin Rocky equated his future success with his ability to use his grades in school, his football prowess, and his imagined military glory with escaping the burden of tribal identification.) This is the witchery that works like a whirlwind to deform sustaining patterns (135–38), and, like Yeats's widening gyre, to decenter and evict those who inhabited them. Had Tayo succumbed to the impulse to kill Emo during a bar brawl, he, too, would have been lost in the vortex. Only by locating Grandmother Spider's unifying design can one rethread his or her way into "the life moving through things," which is consecrated in *Ceremony* as the sunrise that brackets the book-long contest with darkness and serves as the refrain for Tayo's prayer of deliverance.

The recuperative resolve that drives Tayo's ceremony is conditioned by a heritage that respects perpetuation—a "both-and" prescription for personal and racial well-being. Convenient majority opinion to the contrary, Tayo "was not crazy; he had never been crazy": "He had only seen and heard the world as it always was: no boundaries, only transitions through all distances and time" (246). Meanwhile, set as an eternal precedent, the Laguna gods, bent by generations of telling to the same behaviors, amplify the cycles even they cannot arrest. Heaven and earth embrace a Jamesian recognition that the transitions are as genuine as the turns connected. The metaphysical quest does not close. William James explains, "It appears less as a solution, then, than as a program for more work, and more particularly as an indication of the ways in which existing realities may be *changed*" (qtd. in Poirier, *Renewal of Literature* 178).

The Trickster who fattens along the invisible boundaries of several Native American cosmologies plays about the core of things; his forked wishing bone symbolizes "both options and divisions in a continuum . . . the delightful, yet problematic, duality in this world of changes." Fixity desiccates like drought, its natural example. That is why the Trickster's chaos is desirable: it spurs advancement. He "gambols to regenerate the world, to change or make over a reality that is always in flux" (Lincoln, "Native American Literatures" 126). Thus, the stories recounted and counted upon, and which the individual neglects at his peril, are stories of "creation *and* continuation" (*Ceremony* 249; italics mine). A fragment from an Omaha ritual healing confirms this ambiguous posture: "you rest / in the midst of winds" (qtd. in Lincoln, "Native American Literatures" 95).

Individual commitment to the transitional is repeatedly and hearteningly advanced throughout the novel. Uncle Josiah once advised Tayo that "nothing was all good or all bad either; it all depended" (11). Although Tayo rebukes himself for his entanglements with the white world, he comes to understand that disentanglement is not sufficient as an end in itself but only as an initial stage in his convalescence. At first Tayo hopes to subdue his illness by amputating himself from a bewitched society; however, segregation cannot convey his quest any further than that. Because it is born of contempt for the Other, its purchase is exile. Since everything past and present—"this world and the four worlds below," including this recounting (1)—is spun from the All-mind of Thought-Woman, any elimination whatsoever is a sacrilege.

"Nothing is itself taken alone," offers Wallace Stevens in his *Adagia*. "Things are because of interrelations and interactions" (189).[6] Avoidance becomes depletion on every front: the rain stops, gasoline and alcohol give out, and our hero, wracked with delirium and vomiting, realizes that "it took a great deal of energy to be a human being, and the more the wind blew and the sun moved southwest, the less energy Tayo had" (25). The opening sections of *Ceremony* depict him in terms of invisibility and diminishment, the point being that self-protective measures tend toward self-erasure, until "he inhabited a gray winter fog on a distant elk mountain where hunters are lost indefinitely and their own bones mark the boundaries" (15). In short, when refuge is treated as an end in itself, it negates any chance for resurrection. Tayo's longing for a "peaceful silence beneath the sounds of the wind" isolated from human contact and free from human responsibility "was the silence of hard dry clay and old juniper wood bleached white" (21).

One of the saving qualities of Native American tribalism, William Bevis contends, is that it is intrinsically relational. Village and clan are absorbent configurations that defy the white American assumption that "the individual is often the ultimate reality, that therefore individual consciousness is the medium, repository, and arbiter of knowledge, and that our 'freedom' can be hard to distinguish from isolation" (590). Contesting this sterile impasse is what Bevis terms the "transpersonal self," valued by Native Americans for the composite it implies: the self exists through the communal extensions that warrant it. We may remember Patricia Waugh's thesis regarding the "collectivist" heroine whose own relational priorities represent a feminist counterargument against the tradition of the autonomous male hero. His choosing to separate himself from a tarnished society is very different from the marginalization to which minorities (women, Native Americans) find themselves consigned. Furthermore, escape proves to be self-defeating anyway, for it erodes the human context upon which the self relies for nourishment and definition.

Travail comes largely from misguidedness: "only humans resisted what they saw outside themselves. Animals did not resist. But they persisted, because they became part of the wind" (27). The white man abuses the earth by pronouncing it dead. Bombs are only part of it; for instance, there is also Christianity, which enforces the soul's apartheid and violates spirituality by deeming it a separative fact rather than the integrative activity it must be (*Ceremony* 68). The white man's political and cultural encroachments render Native Americans peripheral, then disposable, in that they are deemed worthy to die in the Pacific theater; his linguistic encroachments render them practically illegible. No wonder strategies of aversion and recoil dominate among those who do survive.

This is why Betonie, the old medicine man, is the novel's fulcrum. It is he who articulates and embodies a belief in motion as grace: "Old Betonie might explain it this way—Tayo didn't know for sure: there were transitions that had to be made in order to become whole again, in order to be the people our Mother would remember; transitions, like the boy walking in bear country being called back softly" (170). A subtle overlap in grammatical modification enables boy and country to be called back together. "Relentless motion" is also the lion's defining beauty, "moving like mountain clouds with the wind, changing substance and color in rhythm with the contours of the mountain peaks" (195–96). Pueblo expression accommodates this belief in that "the structure emerges as it is made and you must simply listen and trust" in the evolving meaning (Silko, "Language and Literature" 83). So, too, can the self revive through ongoing revision. It is the redemptive promise of the ritualistic "interval training" upon which Tayo is encouraged to embark: "As far as he could see, in all directions, the world was alive. He could feel the motion pushing out of the damp earth into the sunshine—the yellow spotted snake the first to emerge, carrying this message on his back to the people"

(221). Just as it correlates oral (performative) and written (artifactive) discourses, *Ceremony* realizes Laguna history to be simultaneously an endowment and an enactment.

Unlike Ku'oosh, the medicine man Tayo originally visits, and who endures by repudiating convulsive realities he cannot fathom (36–38), Betonie insists upon an assimilative balance. Tayo encounters him in the midst of his humble plunder of discarded telephone books, old shopping bags, calendars, and Coke bottles—the jetsam of an incursive, spendthrift culture—which in his room establish an intricate ovenbird barricade. Whereas Ku'oosh was baffled and anxious in face of Tayo's confessions, Betonie is composed, even jocular, in face of the task of mediation. His secret is at the heart of the ceremony he prescribes: stories live on in all things, not excluding the white man's debris, and we can tap that animus for our own enlargement and repair. But they live as continua:

> At one time, the ceremonies as they had been performed were enough for the way the world was then. But after the white people came, elements in this world began to shift; and it became necessary to create new ceremonies. I have made changes in the rituals. The people mistrust this greatly, but only this growth keeps the ceremonies strong.
>
> She taught me this above all else: things which don't shift and grow are dead things. They are things the witchery people want. (126)

Tayo's "therapy" is formulated in emulation of this philosophy: "his cure would be found only in something great and inclusive of everything" (126). Betonie counsels Tayo to recognize—and, subsequently, to enter—the timeless patterns of nature which "gathered all things together" (182); the effect of such "gathering" is not a profanation of heritage but, rather, a fortification of its capacities. Flouting the fallacy of we-they oppositions between Indian and white, Betonie proposes what we have referred to previously as a kinetic balance: "But don't be so quick to call something good or bad. There are balances and harmonies always shifting, always necessary to maintain. It is very peaceful with the bears; the people say that's the reason human beings seldom return. It is a matter of transitions, you see; the changing, the becoming must be cared for closely" (130). We are custodians of cyclical changes, Betonie appears to be saying, and maintenance of the shifts is no less crucial than maintenance of the balances, for they are mutually contained and contextualized. In other words, heritage lasts in part because of its plasticity. Risking that heritage in the contemporary arena may invite the threat of relativity, but failing to do so will lead to its vitiation and, ultimately, to its irrelevance. The basis of Tayo's restoration is democratic reintegration, its emblem Betonie's pluralist totem pole.[7]

Betonie's insights and premonitions conspire to establish a discipline for Tayo through which the systematic and the generative aspects of ancestry coalesce. His principal task is to retrieve Josiah's cattle, which after Tayo's enlistment and his uncle's death have been appropriated by white ranchers. Those cattle are more than property; specially bred for the rigors of this part of the country, they duplicate Tayo's own status as a half-breed. The telling point here is that a blend of inheritances is particularly robust; the fading of identifying boundaries is a matter of hybridization, not mongrelization. In brief, these cattle express balance as a genetic imperative. Shadowed and stressed by a variety of oppositions himself, Tayo searches for the cattle in order to converge with the principle they embody.[8] Drawn along the same hunger line, Tayo counts on "the dim memory of direction" (197), which instinctively compels him to that rendezvous and its psychic rewards.

Beneath Betonie's foretold arc of stars, secured by the primordial round of "the four directions" in synthesis, Tayo translates a dead text into "a story he could feel happening" (186). The night sky serves as a galvanic mooring that symbolizes that philosophy: "It was a world alive, always changing and moving; and if you knew where to look, you could see it, sometimes almost imperceptible, like the motion of stars across the sky" (95). Whereas Emo, Harley, and the other wastelanders remain congested by bitter, claustrophobic narratives, Tayo is fortified by a progressive vision. Even the discovery of Ts'eh, who is to become his lover and spiritual guide, is treated as another advent. In her enchanted company Tayo goes beyond the dreamless sleep that represented his initial stage of development to achieve a capacity for projective dreaming which joins him to the momentum of natural forces. The virtue of their lovemaking is the making itself, which is idealized as being both a gathering and a solvency:

> He was afraid of being lost, so he repeated trail marks to himself: this is my mouth tasting the salt of her brown breasts; this is my voice calling out to her. He eased himself deeper within her and felt the warmth close around him like river sand, softly giving way under foot, then closing firmly around the ankle in cloudy warm water. But he did not get lost, and he smiled at her as she held his hips and pulled him closer. He

> let the motion carry him, and he could feel the momentum within, at first almost imperceptible, gathering in his belly. When it came, it was the edge of a steep riverbank crumbling under the downpour until suddenly it all broke loose and collapsed into itself. (180–81)

Not loss but metamorphosis characterizes this passage. From this point on Tayo's growth seems to him to be more a matter of remembrance than of unprecedented learning (219). The witchery of the destroyers manifests itself as a delusion of nonnegotiable factions: starving versus fat, colored versus white, empowered versus disenfranchised, deceptive versus gullible (191). But Ts'eh, angel of repose and incarnation of first principles, is its living refutation.[9] Born into a close-knit family with a diverse lineage, she extends the model of the vital hybrid embodied by Betonie and sought by Tayo; she is the transitive example of the serenity that necessarily succeeds wholesale evacuation of Self and Other.

One by one Tayo's lingering misgivings about his progress are allayed. Even Nature itself dependably intervenes on his behalf. When Tayo encounters a band of loutish cowboys out to harass the trespasser, they are distracted by the sudden appearance of a mountain lion. As the lion entices the cowboys to better game, it simultaneously revives Tayo's commitment to his mission because, hunter and hunter's helper, it reminds him of the motives behind his quest: " 'Mountain lion,' he whispered, 'mountain lion, becoming what you are with each breath, your substance changing with the earth and sky' " (196). When Tayo departs, an enveloping snow falls like a benediction, concealing the lion's scent and Tayo's tracks, as well as duplicating the fertilization ceremony conducted by the questor (the dusting of footprints wth pollen). Significantly, although the snow routs their pursuers, it does not deter Tayo, who trusts to the curve of his own belly to learn the shape of the landscape he must cover (205).

Ts'eh urges Tayo to author himself apart from the foreclosed story structures others mean to foist upon him. "They" are the white authorities—the police who would term his reclamation of the cattle "rustling," the doctors who would delegitimate him as another crazy Indian—but also Emo, their accomplice in divisiveness and hatred. She warns him: "They want it to end here, the way all their stories end, encircling slowly to choke the life away. . . . And they would end the story right here, with you fighting to your death alone in these hills. . . . They'll hunt you down, and take you any way they can. Because this is the only ending they understand" (231–32). Theirs is the killing whirlwind disguised as a resolved circle, which is political tyranny and narrative arrogance.

By contrast, Ts'eh silently directs Tayo's attention to a shooting star, "scattering light behind it like dust on a trail," and Tayo realizes that, "like old Betonie, she could see reflections in sandrock pools of rainwater, images shifting in the flames of juniper fire; she heard voices, low and distant in that night" (232). Truer stories admit what shifts and scatters; in imitation of the stories that still inhere in the natural environment, they are enriched by their ambiguities and openness to additional, future voices. Accordingly, Ts'eh teaches Tayo about transplanting roots that contain "the color of the sky after a summer rainstorm," whereby one disseminates the blessings of renewal (224). To hoard those treasures against dispersion would be to squander their benefits and stifle the future. Sky, rock, and water, not as sterile objects but as balanced entities, consecrate Tayo's expedition and assure him that "he had only to complete this night, to keep the story out of the reach of the destroyers for a few more hours, and their witchery would turn, upon itself, upon them" (247).

In the wake of ceremony "a frail luminous glow" commemorates the rebirth of spirituality. Balance suffuses the landscape: "Yet at that moment in the sunrise, it was all so beautiful, everything, from all directions, evenly, perfectly, balancing day with night, summer months with winter. The valley was enclosing this totality, like the mind holding all thoughts together in a single moment" (237). "This night is a single night; and there has never been any other" (192): the autumnal equinox authenticates Thought-Woman's complex of all, already, always—a multiaxial, growing entirety. Silko's novel braids the primeval with the popular. *Ceremony* stands forth not as a revisionist history but as a visionary compact among living historical presences.

II

Shuttles in the rocking loom of history,
the dark ships move, the dark ships move,
their bright ironical names
like jests of kindness on a murderer's mouth;
plough through thrashing glister toward
fata morgana's lucent melting shore,
weave toward New World littorals that are
mirage and myth and actual shore.
—Robert Hayden, "Middle Passage"

In Silko's *Ceremony* the historical, the legendary, and the personal are mounted as intersecting planes, strung about a mobile and receiving the light in changing alliances and articulations. Recognizing that the alternative is either obliteration or sterility, Charles Johnson also accepts the inevitability of racial interdependency. Indeed, his novels consistently expose the illegitimacy of a so-called separate identity as a form of ontological vanity. For the Allmuseri, the ancient African clan-state he introduces in *Oxherding Tale* (1982) and whose philosophy presides over *Middle Passage* (1990), there are no personal pronouns, no individual experiences or rhetorical allegations of a divisible Absolute (*Oxherding Tale* 97). Reb the Coffinmaker, a descendant of the Allmuseri, who accompanies the hero of *Oxherding Tale* on his flight to freedom, counsels him that he say yes to everything, even to his suffering (76). The Self is always and only the Self enjoined. "I was in the thick of diversity, awash in the world's rich density," exclaims Andrew Hawkins, Johnson's reluctant picaro, whose lesson—Reb the Coffinmaker refers to it as his "life assurance"—is that psychic health is to be found in that very commonwealth of affirmation.

Although he was raised to believe it to be man's destiny to transcend "the polarities, to find the Ground," Andrew's adventures retain their multiplicity and incommensurability (52).[10] But the consolation is that, while nothing is exorcised in the name of racial hygiene, nothing is forfeited either.[11] Bernard W. Bell, in *The Afro-American Novel and Its Tradition*, begins his comprehensive evaluation by attesting to the indispensability of terms such as *socialized ambivalence*, *double vision*, and *double consciousness* (the last the famous coinage belonging to W. E. B. Du Bois from *The Souls of Black Folk* [1903]), whose apparent equivocations indicate that art is generated and can only flourish as a hybrid, whatever its revolutionary agenda might be (xv–xvi). Thus, while the African-American novel originates in a variety of oral and literary traditions of African-American culture, it also is rooted in the history of Western culture—namely, "a racist, capitalist, patriarchal American social arena"—in whose confines African-American identity has been at once shaped and censored. "The Afro-American novel, in other words," Bell concludes, "is not a solipsistic, self-referential signifying system, but a symbolic sociocultural act" (339).[12] What was true for Silko's Pueblo medicine man is true for Johnson's Allmuseri: Otherness is a precondition for the demarcation and, ultimately, the fortification and honest apprehension of one's own cultural inheritances.

In Johnson's first published novel, *Faith and the Good Thing* (1974), the discovery of Faith Cross anticipates and complements Andrew Hawkins's. Leaving Hatten County, Georgia, at the insistence of the vexatious werewitch, Swamp Woman, Faith pursues the grail she hopes will be revealed to her among the gravid shadows of contemporary Chicago. The Good Thing promises to represent the end of bondage to restless questioning—a kind of philosophical manumission. It turns out to be an antiempiricist, postsystematic, all-inclusive embrace of the creative principle which enables Faith to shed history's grim strictures and loosen the hold of circumstance (characterized in the novel by prostitution, poverty, and disease). All too typically, Johnson confesses in *Being and Race*, black fiction resigns itself to the tragedy of black history: "It is full of failures. A catalogue of man's inhumanity to man and woman. Book after book discloses the desperate struggle of a people first to survive against stupendous odds and then to secure the most basic rights in a perpetually hostile environment. Whites in this history act; blacks can only *re*act" (7). But selective refusal of one's history leads to the ritual excision of black consciousness. To rise above this dilemma Faith Cross entertains the prospect of flexible, fluxional experience: "That was responsibility: factoring the possible number of paths to the Good Thing," she concludes, "but not becoming fixed, or held to those paths in her history, or the history of the race. Moving always on . . ." (195). Beauty and wonder disperse the brunt of Fact; Johnson's hero is necessarily a conjure doctor, a shape-shifter, and the Good Thing looms as an endless draw—the call to story.

The trick (for African-American literature regularly employs its traditional Trickster figure too) is to sabotage a history of bondage by mitigating the bondage of history. Robert Hayden's "dark ships" of the slave trade fashion an unforgiving weave as they cross and recross the Atlantic. Replete with ghosts, sorcerors, and all the denizens of legend, Johnson's novels show how that weave may be slackened to admit new stories and to ensure that the "New World littorals" not become "literals" that brook no objection.[13]

The picaresque, especially as it is handled in *Middle Passage*, constitutes a generic dispute with constrictive historical solemnities, in that it embraces discontinuities and mobilizes them as aesthetic and political agents. The picaro makes of his pastlessness an advantage, treating it as the freedom to "pillage" experience (*Middle Passage* 160, 163). Our incorrigible narrator, the canny, corrupt Rutherford Calhoun, relies on the incompleteness and contestability of identity as a means of eluding subjugation;

nevertheless, he comes to realize that it is impossible to renounce every contact he suspects of co-optation. Thus, on the one hand, the artist is held accountable to stories that jeopardize the certification of his people; on the other hand, he hacks away at the ideological roots of enslavement with what Roland Barthes, in his analysis of mythic narrative, describes as "a rhetoric of transmission . . . whose infinitely possible shifts afford the work the responsibility of its choice." In this way art challenges the "privileged object"—conventional conception or authorized story—with infinite "compossibility": "an incessant trial of contiguities, of shifts, of returns, of entrances bearing on denominative enumerations, oneiric fragments, legends, flavors, colors, or simple toponymic noises" ("Literature and Discontinuity" 182, 183). In other words, a book like *Middle Passage* introduces precariousness into the official proceedings of belief, which becomes a matter of continual adjustment of, and to, ever-multiplying perspectives.

Set in 1830, *Middle Passage* tells the story of a recently freed slave, who, the latest in Johnson's collection of philosophically sensitive heroes with trip-hammer hearts, is still running from the responsibilities that ironically inhere in freedom. He is the Trickster as social parasite, who recalls Jean Genet in his faith in thievery as transcendence of mediocrity, expectation, and all the numbing particulars of conventionality; he is "hooked on sensation, you might say, a lecher for perception" (3), which accounts for his blithe dismissal of his childhood training in religion and philosophy at the hands of a liberal-minded master. The immediate manifestations of constraint are a trail of bad paper leading from Rutherford's waterfront extravagances (principally, gambling and women) and the marital aspirations of bookish Isadora Bailey, an island of gentility in the orgiastic wash of New Orleans. When these claims suddenly dovetail into blackmail—Isadora enlists the coercive support of the gangster Papa Zeringue to guarantee wedlock in exchange for her promise to pay off all of Rutherford's debts—our hero lights out for the sea, that measureless invitation to formlessness which dissolves all entailments.

Herman Beavers cleverly observes that Johnson's characters are verbs rather than nouns; they see in the demand to be something "a trap of positionality" whose ironic result is the attrition of possibility and stature ("Denotating the Rising Sun"). Isadora's desire to have and to mold her man—he shudders at the threat of rectitude and the pitiable company of her crippled pets—turns Rutherford into a stowaway aboard the *Republic*. For him the sea is not only a last resort; it is nature's analogue for his own prodigality, in whose "thrashing Void" troublesome claims of station and shore will be overwhelmed (36).

Only after the ship has put out to sea, however, does he discover how truly expensive his action is. The *Republic* is a slaver bound for Africa for a load of prime human cargo. An ugly comment on the so-called republic from which it embarks, the ship teems with wretched refuse—criminals, drunks, and primitives of every stain; indeed, this melting pot is no shining alliance united in freedom but a hodgepodge of contaminants under the vicious, paranoid command of Captain Ebenezer Falcon, a dwarf-sized, pederastic Ahab puffed by misanthropy and rant.[14] Falcon's goal is to Americanize the planet, but his method of extending his *Republic*, like the nation's own, is rapacious and without conscience—piracy justified as manifest destiny (30). And Rutherford, a prisoner of Falcon's whim and soon to be a traitor to his African ancestors, is relegated to the lowest circle of hell: the ship's orlop deck, a foul cavity beneath the waterline.

As the expedition progresses, Falcon takes Rutherford deeper and deeper into his confidence, bragging about the intricacy of his defenses against the Other (such as a series of invisible lethal trip wires awaiting those hoping to burglarize his quarters) and expounding his beliefs regarding the irreconcilable conflicts that constitute the truth of human society and the human mind itself. "Conflict," says he,

> *is* what it means to be conscious. Dualism is a bloody structure of the mind. Subject and object, perceiver and perceived, self and other—these ancient twins are built into the mind like the stem-piece of a merchantman. We cannot *think* without them, sir. . . . They are signs of a transcendental Fault, a deep crack in consciousness itself. Mind was *made* for murder. Slavery, if you think this through, forcing yourself not to flinch, is the social correlate of a deeper, ontic wound. (97–98)

Here is the "logical" extreme of Rutherford's strategic disconnectedness. If all implication is the delusion of soft hearts and soft heads, then the Other is the enemy, and expendable. Falcon has hit upon a cosmic validation of ruthlessness. When the crew plans to mutiny, they verify their captain's Hobbesian sense of human behavior, while he has been spending his waking hours preparing for their predictable capitulation to their own nature.[15] The sea wears away all pretense of allegiance, and, says Rutherford, "leagues from culture or civilization, I saw no point in our perpetuating the lunacies of life on land. . . . No one had the strength to sustain idols of the tribe or cave" (106).

As the sole "Negro" joining this voyage, and an unlicensed crewman at that, Rutherford cringes in the center of the conflicts between his captain and his mates (and later between the slaves in the ship's cramped hold and their white captors)."I could no longer find my loyalties," explains Rutherford, whose very presence on the *Republic* is due to his having tried to flee them. "All bonds, landside or on ships, between masters and mates, women and men, it struck me, were a lie forged briefly in the name of convenience and just as quickly broken when they no longer served one's interest" (92). To be sure, Rutherford trusts in double agency and trades on his several confidences just to stay alive. But, if the sea is a "chaosmos" whose "churning field . . . threw out forms indistinctly" (183), it is also simultaneously and continuously creative. Indistinct forms are still forms; relativized associations still connect. The sea represents a vortical balance between invention and demolition, as Rutherford indicates in his description of its "theater of transformations":

> At my post I was for a time hypnotized by tumbling, opaline blades of ocean, by its vortices that were mirrored in me since we were mainly made of Main, by the way—as the mate said—it seemed to be some monster of energy, without start or finish, a shifting cauldron of thalassic force, form superimposed upon form, which grew neither bigger nor smaller, which endlessly spawned all creatures conceivable yet never consumed itself, and contained a hundred kinds of waters, if one could but see them all. (79)

This characterization prefigures, even renders inevitable, the storms, mutiny, and slave uprising to come. The ship that rides those unpredictable energies is itself a process: its ragged sails and rotted wood have to be repaired or replaced constantly, making it as unstable as the forces that assault it (35–36). *Middle Passage* eventually masquerades as the ship's log, which Rutherford is ultimately assigned and which, conceived as nine linear entries, suggests the reliable gestation of the hero. But the novel belies that self-assured format as it increasingly entertains such "middle passages" as the depiction of the sea, monstrous in part because it offers no evidence of start or finish.

Rutherford's growing recognition of such paradoxical balances is primarily due to the influence of the Allmuseri tribe. Despite their incarceration in the soggy bowels of the *Republic*, Rutherford is acutely aware of their sublime endowments. Keepers of miracles, martial artists of the highest order, they suggest an enduring synthesis that is at once biological, historical, and philosophical, and their profound complementarities oppose Captain Falcon's either-or/us-them bipolar fixities.

Reb the Coffinmaker, an Allmuseri descendant in *Oxherding Tale*, evades the sinister Soulcatcher because there is nothing static in him to grasp. He explains to Andrew Hawkins that "the Real, if it was anything at all to the Allmuseri, was a matter of consent, a shared hallucination" (49); he speaks of his *kra* as an infinitely hostable soul (61). Meanwhile, Andrew comes to understand that fixity ("the Ground") is not something the hero erects against change but, rather, a constraining illusion from which the hero must emerge. Similar subtleties identify the Allmuseri in *Middle Passage:* as fluid personages, they can never be fixed and formulated, a quality that makes their enslavement not just heretical but also a contradiction in terms; yet they permeate whatever and whomever they contact. Just as they prove to be magically undeniable presences, a clan cemented more by vision than by blood (109), so too do they appear to be "a clan distilled from the essence of everything that came earlier" (61).[16]

And, if they are verbs, they are *transitive* verbs. The "teachings" and conduct of the tribesman Ngonyama definitely influence the content and tenor of Rutherford's appraisal. The gnomic Allmuseri language is a language of becoming which resists the stiffness of alphabet and grammatical rule. Gerunds, for example, supplant nouns (a *bed* becomes a *resting*), since the existence of "static substances" is something their vocabulary hardly endures, while verbs inflect according to the composition, even the contour, of each object they act upon; meanwhile, the written language consists of pictograms whose effect is intuitive and subjective (77–78). "It was not, I gathered, a good language for doing analytic work, or deconstructing things into discrete parts," Rutherford thinks (78). As a document developed under the influence of the Allmuseri, his narrative likewise withdraws from absolute interpretations of his adventures. Negative Capability is the only defensible writing posture. Like a navigator in unsettled waters, the writer locates himself provisionally according to a "running fix" (157).

Thanks to the displacements occasioned by Ngonyama, Rutherford scorns himself for his previous assumptions about the nature of mankind: "Stupidly, I had seen their lives and culture as a timeless product, as a finished thing, pure essence of Parmenidean meaning I envied and wanted to embrace, when the truth was that they were process and Heraclitean change, like any men, not fixed but evolving and as vulnerable to metamorphosis as the body of the boy we'd thrown overboard" (124). That boy is the first of the corpses extracted from the mass of Allmuseri below deck. To Captain Falcon the body's cheesing, clumping decay is just the reminder of a bad investment, but to Rutherford, who is engaged to help dispose of it, it is a horrifying lesson about the illusion of separability. Ghastly shards of the rotten body rub off on him, and his reflex is to take a knife to his own flesh, until he is stayed by Ngonyama. Earlier, when Falcon bequeathed to Rutherford a magnetic ring for a customized pistol in exchange for his promise to serve as a spy against the crew, Rutherford was shocked to contemplate the "marriage" of two such disparate minds (58), but he could not deny that he saw something of himself in the captain after all. He also sees himself in Ngonyama, which makes them brethren (124); in fact, Rutherford senses his own spirit taking up residence in the vacant eyes of the corpse that seems annealed to his hand (123). Therefore, whereas Captain Falcon represents and commits himself to separation, "the failure to experience the unity of Being everywhere was the Allmuseri vision of Hell" (65). Believing in his distance is the hallmark of Falcon's presumptuousness and, eventually, what makes him vulnerable to the upheavals to come. By contrast, Ngonyama recognizes that even his enemies are part of his constitution; furthermore, each man killed by the Allmuseri during their takeover alters them spiritually, and sin threatens to wrest them from the abiding snythesis into the Falconian realm of irreconcilable oppositions, for "no leaf fell, no word was uttered or deed executed that did not echo eternally throughout the universe" (140).

As for our narrator: "I found nothing I could rightly call Rutherford Calhoun, only pieces and fragments of all the people who had touched me, all the places I had seen, all the homes I had broken into. The 'I' that I was, was a mosaic of many countries, a patchwork of others and objects stretching backward to perhaps the beginning of time" (162–63). There is remorse here, to be sure, and longing too, but there are also profound compensations: with indebtedness comes connection, compassion—viable sources of equilibrium because they profess identity to be an ongoing, integrated concern. As conditions aboard the *Republic* deteriorate, Rutherford becomes its self-appointed caretaker, salving wounds and offering whatever meager comfort he can. This is not the aggrieved brother who never forgave his elder for refusing their dying master's possessions; Rutherford has matured into obligation.

Or, put another way, by encountering the intricacy of human dependencies, he has become a debtor in a deeper sense than ever before. When he confronts the protean Allmuseri deity, he hears "a thousand soft undervoices" interpenetrating, "each one immanent in the other, none his but all strangely his." Whole populations conspire before him in "the broader, shifting field":

> his breathing blurred in a dissolution of sounds and I could only feel that identity was imagined; I had to listen harder to isolate him from the We that swelled each particle and pore of him, as if the (black) self was the greatest of all fictions; and then I could not find him at all. He seemed everywhere, his presence, and that of countless others, in me as well as the chamber, which had subtly changed. Suddenly I knew the god's name: Rutherford. (171)

That "he" begins as the image of Rutherford's lost father, a slave killed and left to rot (a legacy visited upon his son and the stricken tenants of the dying *Republic*) for running off, but persists as an elemental, ineradicable We that plunges all isolate selves into a true republic of mutuality—the "I am" of Ralph Ellison's *Invisible Man* (1952) redefined as E Pluribus Unum. Every man's story is "unfinished business' until it opens itself up to all the stories that pertain (167); every man is marginal until he embraces the blending whereby he is lost and found. Therefore, neither Falcon's schismatic interpretation of human existence nor Diamelo's exquisitely honed detestation of the white world will suffice. In campaigning to direct the Allmuseri after the uprising, Diamelo equates Ngonyama's reserve with faintheartedness, but his vengeful rages rival and repeat his enemy's advocacy of racial and cultural purity, which *Middle Passage* discredits on both practical and philosophical grounds.

Not everyone is fortified by the melodious guile of the Allmuseri. His categories shattered, Captain Falcon pronounces the end of history, and, in delivering his logbook into the hands of Rutherford Calhoun, he charges him with the task of bringing order in the wake of catastrophe should Rutherford manage to survive it. First Mate Cringle claims the very heavens have mutinied, for the stars themselves seem to have sprung from their sockets (158). And yet both men ironically participate in that mergent vision. Even after his death Falcon still serves as cynosure for the Allmuseri and the crew alike, all of whom absorb the consequences of his death, as they did his prior domination. But it is Cringle who is gathered into the We in the most tangible fashion: in keeping with Cringle's final disposition, the starving few who remain cannibalize his corpse.

The violent, vomitous illness of Rutherford Calhoun exorcises the last separatist vestiges of the erstwhile thief. He prays not for release but for the restoration of the ballasts of home. As the decaying ship finally collapses into the sea, the dashed, miserable citizens of the *Republic* enter the democracy of indistinction, "this chaosmos of roily water and fire" (183). Miraculously, Rutherford is rescued, but he is never returned to old, discarded certainties. The Jamesian with the thievish streak—"Truth is what *works*, pragmatically, in the sphere of commerce," Cringle had once advised him (160), unwittingly acquitting the pickpocket along with the entrpreneur—has, like the Allmuseri, lost the ability to generalize with impunity (194). Former intellectual attachments have succumbed to a Bergsonian flow: "The voyage had irreversibly changed my seeing, made of me a cultural mongrel, and transformed the world into a fleeting shadow play I felt no need to possess or dominate, only appreciate in the ever extended present" (187).

Further disruptions await. The Fury proves providential: Papa Zeringue, who, it has been revealed to Rutherford, kept him tethered because he was part owner of the *Republic* expedition, also presides over the *Juno*, the floating gin palace that has plucked him from drowning. Moreover, Papa is on the verge of a shipboard marriage to Isadora, who, despite her devotion to Rutherford, cannot hold out against Papa's persistent suit. (If Rutherford is Odysseus making his torturous way home, she is the faithful Penelope knitting and unknitting not a shroud but sweaters for her cats to delay Papa's advances.) Rutherford defeats Papa with the selfsame technique of extortion—indeed, the selfsame smug phrases—which Papa had originally leveled against him: in return for funding the surviving Allmuseri and for leaving Rutherford and Isadora alone, Rutherford promises not to broadcast Papa's financial interest in a slave ship. (That Papa's hulking minion, Santo, overhears this agreement and thickly recalls that his grandfather was an Allmuseri suggests that Papa will not escape just reckoning after all.)

All plot lines seem conventionally secured, and we await the celebratory union of the true lovers, yet the intimate rewards of *Middle Passage* are lined by the same contingencies that condition the narrative as a whole. Their long-deferred lovemaking is a clumsy failure, for, as Rutherford realizes, "Desire was too much of a wound, a rip of insufficiency and incompleteness which kept us, despite our proximity, constantly apart, like metals with an identical charge" (208). Rather than conquest, he craves a balanced affirmation, braided faith, or reciprocal ease.[17] Quaking waters wrap the planet, rendering all commitments tentative, chastening the savor of lovers who cannot forget their suffering. Call it the plight of troth that nothing is rescued from the roil, but all must learn to ride it.

So, frail yet hopeful vessels, their urges tempered by the fluxional context they inhabit and imitate, Rutherford and Isadora nestle against alarm.

Notes

1. Leslie Marmon Silko maintains that the tendency to separate oneself from traumatic experience "not only endangers the group but the individual as well—one does not recover by oneself" ("Language and Literature" 86). The reciprocities among man, nature, and their shared past can be seen in the legendary "Chantways" that unite the promise of healing with racial memory (Allen, "Bringing Home the Fact" 576–78). For a gloss on this concept taken from a distant culture, see Bruce Chatwin's investigation of the "songlines" of aboriginal Australians. They likewise constitute an animate map, or animating text.
2. See representative book reviews by Peter J. Beidler, Hayden Carruth, and Elaine Jahner, all of which attest to Silko's stylistic and thematic employment of this method.
3. Programmatic interpretations of so-called political correctness in university curricula may unfortunately ignore the desirability of a mainstream that accepts a diversity of cultural inheritances without eradicating their distinctions. Walter J. Ong advocates an ongoing interaction between minority literatures and the majority culture whereby the maintenance of unfamiliarity (versus disappearance into the melting pot) keeps the whole alive:

    > A minority literature often negotiates for its own identity with the majority culture and constantly redefines itself, ultimately bringing the majority culture to define itself more adequately, too. Cultures, whether majority or minority, are remarkably like persons, born both to isolation and to community. All of us want to realize ourselves as distinct persons, but we also want others—lots of others—to know that we are our own distinct selves. We do not want to be unique all alone. (3–4)

4. Silko's poetry in *Laguna Woman* (1974) complements this aesthetic through its consistent use of the present progressive. In poems such as "Poem for Myself and Mei: Concerning Abortion," "When Sun Came to Riverwoman," and "Poem for Ben Barney," things are always shimmering, spilling, whirling, dancing, spinning, fluttering. Indeed, the volume features the author's drawing of a coiled snake (5) as a sort of emblem for the collection which also recalls the open-ended circle of the Navajo sand painting and its depiction of becoming.
5. Silko's descriptions of the war zone show it to be a place of engulfing terror and confusion, like Tim O'Brien's Vietnam "shit field." The same sensations haunt Tayo when he goes to the bathroom at the bar: "He pushed down on

the handle of the toilet, but it didn't flush; the lid of the toilet tank was leaning against the wall and the floor was covered with dirty water. It was soaking through his boots. The sensation was sudden and terrifying; he could not get out of the room, and he was afraid he would fall into the stinking dirty water and have to crawl through it, like before, with jungle clouds raining down filthy water that smelled ripe with death" (56).

6. See further Wallace Stevens's "July Mountain," which focuses on "Thinkers without final thoughts / In an always incipient cosmos." In *Lyric Contingencies* Margaret Dickie uses excerpts from these two works to begin her analysis of the poet's modern penchant for "staged arbitrariness" (1–4), an interweaving of technique and improvisation which readily applies to the issue of balance at stake in this study.
7. Kenneth Lincoln explains that the Laguna reservation in particular "has evolved adaptively" as "a Pueblo of transitions—geographically, genetically, linguistically, culturally, and historically" (*Native American Renaissance* 233).
8. Silko herself combines Laguna, Mexican, and white ancestries, announcing without apology the unique value of living "somewhere on the fringes of all three" (qtd. in Lincoln, *Native American Renaissance* 224). Betonie, meanwhile, derives from the union between an Indian grandfather and a disgraced Mexican girl, so he also embodies the evolving modulation of heritages. Susan Perez Castillo refers to this interactive phenomenon as being part of the inherently (and desirably) relational quality of life for many Native Americans, who find themselves "shuttling between radically diverse realities": "This diversity can be seen, however, not only as potentially alienating, but also as a source of creative ferment and positive historical change" (289).
9. It is noteworthy that, while the white man's language makes malefic incursions throughout the Indian culture, "Ts'eh" is a nickname for an otherwise unpronounceable name. She is an unassailable mythic fundament protected by her very elusiveness. Compare the characterization of the *ka'tsina* spirit (whom the accused cattle rustler Silva "reveals" himself to be) and his dreamlike insinuations into the narrator's body and consciousness in Silko's "Yellow Woman."
10. Andrew Hawkins is a mulatto, conceived through a drunken swapping of wives between his slave father and his father's master. Thus, like Silko's Tayo, he embodies, however unwillingly, an uneasy balance and spends his childhood poised between the two families and the two races "in their crossfire" (8).
11. This attitude can be related to Johnson's impatience with the concept of Negritude developed during the 1930s and 1940s, which he indicts, as he does all kitsch, for being a "retreat from ambiguity, the complexity of Being occasioned by the conflict of interpretations, and a flight by the black artist from the agony of facing a universe silent as to its sense, where even black history (or all history) must be seen as an ensemble of experiences and

documents difficult to read, indeed, as an experience capable of inexhaustible readings" (*Being and Race* 20).

12. Keith E. Byerman echoes the "double-faced" fact of black art and culture, whereby black and white identify themselves in terms of one another, inextricably bound by their common history and subject to their changing perceptions of that interrelationship (2–5). Byerman theorizes that black folk forms structurally correspond to the need for blacks to equip themselves for functioning with the polarities inherent in their racial history—silence and voice, oppression and freedom, trickster and tricked, and so on—"which can be destructive but also powerfully creative" (3).
13. Hence, Johnson feels smothered by the idea of the political novel, believing it to be guilty of the same sort of dogmatism which presumably inspires its reaction. He prefers, as well as predicts, the growing ascendancy of "a fiction of increasing intellectual and artistic generosity, one that enables us as a people, as a culture, to move from narrow complaint to broad celebration" (qtd. in Monaghan A3).
14. And, if Falcon resembles Ahab, Rutherford echoes Ishmael's realization: "Who aint a slave? Tell me that" (Melville 15). Nor is a captain exempt from that status, as Ahab confesses to Starbuck: "When I think of this life I have led; the desolation of solitude it has been; the masoned, walled-town of a Captain's exclusiveness, which admits but small entrance to any sympathy from the green country without—oh, weariness! heaviness! Guinea-coast slavery of solitary command!" (443).
15. Ironically, Rutherford's persistent attempts to avoid being implicated make him the logical candidate to be forced to kill Falcon. As one of his shipmates contends, "Once we reach New Orleans the rest of us kin sign on to other ships, and Calhoun'll go his own way, like he always done, believin' in nothin', belongin' to nobody, driftin' here and there and dyin', probably, in a ditch without so much as leavin' a mark on the world—or as much of a mark as you can get from writin' on water" (88). Disassociation erodes identity instead of protects it.
16. When Rutherford encounters the Allmuseri deity in the ship's hold he learns that he cannot respond to a single question, whether it be about the tribe or about Rutherford's own life, "without delivering as well the *complete* content of the antecedent universe" to which a given item belongs (169). In other words, and in refutation of Captain Falcon's presumptions, everything exists in context, balanced by many-sided stories with roots of indeterminable reach.
17. The indeterminacy of the end of *Middle Passage* coincides with the resistance to controlling systems, political and aesthetic alike, whose "mechanistic order" sacrifices vitality to predictability. In Byerman's words, "The lack of certainty includes the sense of identity" (5), a situation that, by contrast, black folk culture respects, in that it "provides strategies for endurance and improvement, not for domination. The lesson of the lore is 'making a way of no way,' making the best of conditions rather than presuming to dictate them" (8).

8

MAXIMALIST STORIES, MINIMALIST NOVELS

> Also, the sensual experience of writing a novel is radically different from the sensual experience of writing a story. You're the control freak when you're writing stories and you're the passive aggressive when you're writing a novel.
>
> —Russell Banks, "Talking about American Fiction"

Complaining of poetry, a character in David Foster Wallace's short story collection, *Girl with Curious Hair* (1989), admits, "Even when I like it, it's nothing more than a really oblique way of saying the obvious." Her friend responds, "But consider how very, very few of us have the equipment to deal with the obvious" (qtd. in Levin 31).

In her review of Wallace's book Jenifer Levin highlights this interchange and suggests that the author "might as well be commenting on modern fiction here" (31). The question of how to deal with the obvious is at the core of what has fast become a minor tradition in contemporary American fiction, and, indeed, among detractors the obvious is not only minimalism's principal subject but also its principal restriction. By limiting themselves to aridity of circumstance, outlook, and style, writers such as Frederick Bathelme, Ann Beattie, Raymond Carver, Richard Ford, Mary Robison, and Tobias Woolf (to round up the usual suspects) have achieved an impasse; or, to borrow from a representative denunciation by James Atlas, they discover, as they plink the same single note over and over again, that "less is less" (96–98).

This sort of flat dismissal of flatness is now at least as common as the examples that have incited it, as are the hip characterizations (K-Mart realism, hick chic) designed as euthanasia for a strapped, listless muse starved for vastness and aching for lyricism (the minimalist atmosphere being too thin to support sentiments like that). Minimalist fiction so boils down the world, the argument runs, that it loses the broth.

For the sake of argument let us accept this contention for the moment. If minimalism is in fact a dead-end aesthetic, is it possible to proceed from its models without discarding the philosophy of "the richness of a glimpse" altogether? One way out of this self-imposed monotone, of course, is to embrace the willful variousness and experimental zeal of antirealism in order to break the fixation with so-called neorealism, which has now become a pinched-out claim. Another option is to persist in taking pains with the empirical but to forgo the restraint on data and language which marks minimalism. Donald Barthelme is the prime minister of this recourse, which is also variously practiced by Max Apple, T. Coraghessan Boyle, and David Foster Wallace. Quoting with addictive persistence from the quotidian, these writers achieve a supernatural, defamiliarized version of American society's kitschy fascinations.

Another approach, upon which the balance of this section will focus, is based upon redefining minimalism as a mode of inquiry instead of a stylistic program per se. If we think of minimalism as referring to a set of ways of asking questions about the contemporary world, we may better appreciate the truths it discovers, even as we admit that these truths are to some degree determined by minimalist manners themselves. Furthermore, we may reenergize the visible field of minimalist writing by increasing it to include works whose secular devotion, if not the austerity of their diction, parallels that of the minimalist "canon." Finally, we will see that inordinate attention to the ordinary contents of our world need not necessarily serve satirical ends, as it usually does in the comedies of Donald Barthelme and T. Coraghessan Boyle. It is also possible to take the world at its considerable face value. Thus, Carl Sandburg's query in "Waiting for the Chariot"—"Can bare fact make the cloth of a shining poem?" (l. 1)—can be answered affirmatively for prose as well.

Within their abbreviated settings, however, the texts under discussion tend to foreground an anxiety about their tenure. This is partly due to their "failure" to fit traditional generic categories and partly to their self-conscious incompleteness. Less may be more, yes, but less is also mortal. Like the rogue prince haunted by his supposititious birth, the odd complexes that we call "maximalist stories" or "minimalist novels" feature apologies for their status and undisguised questions about their issue.

Terms such as *maximalist* and *minimalist* are conveniences at best; typically, they are conveniences refused by writers assigned them. The rough coupling of the terms proposed here may intensify instead of subdue the difficulty; however, it may also enable us to appreciate how compatible the aims of the two ends of the spectrum actually may be. Frederick R. Karl is one critic who does not seem to mind using wide nets like these. For him the maximalist novel—he prefers Mega-Novel, which admittedly has the added appeal of the tone otherwise reserved for the movie blockbuster or extravaganza—is itself defined by antithetical tendencies. Whereas its chief feature is its vast scope, it actually shies away from inclusiveness, or, rather, it causes us to focus upon the impossibility of completeness "by stressing associations and composition, the 'drips' rather than the base": "What emerges is not 'content' as we traditionally describe or discuss it, but architecture, form, arrangement, composition, associational matter, mass and cluster" ("American Fictions: The Mega-Novel" 254). Although the novels covered in this chapter do not compete with the Mega-Novel in terms of size, they still demonstrate the same interest in the shape and arrangement of its materials.

A second point of conjunction between the extremes has to do with self-reflexivity. When Karl accepts Faulkner's *A Fable* (1954) as a Mega-Novel he does so on the basis that, despite its relatively shorter length, "it does have the stress on sentences and paragraph problematics connected with the form": "Words, sentences, paragraphs are not utilized chiefly for informational or narrative purposes, but for the quality of the language, or the illumination of the immediate area" ("American Fictions: The Mega-Novel" 251–52). Novels usually referred to as minimalist do not dispense with such concerns in favor of a bland rehearsal of societal phenomena. On the contrary, in the latter instance, just as economy of size bespeaks urgency of vision, to minimalize the verbal arena is not to minimize structural problems.[1] Karl himself proposes as much in his chapter on "The Possibilities of Minimalism" in *American Fictions, 1940–1980*, among which he highlights questioning narrative conventions, corroding the authority of words with irony and the "surrounding blankness," and implying that what really counts is what is left unsaid (384–85). Thus, minimalist texts are pitted "against scale," to use Philip Stevick's phrase in his *Anti-story* anthology (xxii), in a manner that complements what is seen in maximalist counterparts. Both styles may recommend a single attitude that is marked by daring and haunted by failure.

We might begin the examination of individual works of fiction with *Out of Focus* (1985), by the Irish author Alf MacLochlainn, in which an anonymous narrator brings his hypermethodical attentions to bear upon soap containers, the difficulties inherent in propelling a bicycle loaded with a briefcase, and the treasures to be found in the "furry glen" of the recess between the seat and back of a lounge chair (47). MacLochlainn's narrator is an archivist of the proximate world, but he is one whose perceptions are rendered remarkable, or absurd, because his visions are achieved by his peering through (1) his detached watch crystal, (2) the overflow hole of his bathtub, (3) a hollow ballpoint pen barrel, and (4) a gauze bandage. To be sure, he returns *vision* to its optical origins, for injuries to, or willful distortions of, his eyesight lead to his insights, many of which inspire diagrams, exotic imagined inventions, or extended clinical descriptions of anything from comparative brassiere designs to his attempts to manipulate the bathtub taps with his feet.

When he marvels at the impact of the morning sun upon his unprepared eyes—"Quintrillions of those quanticles, of brain-blistering miniatude, were being constantly disgorged from the sun, vomited forth from its forced feeding of itself on itself" (11)—he confesses the indistinguishability of the authentic and the distorted products of his investigations. If this brand of minimalist writing dismantles the conventional hierarchy between the germane and the digressive, *Out of Focus* takes an additional liberty by rendering all images, the clear and the skewed alike, with equal conviction and delineation. In the end, MacLochlainn seems to say, what matters is the intensity of perception, not its empirical reliability, when it comes to extracting narrative potential.

A story by Paul West, "Those Pearls His Eyes" (1988), appears to confirm these findings. An eminent physicist, whose subatomic concerns make those of MacLochlainn's narrator almost Dickensian by comparison, is similarly stricken by a bizarre visual impairment, which in his case causes whatever he sees to be supermagnified, but, although he is overwhelmed and "sore afraid," he too finds the fresh perspective sublime:

> The staples he tried to fit into his stapler were a vermillion ribcage. Outsqueezed toothpaste was a violent quicksand above which he floated weightlessly. Being nylon, his pajamas revealed themselves as an endlessly interlocking grid of repeated capital omegas. The flame from the Bunsen burner in his basement wriggled with two waists and three pelvises. Brass of the ashtray frothed with all colors save red. A coin's nickel was a cliff quarried deep for corpses methodically stacked. The black plastic of his pen flaked, the flake was a squadron of eastward-plunging open-beaked sienna gulls. Out of an oak splinter soared basketwork torsos with maroon breasts. Facing Hannah over the counter between kitchen and living room, he saw himself upside down on her retinas, against a network of blood vessels and one bright spot that was the optic nerve. (144–45)

As the narrator of *Out of Focus* notes when trying to maneuver the dangling filaments of a failing lightbulb to make them adhere to one another, "This would shorten the expectation of life of this poor little filament but after all was I not giving it one crowded hour of glorious life if also an early age without a name?" (10). The "one crowded hour of glorious life" which constitutes *Out of Focus* is too precious to disturb with questions of trustworthiness. Intrigue is its own legitimation.

"I remembered that when I was little," recalls the narrator of Nicholson Baker's *The Mezzanine* (1988), "I used to be very interested in the fact that anything, no matter how rough, rusted, dusty, dirty, or otherwise discredited it was, looked good if you set it down on a stretch of white cloth or any kind of clean background" (38). This same philosophy, whereby it is the quality of regard paid to an object and not the merit of the object itself which redeems it, serves as Baker's formal aesthetic: he exposes the dormant deep structures in which our lives are nested by setting off minute details against the "clean background" of an otherwise nearly plotless novel (a fit successor, to be sure, to the example of *Out of Focus*). As a result, he vouchsafes each of these details its "true status as an object of attention" (38). Moreover, unlike MacLochlainn, Baker does not resort to experimentalism; *The Mezzanine* rivets its speculations to the scraps at hand. But there is no lament over tedium or claustrophobia as there is in "traditional" minimalist literature. On the contrary, because the novel is predicated on so slight a premise—namely, a lunch hour trip to the local drugstore for replacement shoelaces—incidentals and peripherals loom large; the ordinary, fascinating; the quotidian, exotic.[2]

Because he sweats the details so assiduously, sorting out the secret insights of a seemingly mundane, bluntly efficient office world of rush jobs and routine contacts, a persistent hum of amazement courses through *The Mezzanine* which vitalizes observer and observed alike. Belaboring the trivial like some premature archaeologist, Baker's narrator reinvests the environment with consequence in a way similar to that heralded by Donald Barthelme as "a process of accretion": "Barnacles growing on a wreck or a rock. I'd rather have a wreck than a ship that sails. Things attach themselves to wrecks. Strange fish find your wreck or rock to be a good feeding ground; after a while you've got a situation with possibilities" ("An Interview with Donald Barthelme" 34).

In this scaled-down drama how best to put on socks is the stuff of high comedy; the sight of a "wounded" paper bag brings supreme pathos; the peregrinations of a phonograph needle offer picaresque delights. Reaching the end of a roll of adhesive tape causes "shock and grief," while the stapler's failure is an abrupt "betrayal" that provokes a prolonged analysis of the evolution of stapler design from its brontosaural beginnings to today's streamlined conformity (14–15). There are equally impressive pleasures as well, as we witness in this paeon to perforation:

> Perforation! Shout it out! The deliberate punctuated weakening of paper and cardboard so that it will tear along an intended path, leaving a row of fine-haired white pills or tuftlets on each new edge! It is a staggering conception, showing an age-transforming feel for the unique properties of pulped wood fiber. Yet do we have national holidays to celebrate its development? Are festschrift volumes published honoring the dead great in the field? (74)

"Staggered" too by the miracle of Jiffy Pop, Baker's narrator exhumes its inventor for similar worship. In fact, so great is his propensity for being swept away like this that even the principal "tragedy" of the novel—the breaking of both shoelaces during a single day—excites him with the prospect that this simultaneity could show that "the variables of private life" may "seem suddenly graspable and law-abiding" (15).

Although life conspires to desensitize us, plot pounces from everywhere. Every instant is a mystery, every inch a milestone. To blink is to miss a history, whether its euphoria-inducing potential be housed within the Istanbul of the CVS drugstore or the rhythmic physics of the escalator. Swathed within the numberless discoveries that constitute "the often undocumented daily texture" of our culture (41), the narrator finds comfort in design: he inhabits an insistently significant universe whose subtle matrices rustle at the touch of investigation to reveal a Plan that is intricate and everywhere available. The neglected crevices of the day hold proofs of man's elegance and resolve. Wherever we look we witness Creation shaped by Method.

In order to accommodate the swollen wealth of Baker's microhistories *The Mezzanine* is laced throughout with footnotes, many of which burgeon to crowd out the main text. As it does in Nabokov's *Pale Fire* (1963), our reading grows schizophrenic, for the form of the novel compels us to shuttle back and forth in time to the whims of a narrator whose interests are so promiscuous, so distractable, that no narrative line will suffice to hold all of the enthusiasms he trafficks in. But to describe this method in terms of the opposition of the central story and habitual digression would be to impose upon *The Mezzanine* a convention that is inappropriate to the democracy of wonder. Whereas the normal hierarchy relegates footnotes to secondary status—they are, after all, physically subordinated to the main run of text, a sort of occasional reinforcement to help us negotiate when the footing becomes unsteady—here the asides not only take up nearly as much room in the book but also contain some of the most savory revelations. Thus, the surrender of the plot to its tributaries is paralleled by the structural swarming under of text by subtext. Like some insurgency massing in the foothills, minor amusements mount to magnitude on the pages below.

If a morpheme is the smallest unit of language which conveys meaning, *The Mezzanine* is a compact encyclopedia of society's morphemes, modestly dedicated to restoring the novelty that inheres in what most of us barely notice. As far as what sort of person *does* notice, Baker's man-about-town sees himself as

> the sort of person who stood in a subway car and thought about buttering toast—buttering raisin toast, even: when the high, crisp scrape of the butter knife is muted by occasional contact with the soft, heat-blimped forms of the raisins, and when if you cut across a raisin, it will sometimes fall right out, still intact though dented, as you lift the slice. I was the sort of person whose biggest discoveries were likely to be tricks to applying toiletries while fully dressed. (54)

This is a man whose Blakean capacity for seeing a world in a grain of sand is mirrored by his tendency to granulate matters that typically dominate narrative attentions. Thus, he devotes paragraph after paragraph to the minutest rituals; he rhapsodizes about the braided flow of the urinal he uses and thinks it hardly inferior to the ocean breakers commemorated in a poem by Gerard Manley Hopkins; he deems it an honor to use the "best kind" of paper towel in a public restroom; yet he refers to his beloved only as L.

The Mezzanine is not ironic about these affections, however, nor does it cry poverty over its minimalist landscape. Reading from his Penguin paperback of Marcus Aurelius's *Meditations* that "all mortal life" is "transient and trivial," the narrator sternly objects—"Wrong, wrong, wrong! I thought. Destructive and unhelpful and misguided and completely untrue!" (120)—and pits against this sentiment the abiding value of another passage in the book: "Manifestly, no condition of life could be so well adapted for the practice of philosophy as this in which chance finds you today!" (qtd. in *Mezzanine* 124).

The Mezzanine, therefore, proclaims a sizable victory. Baker's prose has a vigor and sinuousness that contradicts, or at least offers an alternative to, the parched last resort complained of by detractors of minimalist fiction. The "thought frequency chart" that concludes the novel, in which earplugs hobnob with career concerns and the shine on moving objects is not less arresting than the subject of marriage, shows how esteem can light anywhere. (Admittedly, Immanuel Kant and how birds regurgitate food to feed their young are tied, earning a scant half-thought per year apiece!)

That the narrator predicts that shoelaces will ultimately outrank Aurelius among his lifetime periodicity ratings is not a mockery of the philosopher so much as a redemption of all of the mind's particulars. The narrator heroizes and affiliates with "that sort of excellent low-key sort of man who achieves little by external standards but who sustains civilization for us by knowing, in a perfectly balanced, accessible, and considered way, all that can be known about several brief periods of Dutch history, or about the flowering of some especially rich tradition of terra-cotta pipes" (123). To know such things is to deem them *worth* knowing, which is to articulate, secure, and vindicate civilization at the same time. To rephrase Robert Frost, there is much indeed to be made of a diminished thing.

Charles Simmons's *Wrinkles* (1978) also discovers momentum and density in life's familiar store. Unlike MacLochlainn and Baker, however, who inflate an hour into a volume, Simmons reverses the process and collapses a lifetime into a few lines. *Wrinkles* consists of forty-four minichapters, one long paragraph apiece, each of which is devoted to individual lifelong concerns, ranging from laughter to betrayal, sex to athletics, deception to drinking, affection to finances. Each chapter takes us from the narrator's childhood past to his present situation then concludes with a (usually grim) prediction about his future.

The novel's tone is one of surrender to entropy. A given section begins with the promise of absorption:

> He had different feelings about each digit. One was perfect and friendly. Its appearance resembled its meaning. Two looked more complicated than it was. . . . (3)

> Cotton was friendly to him, wool was not. (27)

> When he was about to be taken to his first movie he asked his mother what movies were like. "They're dark in one place and light in another," she said. (69)

> He enjoyed the pennies, piling them into stacks, which represented castles, and attacking them with marbles, which represented armies. When he tired of the pennies he asked his

> mother to change them into nickels. He liked the solidity and dull luster of nickels. . . . (127)

The narrator's early fascinations occasionally parallel the promiscuous wonder of Nicholson Baker's protagonist. But Simmons's cannot sustain the "purity of passion" into adulthood, and, as the past tense slides into the present, the narrative voice freezes over with disappointment, disillusionment; weariness and cynicism infect every interest. The future "codas" are generally severe—a series of shrugs, the energies of each topic having succumbed to age, abandonment, or disease:

> He will learn that the brightest boy of the class was an executive in a Maryland engineering firm and is now dead, that the boys ranked second and third at graduation are also dead. He will wonder if there is meaning in this, since he was fourth. (14)

> As time goes on he will realize that his birthdays rather than accomplishments are looked on as postponements. (38)

> His need for exercise and taste for movement will diminish to the point that he will not leave his home on weekends if he can help it. (84)

> . . . he will realize that they had been talking about him and that he is seen as an aging loser whose illusions about himself should not be disturbed. (102)

The satisfactions of childhood—the reassuring feel of wood, the way a blob of mercury reacts to prodding, the obliteration of cigarette butts with a stream of urine—disappear. Meanwhile, the repetitive structure of the novel instructs our expectations: after we witness the way the narrator's attitudes contract in the opening chapters, we understand that each paragraph will end in divorce, disaffection, or ruin.

Nevertheless, that *Wrinkles* is so much darker than the other fictions discussed here actually serves as further evidence of the resiliency and scope of minimalism. The discovery of eulogistic depth at every turn confirms the cash value of ordinary detail as surely as the discovery of comic abundance or historical weight; in his review of *Wrinkles* Anatole Broyard ascribes the book's power to "the poignancy of the unspectacular" (C24). The glum lessons Simmons gleans from experience are more pessimistic than Nicholson Baker's but no less pregnant.

Wrinkles is centripetal: its foiled nostalgia always returns its narrator to an ineluctable present, where he is—like Dickinson's strange, funereal race—"wrecked, solitary, here" ("I Felt a Funeral" l. 16). By contrast, Renata Adler's *Speedboat* (1976) is centrifugal: Jen Fain's private malaise alleges against the century's. Adler's speaker self-consciously speaks for a group; her jaded takes are offered as symptoms of a sullen zeitgeist, the Dispiritedness of the Age. *Speedboat* characterizes "the idiom of our class and generation" as a withered disaffection (177). It is a matter of no bang and all whimper among the palely loitering inhabitants of Adler's novel. Sundry affairs, frets, and vanities have taken their toll, as have society's inflationary, sensationalist manners. In academics, politics, and private parties, "it was in the interest of absolutely nobody to get to the bottom of anything whatever" (84), and crises compost down into personal eccentricities. The result is an erosion of belief and attention. (The Center for Short-Lived Phenomena ideally symbolizes this, and it undoubtedly succumbs to its own premise.)

Wrath, devotion, inspiration, dread—these would require more animation than anyone in the novel can marshal. Whatever excitement arises takes the ironic form of "a frenzy of antipathy and boredom" (90), and in this regard, among the novels treated in this chapter, *Speedboat* most resembles the stereotype disdained by critics of minimalist fiction. Our narrator, a tabloid reporter, campaign speechwriter, and sometime college teacher, deadpans her way through cultural intensities and trendy orientations. She senses that *tepid* and *arguable* should be scribbled in the margins of all of her copy; she is obsessed with the evanescence of all of today's urgent relevancies, which under inspection could disintegrate as readily as a bit of sugar that a raccoon, "in its odd fastidiousness," washes in a brook (7); she "castles" herself into formal restraint and strategic withdrawal because "everyone has the power to call your whole life into question here" (3). Dutifully, she accumulates experience through interviews, travels, and engagements, but the effect of all that input is to level everything out as gossip. Moreover, her alertness to case studies does not exempt Jen Fain, who deems sanity to be "the most profound moral option of our time" (4), from the same seedy bed of therapies:

> Sometimes I miss, or lose, the point. Late-sleeping utopians, especially, persist like mercury. I am a fanatic myself, although not a woman of temperament. I get nervous at scenes. I stole a washcloth once from a motel in Angkor Wat. The bellboy was incensed. I had to give it back. To promote the

> general welfare and secure the blessings of liberty to ourselves and our posterity—I believe all that. I go to parties almost whenever I am asked. I think a high tone of moral indignation, used too often, is an ugly thing. I get up at eight. Quite often now I have a drink before eleven. In some ways, I have overshot my mark in spades. (8)

It is tempting to credit the ennui commons to "the stresses of winding toward the millenium" (13). Regardless, the incommensurability of things makes angst so familiar as to disarm its energies. People crowd one another on the window ledge and set up drinks there. All sorts of outrage are received in an atmosphere of sublime acknowledgment—indulgence that falls just short of endorsement—which is the mark of well-educated urban unease: "Situps aside, it is possible that we are really a group of invalids, hypochondriacs, and misfits" (176).

Like Simmons, Adler deploys her narrative in small bursts that, in the case of this novel, approximate a collage of the continuous present—a structural equivalent, perhaps, of Fain's comment that "there are given things, all strewn and simultaneous" (41). Tonal congruence replaces plot development as the narrative glue, so that, in keeping with the title, progress seems buffeted and glancing as we are conveyed from textual island to island.[3] There are several preemptive ripples in the daze which masquerade as cumulative insights or moments of prophecy but which in the end effect little change:

> None of us is quite leading the life we were at all prepared for. (23)

> It is possible that we have, separately, acquired the capacity to say a qualified No to any going, too going, concern. (23)

> I think when you are truly stuck, when you have stood still in the same spot for too long, you throw a grenade in exactly the spot you were standing in, and jump, and pray. It is the momentum of last resort. (27)

> Lonely people see double entendres everywhere. (36)

> The pressures were wrong. There was just enough money and not enough time. (47)

> Although altogether too much of life is mood. (64)

> We may win this year. We may lose it all. It is not going as well as we thought. Posterity, anyway, does not know everything. (91)
>
> "I can't believe it," people said almost with passion. It was that year's version of hello. (115)
>
> There is no conceivable proper answer. It all ends in disaster anyway. (136)
>
> It is no accident that boredom and cruelty are great preoccupations in our time. (137)
>
> People seem to be unhappy in so many different ways. (152)

While it occasionally appeals to forthrightness and altruism, to the need to "pick up that check" when it comes to relationships, political commitment, and artistic integrity (31), and thereby achieve some positive extension of self, *Speedboat* comes down to a series of elliptical allegories of authorial fecklessness. Our narrator couches her apologies in several symbolic counterparts. There is the difficulty she has in maneuvering an airplane: "I land funny. Not roughly or dangerously, just a bit canted or askew," she confesses, blaming her fear of crosswind gusts and her having concentrated too gravely on *arrival* when all she has to do is touch down (70). Trying to assemble a rifle, she admits that "putting the damn thing together was and, I guess, always will be one of those simple operations of life that seem to complicate themselves altogether out of my range" (122). She ruefully recalls a course in poetry in which her professor warned that "synonymy" and "contexture," which serve as the subtle logical and emotional connections upon the associative plane of language, can in the case of certain speech disorders break down into useless repetition and rambling, causing "a word heap" (161).

Speedboat lacks the elegiac tenderness of *Wrinkles*, much less the affirming eagerness of *The Mezzanine*, and the selected passages just reviewed indicate the novel's self-consciousness about its filibustering while its audience shift in their chairs. What the novel does present with vigor is another formal equivalent for the balance between maximalist evidentiary procedures and minimalist concentration. While "the equations are statelier" in other fictions between plot strands and attendant insights (170), versus the irreparably cellular quality of *Speedboat*, "maybe there are stories, even, like solitaire or canasta; they are shuffled and dealt, then they do or they do not come out. Or the deck falls on the floor" (171).

Speedboat ends with a wistful reference to writing that "stops right on a dime" (178), for which Adler has substituted a novel that confides its imprecisions with meticulous resolve. Her best guess is that the truth of things lies where intelligence runs abruptly up against them, where rock stops the spade, and nothing budges.

Next we might consider the example of Stephen Dixon, who offers in *Work* (1977) an aural corollary for the visual fascinations of *Out of Focus* and *The Mezzanine*. *Work* follows one Claude Martez, a would-be actor forever between engagements, through a series of tenuous trades, including substitute teacher, movie usher, artists' model, department store demonstrator, waiter, and bartender. Dixon's New York is a city of scroungers, hustlers, and hangers-on, and our protagonist moves among them like the quintessential temporary—an inveterate stand-in, a last-minuteman—foundering at the edge of financial security while awaiting experience's casting call.

What charges otherwise anonymous, menial jobs with interest is language. *Work* is shot through with all manner of urban lingos and protocols, loaded with inside dope and coded cryptics rich enough to satisfy any semiotician: the short-order cook's arcana, the gambler's savvy, the barman's voodoo. Cabbies declaim like manic Ciceros, while busboys rehearse their methods like warriors plotting battle campaigns. Everyone is churning words at once. If MacLochlainn and Baker are transported by objects, Dixon is in love with argots and the oddities of diction that is just enough out of joint to suggest that we have tapped into something mysterious:

> "I've waited on tables, know what's doing in back, did some shortorder cooking for a luncheonette several years ago and am honest and clean and reliable and really need a job."
>
> "How several?" (16)

> Hey, get off it with the holier than flagpole art or whatever thou art routine is, saluting it like that. (24)

> So I think if you don't really sell yourself like where they'll almost carve out a spot for you when none was there before, you're not going to get a job. That's my personal opinion and I know hard as nails. (25)

> And Hans asked me to tell you to forget your drink date at 5 with him as he'll be tied up in meetings till tonight. To cancel your drink date I mean. Which is why he couldn't call. You.

> Had me. Rushed this but seems I've made it. Sorry again for you and Miss Kantor and have a nice day. Sorry you had to hear it this way I mean and that you know her. Know her to hear it. Forget it. (29)

> What you mean and what puts us the understaff back 20 years from yesterday and 10 from tomorrow and the union we're trying to force in here is 2 different classic comics, so don't go fucking martyring for your own fucking cause, no disrespect unmeant. Peter's upset and damn good reason to be so throw him a punch, brother. Each counts. (34)

Words are hawked and spat rather than shared. Dixon's people most often react in captions. (Ironically, one of Claude's fizzled job opportunities is writing captions for a book on the history of film.) Sensibilities all seem stammered out, and ellipses litter the pages of *Work* like birdseed on the sidewalk. As Jerome Klinkowitz contends, Stephen Dixon is a phenomenological realist whose data are soliloquies and dialogues routine as any day shift; however, he manages to find even beneath the underbelly of the city's economy that words glitter with "self-apparent" richness (*The Self-Apparent Word* 98–101). Urgency percolates in every corner of contemporary culture; a ubiquitous interest guarantees its own rewards.

Perhaps nothing so accurately encapsulates the uneasy negotiations between minimalist and maximalist impulses as Ronald Sukenick's paradoxical title *The Endless Short Story* (1986). The suggestion it carries of a perpetuated end, of the imposition of formal restraint upon a readiness to dilate in unexpected directions, prepares us for a fiction that, while it defies circumscription, steers itself into a clutch of unresolved middles. Operating on the assumption that "the minimum is included in the maximum" (117), *The Endless Short Story* (which earns the chummy personification "ESS" late in the book) seeks to "ride the breaking wave just right" so that "the wave would never break" (17). In an appreciation of fellow Fiction Collectivist Steve Katz, Sukenick describes this as writing "like a seal with the ball continually about to fall off its nose" ("The New Tradition" 211). Sukenick perches the ESS, that risky vessel, atop the always disintegrating, always renewing crest, where plan and digression, "lethal certitude and aggravating confusion" mingle as unpredictably as they do in the real world (128), whose self-contradictory "discipline of inclusion" the Surfictionist emulates.[4]

Sukenick's commitment to the "endless" half of the equation is well known. Sukenick himself eagerly and famously campaigns for the shattering of conventional generic containments in the essays collected in *In Form: Digressions on the Act of Fiction* (1985). "Act," "experience," "process," "energy," "displacement," and "flux" echo throughout the collected criticism on behalf of a general defense of improvisation against the tide of stale, static formulas. "You practice a discipline of reduction I of addition," Sukenick explains. "You pursue essentials I ride with the random. You cultivate separation I union. You struggle toward stillness I rest in movement" (*Endless Short Story*, back cover). A joyful impudence runs through the fiction and criticism alike, and its burden is that anything that compromises the novelty of the novel or its freedom to generate is inimical to the engaged writer.

The Endless Short Story is obviously leashed to these beliefs. From its opening words, "to continue" (an homage to *Finnegans Wake* and its inaugural dip into the river of experience), Sukenick triggers all sorts of antigravity devices to reduce the friction of the realist page. There is the pastlessness of the book's slivered entities and the cartoon exuberance (and vulgarity) of the extemporaneous activities of Pickles Pecker Prince von Mocassin, I. Seymour Hare, Dong Wang, Claude Balls, and I. Bitchakokoff (the Marxist theorist, no less)—all of them "loose ends of a petty denouement" (45). There is the studied resistance to teleology, inductive fact gathering, and intentionality: "your trip traces trivial continuities among grandiose disruptions sucks venom finds oil wells in flower pots politicizes ganglia make something of it" (48). Symbols are disparaged for their pretense of being intrinsic to the work at hand. They are exposed as a belated forensic superimposition and parodied mercilessly:

> he goes down to the beach to lo
> ok for omens he finds a dead fish some
> broken shells gulls flying children play
> ing t he children are beautiful he watch
> es them awhile the fish doesn't know th
> at it's dead the shells don't know that
> they're broken nor the gulls that they're
> flying or if they do they don't think ab
> out it
>
> (13)

> Each bird appeared on his lower lip, peered around and leaped into the air unfurling into a colorful symbol of mutability, metamorphosing quickly into a wide variety of dissa and data. In fact, blimey! everything began turning into everything else.

> The trees turned into snow sculptures and the fish turned into skaters skating on the icy river to a Strauss waltz. The blue sky turned grey and the air turned into tinsel. (124–25)

Circling the drain with the rest of the fragile cast is Aziff, whose name ("as if") and fate serve as another warning regarding the hazards of promiscuous, uninhibited connections, be they sexual or symbolic. Accordingly, ignorance is postulated as a sounder tactic for accommodating the strains of a text whose "syntax coils and weaves dangerously like a green mamba in the bush seeking release from the tedium of prefabrication" (*Endless Short Story* 97).

This is the infamous Ronald Sukenick: flouter of poetical correctness, ardent polemicist of the avant-garde, traverser of alphabet rapids. Let others "stutter off in the clumsy Model T of analysis" (*Endless Short Story* 132); he will brave bliss: "Meaning does not pre-exist creation and afterward it may be superfluous" ("Thirteen Digressions" 32). Or, for those who fail to heed a similar dismissal in the novel of "the necessity or even the profit of explanations," Sukenick parodies teleological pretensions by serving them up in useless lumps:

> Uncle Don is full of answers   here are s
> ome of them   it's behind the radio   the
> square root of seven   Helena   Maxine Pat
> ty and Laverne   Petrarch   a fat oranguta
> ng   a garbage truck   the Dutchess of Mal
> fi   no trespassing
>
> (20–21)

But, as we tour this lexical minefield that is more "attuned to energies / than comprehensions" (33), the skittish pages often betray formal pretexts. The "conjunctions of chance" are not to be eschewed for their arbitrary origins (41). *The Endless Short Story*, for all its vaunted aleatory freedom, is channeled through altered margin settings like canal locks, driven into quilted boxes, hammered into filagreed columns of thought; excesses are quarantined, experiences sectored, words assigned to specific barracks. Characters migrate and mutate, but they are also either segregated or forced to rendezvous at assigned textual contact points. In other words, contesting concepts such as the book as black hole or plot as sightless safari are the patterns and premises of authorial control. Call it the inescapable "withness" of form, which, like Delmore Schwartz's "heavy bear" of a body, lurches along with his purer aspect: "Clumsy and lumbering here and there, / The central ton of every place" (ll. 3–4).

Thus, among the "exhilarating contradictions" that texturize the mysterious goings-on in *The Endless Short Story* the most subtle may be the coded quality of its improvisational vigor (106). Although the question posited within the fiction is "can deliberation deliver us from liberation?" (88), the fact of the matter appears to be that neither deliberation nor liberation is at stake here. Instead, a dynamic polarity between these claims upon, and by, consciousness is asserted, and with surprising consistency. For example, there are loaded paradoxes to reckon with: phrases such as "inescapable sequence of discontinuous fragments" (102) and the motto Perspective and Schizophrenia (27); the concurrent addiction to surfaces and contentions that we have never left the depths, or that depths have been effectively transported to surface level (10, 16); the hope that pure fact will act as an antidote to ambiguity, coupled with the belief that the only way to approach the truth is to discard the tape recorders and make it up (26, 85). On the one hand, sentences die out as though the author were lighting one bad fuse after another, but we are advised that these "terminals initiate agenda of chance" (40). As we alternately stagger or skid through the odd sculptings of typography, we, along with the self-confessing text, "crave expansive continuities," even as we acknowledge the "terminal prosody of event" (44)[5]

All of these instances support the notion that the "flux" we find in *The Endless Short Story*

> is no mere op
> en ended leak like leak to whe
> re but a see-saw
>
> (110)

And would it be unseemly to suggest, amid all the typological idiosyncracies and theoretical grandstanding in the novel, that there is more than a little mischief at work in the contradictions Sukenick employs?—that, while the realists are trying to get dinner on the table, he is out running around the neighborhood, ringing all the doorbells on the block? After announcing that "the important thing" is to "keep it open" and "evade connections," Sukenick suggests that it is, rather, "to outthink premeditation"—a doomed sort of logic by definition—then "to pursue the continuum," which forgoes the original advice in favor of a discrete plan. In the end he capitulates to the dilemma: "the important thing is to annihilate the important thing" (116). Because the big picture is that there is no big picture, offers Dong Wang, we keep painting it.

Does the inevitability of formal impingement on improvisation constitute one of those "exhilarating contradictions" after all? "I rest in movement," Sukenick teases, adopting that paradoxical balance as an aesthetic stance. Indeed, careful examination of *In Form* corroborates the interrelationship—the *desirability* of the interrelationship—between the experiential and the artifactive natures of fiction. "The essential story that fiction tells is that of motion and stasis," Sukenick asserts in "Twelve Digressions toward a Study of Composition" (9); later in that same essay he identifies the dependence of language on experience as fundamental to its "health," but he goes on to voice concern over sustaining its "integrity as artifact" while it undergoes experiential contacts (11). In another context Sukenick elaborates on this conundrum when he champions the "cyclical" traits of language, whereby figurations devolve into phenomena, which, in turn, fraught with design, renovate subsequent figures ("Cross Examination" 146).[6] In fact, he explains, this theoretical waffling is not really the artist's compromise so much as the revealed character of all linguistic enterprises:

> In fact, to tell you the truth, I think what improvisation really depends on is the fact that the mind wants release from larger structures. It simply cannot be unstructured. . . . Our minds are very organized and what you are doing when you are improvising is removing the larger structures as you are releasing other structures, structures you did not know were there are therefore structures that are real discoveries and can be very useful. (149)

By this reasoning minimalist retentiveness can be more than just an unavoidable restraint upon a better-ventilated page. It can provide the comforts of embracing craft. To apply William Gass's convenient expressions, data-crazed Thicks eventually welcome the applications of bracketing Thins ("Representation and the War for Reality" 93–95).

Sukenick justifies deformation because it occasions new postures. One evident result of this method in the criticism is the development of synthetic sophistries such as "the form is closed so it can open to new material" ("Cross Examination" 135). Arbitrariness need not refer to the abolition of structure; instead, it may refer to the adoption of arbitrary structures as means of breaking against the grain of the medium. Whatever privileged liberation the so-called performative text endows itself with, there remains a tension between the text as an example of an ongoing performance and the text as evidence of a completed (and now published) performance (Mellard 140). Consequently, improvisation is inevitably practiced within and against structures, not in lieu of them ("Cross Examination" 138).[7]

Toiling "at the interface of system and disorder, form and chaos, meaning and meaninglessness," where art of necessity must "constantly define and de-define itself" ("Twelve Digressions" 12), Sukenick carves fluid icons: his plots are assembled like clouds that scud and avalanche along (*Out* 74); his characters are victims of "terminal identity fission" (*Death of the Novel* 26)—provisional recombinant entities, or "dialectical fragments" ("Cross Examination" 123); even his metaphors are staged to be struck, their achievements carrying built-in "impermanent validity" (151). We might call into evidence a comparable contrast advanced by Robert Frost, according to whose principles the artwork "must ride on its own melting" ("Figure a Poem Makes" 128).

The Endless Short Story tends to be a bit more strident on the subject—"what do we do when a form restrains our intelligence get rid of it I say so with history" (101)—but, again, further investigation into the novel reveals Sukenick's preoccupation, and compliance, with the artifactive/experiential yoking. Fragments settle into sequences that surrender to rupture or, at the very least, in keeping with the Mosaic Law Sukenick articulates in *98.6* (1975), eschew seamless assimilations that would cause their diverse origins to vanish. While rivers stall at terminals, lush, foresty script petrifies and thaws, until

> incertitudes
> of travel become a
> prosody of experienc
> e a measure of ident
> ity.
>
> *Endless Short Story* (115)

But let us never forget that stagnation kills. All habit must be clawed off to expose the hidden potentialities of the word: "the trick is to keep the song going keep improvising when the song stops you die" (93). Sukenick racks his focus to accommodate arrangement and flow and leaves us, in *The Endless Short Story*, with a restless hybrid: formed endlessness, or better, to employ one of the titles in his *Death of the Novel* (1969), "Permanent Crisis." Appropriately, what clarification he offers takes the shape of oblique, relentless testimony: "In the mountains there are many energies. The energy of the cosmic rays stream [*sic*] through you, the energy of the granite irradiates you, the push and pull of the moon, the lucid confusion of the stars" (36). A lucid confusion: Sukenick's goal, informed perhaps by Roland Barthes's approval in *The Pleasure of the Text* (1975) of "texts of bliss," is vertiginous delight before the renewing crisis of language (Barthes 14). *The Endless Short Story* emphasizes how fiction is a caged progress watched beneath the "jelling" presence of analysis, but analysis that nonetheless respects and accedes to universal dispersion (*Endless Short Story* 6).

Margins between literary categories are especially conducive to critical inversions. There is something at once defiant and nervous about the minimalist novel, whose assaults on both flanks remind us of discussions of postmodernism's obsession with thresholds. Consider Paul Ricoeur's disquiet in response to the changes he detects in the stories that speak contemporary Western culture:

> Nothing excludes the possibility that the metamorphosis of narrative plot should somewhere confront a limit beyond which we could no longer acknowledge the formal principle of temporal configuration (between past, present and future) which makes narrated history into a unified and complete story. And yet . . . and yet. Maybe it is necessary, *in spite of everything*, to continue to have confidence in the need for concordance which still structures the expectancies of today's readers, to continue to believe that new forms of narrative . . . would testify that the narrative function is capable of metamorphosis without actually dying. (qtd. in Kearney 315)

Perhaps to help substantiate Ricoeur's deference to "necessity," all of the fictions viewed in this chapter contribute to a definition of minimalism which emphasizes concentration rather than attenuation. Their authors appear to share the belief that the work of salvage begins with taking grafts from the world's humblest locations. In this regard we might return to Robert Frost and recall his faith in the sheer availability of the "forms" that persevere, conferring order and sanity against the pressure of "larger excruciations": "Fortunately, too, no forms are more engrossing, gratifying, comforting, staying than those lesser ones we throw off, like vortex rings of smoke . . . a basket, a letter, a garden, a room, an idea, a picture, a poem" (To *The Amherst Student* 113). Frost includes his own creative formulations (an idea, a poem) among the things whose quiet consequentiality consoles us. In doing so he implies that humility best suits the verbal object as well. He also foreshadows the minimalist creed, whose best-known articulation belongs to Raymond Carver: "It's possible, in a poem or short story, to write about commonplace things and objects using commonplace but precise language, and to endow those things—a chair, a window curtain, a fork, a stone, a woman's earrings—with immense, even startling power" ("On Writing" 15).

In other words, the artist's often anonymous but essential task is to employ the "lesser forms" around him or her as fortifications against evanescence. But to resort to minimalism is not to minimize this operation. As Alvin Greenberg declares, "Brevity is the face of mortality" (230): minimalist writers engage mortality not only as a thematic issue, scanning like gleaners in the wake of what other books miss, but also as an artistic principle. The compatibility of Frost's and Carver's lists, as well as the confidence their modest particulars inspire in both authors, suggests that simple objects and events, enclosed in simple prose, offer abiding consolation.

"I embrace the common, I explore and sit at the feet of the familiar, the low," announces Emerson in "The American Scholar," which is animated by a belief in a circumambient spiritual cause that redeems "the suburbs and extremities of nature" and leaves "every trifle bristling" with rich design (61). Nevertheless, these simple forms need not be ground to formula to achieve this goal. Revising our understanding of what constitutes literary minimalism, so as to include the panoramic fervor that may ironically contribute to its surprising density, will help us to appreciate how its characteristics are as subtle and as various as its contents.

Notes

1. See also my introduction to *Understanding Raymond Carver*, "Connoisseur of the Commonplace" (1–20), in which I contend that minimalism joins with other more overtly experimental fictional forms in foregrounding and struggling with the intricacies of craft.
2. For those Spartans who seek even greater reductive discipline than this, Baker's second novel, *Room Temperature*, shrinks the time frame still further, from a lunch hour to twenty minutes.
3. So it is that Joseph Epstein sardonically offers that, in *Speedboat* and *Pitch Dark*, Renata Adler "has written, in fact, two novels but no narratives" (63).
4. Surfiction "proposes a new kind of 'realism' which is true to life by *being* it," writes Peter Quartermain (66). I would suggest that Sukenick qualifies this opinion by leaving his procedural scaffolding in plain view. For an overview of Surfictionist principles, see Quartermain's composite review of texts by four members of the Fiction Collective, "Trusting the Reader."

5. For further graphic evidence of Sukenick's ingenious methods for policing our reading experience, see in particular "Momentum" (in *Death of the Novel*) and *Out*, neither of which hides the attempt to maneuver our speed through it.
6. It should be noted for clarification that "Cross Examination" represents Sukenick's weaving together of seven different interviews with seven different "interrogators" over the course of a dozen years (1970–82). Combined in this fashion, they testify to the endurance of these themes in Sukenick's imagination over the course of his career, as they persist in bolstering and bothering his compositions.
7. Jerry A. Varsava also recognizes this characteristic in Sukenick's critical pronouncements:

> Though by admission not a formalist, Sukenick voices a radical rhetoric that often inadvertently suggests as much. . . . In continually straining to discredit the mimetic theory behind nineteenth-century realism, he often obscures the referential bias of his own theory of representation. While one admits the difficulty, perhaps even the impossibility, of dealing with literary aesthetics in a systematic, "consistent" way, metacritical awareness of self-contradiction would make various of the essays of *In Form* more persuasive and establish the "order in disorder" Stevens talks about. (33)

I would contend, on the contrary, that what Varsava sees as unreliable logic is in fact evidence of a perpetually emerging equilibrium, one whose slippages are deliberately advanced after all. In his review of Jerzy Kutnik's study of Sukenick and Federman, Marek Wilczynski cautions against any interpretation of literary performance that neglects the problematical overlaps between the act and its "trace" (152–57). Again, I submit that Sukenick not only acknowledges them but, indeed, risks his productions on such instabilities.

Works Cited

Aaron, Daniel. "How to Read Don DeLillo." Lentricchia 67–81.

Ackerman, Diane. *A Natural History of the Senses*. New York: Random House, 1990.

Adler, Renata. *Speedboat*. New York: Random House, 1976.

Albee, Edward. *Tiny Alice*. New York: Atheneum, 1965.

Allen, Paula Gunn. "The Autobiography of a Confluence." Swann and Krupat, *I Tell You Now* 141–54.

———. "Bringing Home the Fact: Tradition and Continuity in the Imagination." Swann and Krupat, *I Tell You Now* 563–79.

Angell, Roger. "Box Scores." *The Summer Game* 3–5.

———. "The Cool Bubble." *The Summer Game* 125–39.

———. "The Interior Stadium." *The Summer Game* 291–303.

———. *The Summer Game*. New York: Viking, 1972.

Armstrong, Paul B. "Play and Cultural Differences." *Kenyon Review* 13 (1991): 157–71.

Atlas, James. "Less Is Less." *Atlantic* June 1981: 96–98.

Attridge, Derek. "Joyce the Post: A Retrospective Arrangement." Paper presented at the Modern Language Association Convention. Chicago, 29 December 1990.

Auster, Paul. "Disappearances." *Ground Work* 61–68.

———. "From Cakes to Stones: A Note on Beckett's French." *Ground Work* 147–52.

———. *Ground Work: Selected Poems and Essays, 1970–1979*. London: Faber and Faber, 1990.

———. *The Music of Chance*. New York: Viking, 1990.

———. "The Novelist Out of Control." Interview by Michael Freitag. *New York Times Book Review* 19 March 1989: 9.

———. "Pages for Kafka on the fiftieth anniversary of his death." *Ground Work* 116–18.

———. "Spokes." *Ground Work* 3–6.

Bailey, Peter J. *Reading Stanley Elkin*. Urbana: University of Illinois Press, 1985.

Baker, Houston A., Jr., ed. *Three American Literatures*. New York: Modern Language Association of America, 1982.

Baker, Nicholson. *The Mezzanine*. New York: Weidenfeld & Nicholson, 1988.

———. *Room Temperature*. New York: Grove Weidenfeld, 1990.

Barrow, John D. *Theories of Everything: The Quest for Ultimate Explanation*. New York: Oxford University Press, 1991.

Barth, John. *Giles Goat-Boy; or, The Revised New Syllabus*. Garden City, N.Y.: Doubleday, 1966.

———. "How to Make a Universe." *The Friday Book: Essays and Other Nonfiction.* New York: G. P. Putnam's, 1984. 13–25.

———. "Lost in the Funhouse." *Lost in the Funhouse: Fiction for Print, Tape, Live Voice.* New York: Doubleday, 1969. 72–97.

Barthelme, Donald. "An Interview with Donald Barthelme." With Larry McCaffery. *Anything Can Happen: Interviews with Contemporary American Novelists.* Ed. Tom LeClair and Larry McCaffery. Urbana: University of Illinois Press, 1983. 32–44.

———. "See the Moon?" *Sixty Stories.* New York: Dutton, 1982. 97–107.

Barthes, Roland. "Literature and Discontinuity." *Critical Essays.* Trans. Richard Howard. Evanston, Ill.: Northwestern University Press, 1972. 171–83.

———. *The Pleasure of the Text.* Trans. Richard Miller. New York: Hill and Wang, 1975.

Beavers, Herman. "Denotating the Rising Sun: Modulations of East and West in the Fiction of Charles Johnson." Paper presented at the Modern Language Association Convention. San Francisco, 28 December 1991.

Beckett, Samuel. *Molloy.* Trans. Patrick Bowles and the author. *Three Novels: Molloy, Malone Dies, The Unnamable.* New York: Grove, 1955. 7–176

———. *The Unnamable.* Trans. by the author. 289–414.

———. *Waiting for Godot.* New York: Grove, 1954.

———. *Worstward Ho!* New York: Grove, 1983.

Beckett, Samuel, and George Duthuit. "Three Dialogues." *Samuel Beckett: A Collection of Critical Essays.* Ed. Martin Esslin. Englewood Cliffs, N.J.: Prentice-Hall, 1965. 16–22.

Beidler, Peter G. Review of *Ceremony*, by Leslie Marmon Silko. *American Indian Quarterly* 3 (1977–78): 357–58.

Bell, Bernard W. *The Afro-American Novel and Its Tradition.* Amherst: University of Massachusetts Press, 1987.

Bell, Madison Smartt. "Poker and Nothingness." *New York Times Book Review* 4 November 1990: 15–16.

Bellow, Saul. *Herzog.* New York: Viking, 1964.

———. *Seize the Day.* New York: Viking, 1974.

Bevis, William. "Native American Novels: Homing In." Swann and Krupat, *Recovering the Word* 580–620.

Black Elk Speaks: Being the Life Story of a Holy Man of the Oglala Sioux. Trans. John G. Neihardt. 1932. Reprint. New York: Pocket, 1972.

Blades, John. "E. L. Doctorow—Reinventing Fiction with Every Book." *Chicago Tribune* 11 November 1984, sec. 13: 13–14.

Borges, Jorge Luis. "The Circular Ruins." *Labyrinths.* Ed. Donald A. Yates and James E. Irby. Trans. James E. Irby. New York: New Directions, 1964. 45–50.

Boyers, Robert. "The Avant-Garde." *The Columbia History of the American Novel.* Ed. Emory Elliott et al. New York: Columbia University Press, 1991. 726–51.

Boyle, T. Coraghessan. "The Hector Quesadilla Story." *Greasy Lake and Other Stories.* New York: Viking, 1985. 83–95.

Broyard, Anatole. Review of *Wrinkles*, by Charles Simmons. *New York Times*, 16 November 1978: C24.

Byerman, Keith E. *Fingering the Jagged Grain: Tradition and Form in Recent Black Fiction*. Athens: University of Georgia Press, 1985.

Calvino, Italo. *Invisible Cities*. Trans. William Weaver. San Diego: Harcourt Brace Jovanovich, 1974.

Carruth, Hayden. "Harmonies in Time and Space." *Harper's* June 1977: 80–82.

Carver, Raymond. "On Writing." *Fires: Essays, Poems, Stories*. Santa Barbara, Calif.: Capra, 1983. 13–18.

Castillo, Susan Perez. "Postmodernism, Native American Literature and the Real: The Silko-Erdrich Controversy." *Massachusetts Review* 32 (1991): 285–94.

Chatwin, Bruce. *The Songlines*. New York: Viking/Penguin, 1987.

Chénetier, Marc. " 'The Pen and the Skin': Inscription and Cryptography in John Hawkes's *Second Skin*." *Review of Contemporary Fiction* 3.3 (1983): 167–77.

Conte, Joseph M. *Unending Design: The Forms of Postmodern Poetry*. Ithaca, N.Y.: Cornell University Press, 1991.

Coover, Robert. "The Kid." *A Theological Position: Plays*. New York: Dutton, 1972. 13–75.

———. "The Magic Poker." *Pricksongs and Descants*. New York: Dutton, 1969. 20–45.

———. *The Universal Baseball Association, Inc., J. Henry Waugh, Prop*. New York: Random House, 1968.

———. *Whatever Happened to Gloomy Gus of the Chicago Bears?* Interlaken, N.Y.: Linden, 1987.

Cope, Jackson I. *Robert Coover's Fictions*. Baltimore and London: Johns Hopkins University Press, 1986.

cummings, e. e. "O sweet spontaneous." *Complete Poems, 1913–1962*. New York: Harcourt Brace Jovanovich, 1968. 46.

DeLillo, Don. "An Interview with Don DeLillo." By Tom LeClair. LeClair and McCaffery. 79–90.

———. *Libra*. New York: Viking, 1988.

———. *Mao II*. New York: Viking, 1991.

———. *The Names*. New York: Alfred A. Knopf, 1982.

———. " 'An Outsider in This Society': An Interview with Don DeLillo." By Anthony DeCurtis. Lentricchia 43–66.

———. *Ratner's Star*. New York: Alfred A. Knopf, 1976.

———. *White Noise*. New York: Viking, 1985.

Dickie, Margaret. *Lyric Contingencies: Emily Dickinson and Wallace Stevens*. Philadelphia: University of Pennsylvania Press, 1991.

Dickinson, Emily. "I felt a Funeral, in my Brain." *The Poems of Emily Dickinson*. Ed. Thomas H. Johnson. 3 vols. Cambridge: Harvard University Press, 1963. 1:199–200.

———. "Two Lengths has every Day." *Poems of Emily Dickinson*. 3:898–99.

Dixon, Stephen. *Work*. Ann Arbor: Street Fiction, 1977.
Doctorow, E. L. *Billy Bathgate*. New York: Random House, 1989.
———. *The Book of Daniel*. New York: Random House, 1971.
———. "False Documents." *American Review* 26 (1977): 215–32.
———. *Lives of the Poets: Six Stories and a Novella*. New York: Random House, 1984.
———. *Ragtime*. New York: Random House, 1974.
———. *Welcome to Hard Times*. New York: Simon and Schuster, 1960.
Donne, John. "A Valediction: Forbidding Mourning." *John Donne's Poetry*. Ed. A. L. Clements. New York: W. W. Norton, 1966. 28–29.
Dougherty, David C. *Stanley Elkin*. Boston: G. K. Hall / Twayne, 1991.
DuBois, W. E. B. *The Souls of Black Folks: Essays and Sketches*. New York: Johnson Reprint Co., 1968.
Eliot, T. S. *Burnt Norton*. In *The Complete Poems and Plays, 1909–1950*. New York: Harcourt, Brace and World, 1962. 117–22.
———. *East Coker*. *Complete Poems and Plays*. 123–29.
———. "*Ulysses*, Order, and Myth." *Selected Prose*. Ed. Frank Kermode. London: Faber, 1975. 175–78.
Elkin, Stanley. *A Bad Man*. New York: Random House, 1967.
———. *The Bailbondsman*. In *Searches and Seizures*. Boston: David R. Godine, 1973. 3–126.
———. *Criers and Kibitzers, Kibitzers and Criers*. New York: Random House, 1965.
———. *The Dick Gibson Show*. New York: Random House, 1971.
———. *The Franchiser*. Boston: David R. Godine, 1976.
———. *George Mills*. New York: E. P. Dutton, 1972.
———. "I Look Out for Ed Wolfe." *Criers and Kibitzers*, 37–66.
———. "An Interview with Stanley Elkin." By Jay Clayton. *Contemporary Literature* 24 (1983): 1–11.
———. "An Interview with Stanley Elkin." By Scott R. Sanders. *Contemporary Literature* 16 (1974): 131–45.
———. Introduction to *The Best American Short Stories: 1980*. Ed. Stanley Elkin and Shannon Ravenal. Boston: Houghton Mifflin, 1980. ix–xx.
———. *The Living End*. New York: Dutton, 1979.
———. *The MacGuffin*. New York: Simon and Schuster / Linden, 1991.
———. *The Magic Kingdom*. New York: E. P. Dutton, 1985.
———. "The Making of Ashenden." *Searches and Seizures*. 129–88.
———. "On a Field, Rampant." *Criers and Kibitzers* 153–96.
———. "Plot." *SubStance* 27 (1980): 70–74.
———. "A Poetics for Bullies." *Criers and Kibitzers* 197–217.
Ellison, Ralph. *Invisible Man*. New York: Random House, 1952.
Emerson, Ralph Waldo. "The American Scholar." *Selected Writings of Emerson*. Ed. Donald McQuade. New York: Random House, 1981. 43–63.
Epstein, Joseph. "The Sunshine Girls." *Commentary* June 1984: 62–67.
Faulkner, William. *A Fable*. New York: Random House, 1954.

———. *As I Lay Dying*. New York: Random House, 1964.

———. *The Sound and the Fury*. New York: Random House, 1967.

Federman, Raymond. "Fiction in American Today or the Unreality of Reality." *Indian Journal of American Studies* 14.1 (1984): 5–16.

Frost, Robert. "Birches." *Collected Poems of Robert Frost*. New York: Henry Holt, 1930. 152–53.

———. "The Figure a Poem Makes." *Robert Frost on Writing*. 125–28.

———. *Robert Frost on Writing*. Ed. Elaine Barry. New Brunswick, N.J.: Rutgers University Press, 1973.

———. "To Amy Bonner." Letter of 7 June 1937 in *Robert Frost on Writing*. 76.

———. To *The Amherst Student*. Letter in *Robert Frost on Writing*. 112–14.

Fulton, Alice. Afterword to "Everyone Knows the World Is Ending." In *Ecstatic Occasions, Expedient Forms: Sixty-five Leading Contemporary Poets Select and Comment on Their Poems*. Ed. David Lehman. New York: Collier Macmillan, 1987. 50–53.

Gass, William H. Foreword to *The Franchiser*. By Stanley Elkin. Boston: David R. Godine, 1980. vii–xv.

———. "In the Heart of the Heart of the Country." *In the Heart of the Heart of the Country and Other Stories*. New York: Harper and Row, 1968. 172–206.

———. "The Medium of Fiction." *Fiction and the Figures of Life*. New York: Alfred A. Knopf, 1970. 27–33.

———. *Omensetter's Luck*. New York: New American Library, 1966.

———. "Representation and the War for Reality." *Habitations of the Word: Essays*. New York: Simon and Schuster, 1985. 73–112.

Gergen, Kenneth J. *The Saturated Self: Dilemmas of Identity in Contemporary Life*. New York: Basic Books, 1991.

Gerlach, John. *Toward the End: Closure and Structure in the American Short Story*. University: University of Alabama Press, 1985.

Gleick, James. *Chaos: Making a New Science*. New York: Viking, 1987.

———. Text to *Nature's Chaos*. By Eliot Porter (photographs) and James Gleick. Ed. Janet Russek. New York: Viking, 1990.

Goldbarth, Albert. "The Nile." *Heaven and Earth: A Cosmology*. Athens: University of Georgia Press, 1991. 15–20.

Gordon, Lois. *Robert Coover: The Universal Fictionmaking Process*. Carbondale: Southern Illinois University Press, 1983.

Graham, Jorie. "The Geese." *Hybrids of Plants and Ghosts*. Princeton, N.J.: Princeton University Press, 1980. 38–39.

———. "The Lady and the Unicorn and Other Tapestries." *Erosion*. Princeton, N.J.: Princeton University Press, 1983. 37.

Greenberg, Alvin, "Why Is the Short Story Short and the Short-Short Even Shorter?" *Sudden Fiction: American Short-Short Stories*. Ed. Robert Shapard and James Thomas. Layton, Utah: Gibbs M. Smith, 1986. 230–31.

Greiner, Donald J. *Understanding John Hawkes*. Columbia: University of South Carolina Press, 1985.

Hadas, Pamela White. "Green Thoughts on Being in Charge: Discovering Joseph McElroy's *Plus*." *Review of Contemporary Fiction* 10.1 (1990): 140–55.
Hamilton, Edith. *Mythology*. Boston: Little, Brown, 1942.
Hansen, Arlen J. "The Dice of God: Einstein, Heisenberg, and Robert Coover." *Novel* 10.1 (1976): 49–58.
Harpham, Geoffrey Galt. "E. L. Doctorow and the Technology of Narrative." *PMLA* 100 (1985): 81–95.
Hassan, Ihab. "Pluralism in Postmodern Perspective." *Critical Inquiry* 12 (1986): 503–20.
Hawkes, John. *Adventures in the Alaskan Skin Trade*. New York: Simon and Schuster, 1985.
———. *The Blood Oranges*. New York: New Directions, 1971.
———. *Death, Sleep and the Traveler*. New York: New Directions, 1974.
———. "John Hawkes: An Interview." By John Enck. *Wisconsin Studies in Contemporary Literature* 6 (1965): 141–55.
———. *The Lime Twig*. New York: New Directions, 1961.
———. "Response to Richard Yarborough." *Mosaic* 8.1 (1974): 63–65.
———. *Second Skin*. New York: New Directions, 1964.
———. *Travesty*. New York: New Directions, 1976.
Hayden, Robert. "Middle Passage." *Collected Poems*. Ed. Frederick Glaysher. New York: Liveright, 1985. 48–54.
Hayles, N. Katherine. *The Cosmic Web: Scientific Field Models and Literary Strategies in the Twentieth Century*. Ithaca and London: Cornell University Press, 1984.
Heaney, Seamus. "Waterfall." *Death of a Naturalist*. London: Faber and Faber, 1966. 40.
Heller, Joseph. *Catch-22*. New York: Simon and Schuster, 1961.
Hemingway, Ernest. *The Sun Also Rises*. New York: Scribner's, 1954.
Hofstadter, Douglas R. *Gödel, Escher, Bach: An Eternal Golden Braid*. New York: Basic Books, 1979.
Hollander, John. "The Great Bear." *Spectral Emanations: New and Selected Poems*. New York: Atheneum, 1978. 223–25.
Honig, Edwin. "Jawing of Genesis." *Gazabos*. New York: Clarke and Way, 1959. 3.
Huizinga, Johan. *Homo Ludens: A Study of the Play-Element in Culture*. Trans. R. F. C. Hull. London: Routledge, 1949.
Hutcheon, Linda. *The Politics of Postmodernism*. London and New York: Routledge, 1989.
Irving, John. *The World According to Garp*. New York: E. P. Dutton, 1978.
Jahner, Elaine. "All the World's a Story." *Prairie Schooner* 51 (1977–78): 415–16.
James, William. "Bergson and His Critique of Intellectualism." In *The Writings of William James*. Ed. John J. McDermott. New York: Random House, 1967. 561–81.
———. "Pragmatism and Humanism." *Writings of William James* 449–61.

———. "Pragmatism and Radical Empiricism." *Writings of William James* 311–17.
———. "The Types of Philosophic Thinking." *Writings of William James* 482–96.
———. "What Pragmatism Means." *Writings of William James* 376–90.
Johnson, Charles. *Being and Race: Black Writing since 1970*. Bloomington: Indiana University Press, 1988.
———. *Faith and the Good Thing*. New York: Viking, 1974.
———. *Middle Passage*. New York: Macmillan, 1990.
———. *Oxherding Tale*. Bloomington: Indiana University Press, 1982.
Jouve, Nicole Ward. "Too Short for a Book?" *Re-reading the Short Story*. Ed. Clare Hanson. New York: St. Martin's Press, 1989. 34–44.
Joyce, James. "The Dead." *Dubliners*. Ed. Robert Scholes and A. Walton Litz. New York: Viking, 1969. 175–224.
———. *Finnegans Wake*. New York: Viking. 1959.
———. *A Portrait of the Artist as a Young Man*. Ed. Chester G. Anderson. New York: Viking, 1968.
Kafalenos, Emma. "From the Comic to the Ludic: Postmodern Fiction." *International Fiction Review* 12.1 (1985): 28–31.
Karl, Frederick R. "American Fictions: The Mega-Novel." *Conjunctions* 7 (1985): 248–60.
———. *American Fictions, 1940–1980: A Comprehensive History and Critical Evaluation*. New York: Harper and Row, 1983.
Kawin, Bruce F. *The Mind of the Novel: Reflexive Fiction and the Ineffable*. Princeton, N.J.: Princeton University Press, 1982.
Kazin, Alfred. *An American Procession: The Major American Writers from 1830 to 1930—The Crucial Century*. New York: Alfred A. Knopf, 1984.
Kearney, Richard. *The Wake of the Imagination: Toward a Postmodern Culture*. Minneapolis: University of Minnesota Press, 1988.
Keats, John. *The Letters of John Keats, 1814–1821*, vol. 1. Ed. Hyder Edward Rollins. Cambridge: Harvard University Press, 1958.
Kermode, Frank. "Fictions." *The Sense of an Ending: Studies in the Theory of Fiction*. New York: Oxford University Press, 1967. 35–64.
Klinkowitz, Jerome. *The Life of Fiction*. Urbana: University of Illinois Press, 1977.
———. *The Self-Apparent Word: Fiction as Language / Language as Fiction*. Carbondale: Southern Illinois University Press, 1984.
Knapp, Bettina. *Women in Twentieth-Century Literature: A Jungian View*. University Park: Pennsylvania State University Press, 1987.
Kutnik, Jerzy. *The Novel as Performance: The Fiction of Ronald Sukenick and Raymond Federman*. Carbondale: Southern Illinois University Press, 1986.
LeClair, Tom. *The Art of Excess: Mastery in Contemporary American Fiction*. Urbana: University of Illinois Press, 1989.
———. *In the Loop: Don DeLillo and the Systems Novel*. Urbana: University of Illinois Press, 1987.
———. "The Systems Novel." Review of *Prisoner's Dilemma*, by Richard Powers. *New Republic* 25 April 1988: 40–42.

Leithauser, Brad. *Hence*. New York: Viking/Penguin, 1989.

Lem, Stanislaw. "The Princess Ineffable." *The Mind's I: Fantasies and Reflections on Self and Soul*. Ed. Douglas R. Hofstadter and Daniel C. Dennett. New York: Basic Books, 1981. 96–99.

Lentricchia, Frank, ed. *Introducing Don DeLillo*. Durham, N.C.: Duke University Press, 1991.

Levin, Jenifer. "Love Is a Federal Highway." Review of *Girl with Curious Hair*, by David Foster Wallace. *New York Times Book Review* 5 November 1989: 31.

Lévi-Strauss, Claude. *The Savage Mind*. Trans. George Weidenfeld and Nicolson Ltd. Chicago: University of Chicago Press, 1966.

Lincoln, Kenneth. "Native American Literatures: 'old like hills, like stars.' " *Three American Literatures*. Ed. Houston A. Baker, Jr. New York: Modern Language Association of America, 1982. 80–167.

———. *Native American Renaissance*. Berkeley: University of California Press, 1983.

Lohafer, Susan, ed. *Coming to Terms with the Short Story*. Baton Rouge: Louisiana State University Press, 1983.

Lohafer, Susan, and Jo Ellyn Clary, eds. *Short Story Theory at a Crossroads*. Baton Rouge: Louisiana State University Press, 1989.

Luscher, Robert M. "The Short Story Sequence: An Open Book." Lohafer, *Coming to Terms* 148–67.

MacLochlainn, Alf. *Out of Focus*. Elmwood Park, Ill.: Dalkey Archive, 1985.

MacShane, Frank. "American Indians, Peruvian Jews: *Ceremony*." *New York Times Book Review* 12 June 1977: 15, 33.

Mallon, Anne-Marie. "Sojourning Women: Homelessness and Transcendence in *Housekeeping*." Critique 30 (1989): 95–105.

Mann, Susan Garland. *The Short Story Cycle: A Genre Companion and Reference Guide*. Westport, Conn.: Greenwood Press, 1989.

Martin, Ronald E. *American Literature and the Destruction of Knowledge: Innovative Writing in the Age of Epistemology*. Durham, N.C.: Duke University Press, 1991.

Marvell, Andrew. "A Dialogue between the Soul and Body." *The Metaphysical Poets*. Ed. Helen Gardner. Harmondsworth, Middlesex: Penguin, 1957. 243–45.

———. "The Garden." Gardner 253–56.

McClure, John A. "Postmodern Romance: Don DeLillo and the Age of Conspiracy." Lentricchia 99–115.

McElroy, Joseph. "Holding With Apollo 17." *New York Times Book Review* 28 January 1973: 27–29.

———. "An Interview with Joseph McElroy." By Tom LeClair. *Anything Can Happen* 235–51.

———. "John Graham Interview." *Review of Contemporary Fiction* 10.1 (1990): 23–32.

———. *Lookout Cartridge*. New York: Alfred A. Knopf, 1974.

———. "Neural Neighborhoods and Other Concrete Abstracts." *TriQuarterly* 34 (1975): 201–17.

———. *Plus*. 1976. Reprint. New York: Carroll and Graf, 1987.

Meese, Elizabeth A. *Crossing the Double-Cross: The Practice of Feminist Criticism*. Chapel Hill: University of North Carolina Press, 1986.

Mellard, James M. *The Exploded Form: The Modernist Novel in America*. Urbana: University of Illinois Press, 1980.

Melville, Herman. *Moby-Dick*. Ed. Harrison Hayford and Hershel Parker. New York: W. W. Norton, 1967.

Menand, Louis. "Market Report." Review of *Mao II*. *New Yorker* 24 June 1991: 81–84.

Metcalf, Rory Rebecca, and Gael Montgomery. "Names of the Game." *Village Voice* 26 August 1986: 130.

Miller, Alicia M. "Power and Perception in *Plus*." *Review of Contemporary Fiction* 10.1 (1990): 173–80.

Molesworth, Charles. "Don DeLillo's Perfect Starry Night." Lentricchia 143–56.

Momaday, N. Scott. "The Man Made of Words." *The Remembered Earth: An Anthology of Contemporary Native American Literature*. Ed. Geary Hobson. Albuquerque: Red Earth Press, 1979. 162–72.

Monaghan, Peter. "Winner of National Book Award Won't Be a 'Voice of Black America.' " *Chronicle of Higher Education* 16 January 1991: A3.

Moore, Marianne. "Poetry." *Collected Poems*. New York: Macmillan, 1961. 40–41.

Morace, Robert A. "Robert Coover, The Imaginative Self, and the 'Tyrant Other.' " *Papers in Language and Literature* 21 (1985): 192–209.

Morowitz, Harold J. "The Sport of Eggheads." *The Thermodynamics of Pizza: Essays on Science and Everyday Life*. New Brunswick, N.J.: Rutgers University Press, 1991. 201–206.

Nabokov, Vladimir. *Pale Fire*. New York: Lancer, 1963.

Nemerov, Howard. "Figures of Thought." *The Collected Poems of Howard Nemerov*. Chicago: University of Chicago Press, 1977. 472.

O'Brien, Tim. "An Interview with Tim O'Brien." By Larry McCaffery. LeClair and McCaffery 262–78.

———. "An Interview with Tim O'Brien." By Martin Naparsteck. *Contemporary Literature* 32 (1991): 1–11.

———. *Going after Cacciato*. New York: Dell, 1978.

———. *The Things They Carried*. Boston: Houghton Mifflin / Seymour Lawrence, 1990.

Ong, Walter J. "Introduction: On Saying We and Us to Literature." Baker, *Three American Literatures* 3–7.

Otto, Walter F. *The Homeric Gods: The Spiritual Significance of Greek Religion*. Trans. Moses Hadas. New York: Farrar, Straus and Giroux, 1978.

Peterson, Ivars. *Islands of Truth: A Mathematical Mystery Cruise*. New York: W. H. Freeman, 1990.

Pinter, Harold. *The Birthday Party and Other Plays*. London: Methuen, 1960.

Plagens, Peter. "The Last Modernist." *Newsweek* 10 February 1992: 60–61.

Plath, Sylvia. "Johnny Panic and the Bible of Dreams." *Johnny Panic and the Bible of Dreams: Short Stories, Prose and Diary Excerpts*. New York: Harper and Row, 1979. 152–66.

Poirier, Richard. *The Renewal of Literature: Emersonian Reflections*. New York: Random House, 1987.

———. *A World Elsewhere: The Place of Style in American Literature*. New Haven, Conn.: Yale University Press, 1972.

Porush, David. *The Soft Machine: Cybernetic Fiction*. New York: Methuen, 1985.

Powers, Richard. *Prisoner's Dilemma*. New York: Macmillan, 1988.

———. *Three Farmers on Their Way to a Dance*. New York: McGraw-Hil, 1985.

Pynchon, Thomas. *V.* 1963. Reprint. New York: Bantam Books, 1964.

Quartermain, Peter. "Trusting the Reader." *Chicago Review* 32.2 (1980): 65–74.

Rabelais, François. *Gargantua and Pantagruel*. Trans. Burton Raffel. 1532–52. Reprint. New York: W. W. Norton, 1990.

Ravits, Martha. "Extending the American Range: Marilynne Robinson's *Housekeeping*." *American Literature* 61 (1989): 644–66.

Rhinehart, Luke. *The Dice Man*. New York: Dell, 1971.

Robertson, Mary F. "The 'Crisis in Comedy' as a Problem of the Sign: The Example of Hawkes's *Second Skin*." *Texas Studies in Literature and Language* 26 (1984): 425–54.

Robinson, Marilynne. *Housekeeping*. New York: Farrar, Straus and Giroux, 1980.

———. Interview by Kay Bonetti. Audiocassette. American Audio Prose Library, 1989.

———. "Writers and the Nostalgic Fallacy." *New York Times Book Review* 13 October 1985: 1, 34–35.

Roethke, Theodore. "The Waking." *The Collected Poems of Theodore Roethke*. Garden City, N.Y.: Doubleday, 1966. 108.

Ruddick, Lisa. "Fluid Symbols in American Modernism: William James, Gertrude Stein, George Santayana, and Wallace Stevens." *Allegory, Myth, and Symbol*. Ed. Morton W. Bloomfield. Cambridge: Harvard University Press, 1981. 335–53.

Saltzman, Arthur M. *Designs of Darkness in Contemporary American Fiction*. Philadelphia: University of Pennsylvania Press, 1990.

———. *Understanding Raymond Carver*. Columbia: University of South Carolina Press, 1988.

——. "Where Words Dwell Adored: An Introduction to William Gass." *Review of Contemporary Fiction* 11.3 (1991): 7–14.

Sandburg, Carl. "Waiting for the Chariot." *The American Tradition in Literature*. Ed. George Perkins et al. 6th ed. 2 vols. New York: Random House, 1985. 2:1018.

Scholes, Robert. *The Fabulators*. New York: Oxford University Press, 1967.

Schwartz, Delmore. "The Heavy Bear Who Goes with Me." In Perkins et al., *American Tradition in Literature*, 2:1537–38.

Shapard, Robert, and James Thomas, eds. *Sudden Fiction: American Short-Short Stories*. Layton, Utah: Peregrine Smith, 1986.

Shaw, George Bernard. *The Doctor's Dilemma.* 1913. Reprint. Baltimore: Penguin, 1965.
Shaw, Valerie. *The Short Story: A Critical Introduction.* London and New York: Longman, 1983.
Shelton, Frank W. "Humor and Balance in Coover's *The Universal Baseball Association.*" *Critique* 15 (1975): 78–90.
Silko, Leslie Marmon. *Ceremony.* New York: Viking / Penguin, 1977.
———. "The Fourth World." *Artforum* 27 (1989): 124–27.
———. *Laguna Woman.* Greenfield Center, N.Y.: Greenfield Review Press, 1974.
———. "Language and Literature from a Pueblo Indian Perspective." *Critical Fictions: The Politics of Imaginative Writing.* Ed. Philomena Mariani. DIA Center for the Arts Discussions in Contemporary Culture no. 7. Seattle: Bay Press, 1991. 83–93.
———. "Stories and Their Tellers—A Conversation with Leslie Marmon Silko." With Dexter Fisher. *The Third Woman: Minority Women Writers of the United States.* Ed. Dexter Fisher. Boston: Houghton Mifflin, 1980. 18–23.
———. "Yellow Woman." *Storyteller.* New York: Seaver, 1981. 54–62.
Simmons, Charles. *Wrinkles.* New York: Farrar, Straus and Giroux, 1978.
Sollers, Werner. "Introduction: The Invention of Ethnicity." *The Invention of Ethnicity.* Ed. Werner Sollers. New York: Oxford University Press, 1989. ix–xx.
Sontag, Susan. "Review of *Second Skin.*" *The Merrill Studies in* Second Skin. Ed. John Graham. Columbus, Ohio: Charles E. Merrill, 1971. 3–5.
Sorrentino, Gilbert. "The Moon in Its Flight." *New American Review* 13 (1971): 153–63.
Spariosu, Mihai. "Literature and Play: History, Principles, Method." *Literature, Mimesis and Play.* Tubingen, Germany: Narr, 1982. 13–52.
Sperry, Stuart M. *Keats the Poet.* Princeton, N.J.: Princeton University Press, 1973.
Stein, Gertrude. "Manguin a Painter." *Portraits and Prayers.* New York: Random House, 1934. 54–56.
———. "Pictures." *Lectures in America.* New York: Random House, 1962. 59–90.
———. *Tender Buttons.* 1914. Reprint. Los Angeles: Sun and Moon Press, 1992.
Steiner, Wendy. "Postmodernism and the Ornament." *Word and Image* 4 (1988): 60–66.
Stevens, Wallace. *Adagia. Opus Posthumous: Revised, Enlarged, and Corrected Edition.* Ed. Milton J. Bates. New York: Alfred A. Knopf, 1989. 184–202.
———. "The Bed of Old John Zeller." *The Collected Poems of Wallace Stevens.* New York: Alfred A. Knopf, 1954. 326–27.
———. "Chaos in Motion and Not in Motion." *Collected Poems.* 357–58.
———. "July Mountain." *Opus Posthumous.* 140.
———. "On the Road Home." *Collected Poems.* 203–4.
———. "An Ordinary Evening in New Haven." *Collected Poems.* 465–89.
———. "Six Significant Landscapes." *Collected Poems.* 73–75.

———. "The Snow Man." *Collected Poems.* 54.

———. "Sunday Morning." *Collected Poems.* 66–70.

Stevick, Philip. Introduction to *Anti-Story: An Anthology of Experimental Fiction.* Ed. Philip Stevick. New York: Macmillan / Free Press, 1971. ix–xxiii.

Sukenick, Ronald. "Cross Examination." *In Form* 105–55.

———. *The Death of the Novel and Other Stories.* New York: Dial, 1969.

———. *The Endless Short Story.* New York: Fiction Collective, 1986.

———. *In Form: Digressions on the Act of Fiction.* Carbondale: Southern Illinois University Press, 1985.

———. "The New Tradition." *In Form* 201–13.

———. *98.6.* New York: Fiction Collective, 1975.

———. *Out.* Chicago: Swallow Press, 1973.

———. "Thirteen Digressions." *In Form* 16–33.

———. "Twelve Digressions Toward a Study of Composition." *In Form* 3–15.

Swann, Brian, and Arnold Krupat, eds. *I Tell You Now: Autobiographical Essays by Native American Writers.* Lincoln: University of Nebraska Press, 1987.

———. *Recovering the Word: Essays on Native American Literature.* Berkeley: University of California Press, 1987.

"Talking About American Fiction." *Salmagundi* 93 (Winter 1992): 61–77.

Tanner, Tony. *City of Words: American Fiction, 1950–1970.* London: Jonathan Cape, 1971.

———. *The Reign of Wonder: Naivety and Reality in American Literature.* London: Cambridge University Press, 1965.

———. "Toward an Ultimate Topography: The Work of Joseph McElroy." *TriQuarterly* 36 (1976): 214–52.

Thoreau, Henry D. *Walden.* Ed. J. Lyndon Shanley. Princeton, N.J.: Princeton University Press, 1971.

Tolstoy, Leo. *War and Peace.* Ed. George Gibian. Trans. Louise and Aylmer Maude. New York: W. W. Norton, 1966.

Updike, John. "Packed Dirt, Churchgoing, a Dying Cat, a Traded Car." *Pigeon Feathers and Other Stories.* New York: Alfred A. Knopf, 1962. 246–79.

van Delden, Maarten. "Modernism, the New Criticism, and Thomas Pynchon's *V.*" *Novel* 23.2 (1990): 117–36.

Varsava, Jerry A. *Contingent Meanings: Postmodern Fiction, Mimesis, and the Reader.* Tallahassee: Florida State University Press, 1990.

Vonnegut, Kurt, Jr. *Slaughterhouse-Five.* New York: Dell, 1969.

Wallace, David Foster. *Girl with Curious Hair.* New York: Avon, 1989.

Waugh, Patricia. *Feminine Fictions: Revisiting the Postmodern.* London: Routledge, 1989.

Weelen, Guy. *Miro: 1940–1955.* New York: Tudor, 1960.

West, Paul. "Those Pearls His Eyes." *The Universe, and Other Fictions.* Woodstock, N.Y.: Overlook Press, 1988. 133–48.

———. *The Women of Whitechapel and Jack the Ripper.* New York: Random House, 1991.

Wiget, Andrew. *Native American Literature.* Boston: G. K. Hall, 1985.
Wilbur, Richard. "Juggler." *The Poems of Richard Wilbur.* New York: Harcourt, Brace and World, 1963. 130.
Wilczynski, Marek. "American Innovative Fiction." Review of *The Novel as Performance*, by Jerzy Kutnik, and *Literary Disruptions*, by Jerome Klinkowitz. *Contemporary Literature* 30.1 (1989): 151–59.
Wilde, Alan. *Horizons of Assent: Modernism, Postmodernism, and the Ironic Imagination.* Baltimore: Johns Hopkins University Press, 1981.
———. *Middle Grounds: Studies in Contemporary American Fiction.* Philadelphia: University of Pennsylvania Press, 1987.
Williams, William Carlos. *Paterson.* New York: New Directions, 1963.
———. "The Work of Gertrude Stein." *Imaginations.* Ed. Webster Schott. New York: New Directions, 1970. 346–53.
Wineapple, Brenda. "Robert Coover's Playing Fields." *Iowa Review* 10 (1979): 66–74.
Woolf, Virginia. *To the Lighthouse.* New York: Harcourt, Brace and World, 1927.
Wordsworth, William. "Mutability." *The Poetical Works of William Wordsworth.* Ed. Thomas Hutchinson. London: Oxford University Press, 1920. 449.
Wright, Austin M. "Recalcitrance in the Short Story." Lohafer, *Coming to Terms* 115–29.
Yeats, William Butler. "Byzantium." *The Collected Poems of W. B. Yeats.* New York: Macmillan, 1956. 243–44.
———. "Sailing to Byzantium." *Collected Poems* 191–92.
Zolbrod, Paul G. "When Artifacts Speak, What Can They Tell Us?" Swann and Krupat, *Recovering the Word* 13–40.

Index

Note: Titles of individual works are listed by author.